Acclaim for *Rise* by Cara Brookins

"This rousing memoir beautifully illustrates how one family can look apprehension dead in the eye and scoff at it. For readers looking for inspiration to accomplish a daunting task, they need look no further than Brookins's highly engaging and encouraging book." —*Booklist*

"A tough, honest memoir. Brookins deftly narrates the extreme learning curve her family experienced while putting a family back together again." —*Publishers Weekly*

"Cara Brookins turned trauma into power and fear into courage. Her extraordinary memoir tells the story of her resurrection from victim of domestic abuse to badass mom with a hammer and a carpenter's square." —John Grogan, #1 *New York Times* bestselling author of *Marley & Me*

"*Rise* is a compelling story, lovingly told, that will uplift and inspire readers whatever their circumstances." —Martha Beck, *New York Times* bestselling author of *Finding Your Own North Star*

"Sometimes the universe puts us in a bad place and dares us to fight our way out. Cara Brookins did just this. We should all be as strong as her." —Tom Hart, #1 *New York Times* bestselling author of *Rosalie Lightning*

"At once heartbreaking and deeply inspiring, readers will be torn between believing Cara is a one-of-a-kind hero, and that anyone can be." —Hilary Liftin, coauthor of the *New York Times* bestseller *sTORI Telling*

"It has been a very long time since I have read a book as singular and as profoundly moving as *Rise*. *Rise* gives new meaning to the concepts of heroism and sacrifice, and it is a remarkable construct in itself."

—Les Standiford, author of *Water to the Angels*

Rise

HOW A HOUSE
BUILT A FAMILY

CARA BROOKINS

St. Martin's Press   New York

www.stmartins.com

Designed by Meghan Day Healey

The Library of Congress Cataloging-in-Publication Data is available upon request.

ISBN 978-1-250-09566-4 (hardcover)
ISBN 978-1-250-09567-1 (e-book)

Our books may be purchased in bulk for promotional, educational, or business use. Please contact your local bookseller or the Macmillan Corporate and Premium Sales Department at 1-800-221-7945, extension 5442, or by e-mail at MacmillanSpecialMarkets@macmillan.com.

First Edition: January 2017

10 9 8 7 6 5 4 3 2 1

To my parents, Virginia Barrette and Bruce Puttkammer,

who told me I could do anything.

Life would have been easier—though less exciting—

if I hadn't believed you.

Contents

Our task was both extreme and simple.
My family needed sanctuary.
So we built it.

 A House

The house stands sturdy and straight. To us—my four children and me—it is a marvel, as surreal and unlikely as an ancient colossus. It is our home, in the truest sense. We built it. Every nail, every two-by-four, every three-inch slice of hardwood flooring has passed through our hands. Most pieces slid across our fingers multiple times as we moved material from one spot to another, installed it, ripped it out, and then tried again. Often the concrete and wood scraped flesh or hair, snagging physical evidence and vaulting it into the walls. Sometimes bits of wood or slivers of metal poked under our skin. I have shavings of house DNA permanently embedded inside my palm and dimpled forever in my left shin. The house wove us all together in this painful and intimate union, until we were a vital part of one another.

The idea of building our own home was not born out of boredom, but rose as the only possible way to rebuild my shattered family while we worked through the shock waves of domestic violence and mental illness. The dangers of our past were more difficult to leave behind than we ever imagined.

I groped for something that would weave us together with a sense of purpose, something large and profound. We needed a place to live, and one fall evening I imagined us working together, building our place, taking small pieces and fastening them together until they had grown into something much bigger than ourselves. The next day I discussed the idea with my three older children, and by that afternoon we had decided to do it.

I didn't know yet how to frame a window or a door, how to snake pipes and wires through a wall, or how to draw up blueprints and obtain permits. But I knew my kids, and I knew we needed this.

We thought the beautiful metaphor of rebuilding our family while we were building a house would make both tasks easier. We believed we were starting at the bottom and could only rise up from that humble spot. We imagined we'd feel powerful and big because we were doing something profound.

We were wrong on all accounts.

Nothing makes a person feel smaller, weaker, or more insubstantial than taking on one thousand times more than you can handle. Building a house was the most difficult challenge we'd ever face, and so was rebuilding our family amid the trauma of abuse. We were nowhere near the bottom, but we would find it before we found the top.

One board at a time, we built a house.

And in the end, we discovered a home.

−2−

Bad Habits

I had been married for a year and a half and was nineteen when my first child, Hope, was born. From the first time I held her, I knew I would do anything to give her a family with both a mom and a dad. My own parents were long divorced, so I knew how torn in two a kid could feel. Years later, and with three kids in tow, it wasn't especially surprising that I married again after the failed marriage to my high-school sweetheart turned military world traveler, but after I had narrowly escaped Adam's schizophrenia, it surprised everyone when I married Matt.

For some people, the third time's a charm. But for other, hardheaded people, that's just how many times it takes to learn a lesson.

Matt was younger than me but said he was eager to be a dad to my kids—I had three by then—and to have a child with me. He was controlling, manipulative, and violent within a few months of our marriage. He always had a good reason, a solution, and it always pointed to something that he found wrong with me. Even after he started drinking heavily and experimenting with a variety of drugs, I believed that things would get better, that we might be happy, that the mother hen of the universe wouldn't send me another bad egg.

I went to sleep every night expecting to wake up to his apologies, to a happy family, to an alternate reality.

But what woke me was the sound of his breath, ragged, uneven, and no more than six inches from my face in our dark bedroom. He sucked in each lungful through his teeth and then pushed it out the same way. "Fi," it said on the way in, and "Fah" on the way out. How many times had I heard that rhythm? Too many. But not enough. Because here I was again, Matt's hands around my throat, his vodka breath drying my eyes, and that heartbeat-steady sound that woke me even before I felt his right hand scoop under my neck and the left hand close over my throat.

No snooze button on this alarm. "Fi-fah. Fi-fah. Fi-fah."

My heart thumped a dozen times with each fierce breath. And my own breathing went so shallow I wondered if it would just stop altogether, wondered if I wanted it to. He wasn't cutting off my air supply. No, not that. He wasn't trying to kill me, for God's sake. It wasn't until the third—no, maybe it was the fourth—time that I figured that out. Mustn't kill Cara. He just wanted to let me know that he could. Any time he wanted to, he could kill me.

A bit of spittle flew out between his clenched teeth and landed as gentle as a snowflake below my left eye. He squeezed tighter. It would be another turtleneck day. *Had I washed the brown one?* His thumbs would leave two perfect blue ovals on the left side of my neck, tilted out like tiny butterfly wings. The thick fingertips were stacked on the other side, where the bruise would form a long, jagged line, more like the very hungry caterpillar.

Real terror doesn't come at you like a fist in the middle of an argument, or a thump on the back of the head after you do something stupid. You can see those coming. Real terror is going to sleep thinking everything is fine at the end of an ordinary day, a day where you laughed over dinner and watched a late movie, and then waking up to this reminder that you don't have to wake up. Not ever. Not if he doesn't want you to.

His nose and the angle of his jaw looked foreign in the thick shadows, as though his German bloodline were written in an ink visible only by moonlight after being submerged in vodka and the hot breath of his rage.

His strawberry-blond hair, cropped short like he was preparing for a Special Forces mission, glistened with a light sheen of sweat. If his hands were free just then he would have wiped a palm back over his head and flexed strong jaw muscles in a way that had once made me say, "Oh, my." His brow was low, shadowing his eyes into a dark mask. I tried to imagine his wispy, red-yellow eyelashes winking at me over a grin that meant it was all a joke. Just pretend. All in fun. He'd draw up the left side of his mouth in a smile wickedly handsome enough to make women want him and men want to be him.

Like he was reading my mind, his mouth pulled into that half smile, but paired with the intensity of his dark eyes, it was cruel, not a joke after all.

I froze. And I hoped. I hoped this would be one of the simple nights where reminding me my fragile life was in his hands was all he was after. Even when his fingers tightened and I realized that it wasn't, that instead it was going to be one of the long nights he would later say he didn't remember, even then I found things to hope for. Mostly, I hoped the kids would sleep through it, the four amazing little people who kept me drawing breath down through the circle of his hands.

My arms tingled, the nerves jumping with fire from the crushed pressure points on the sides of my neck. Hoping failed, and with barely a nod to the subtle difference between the blackjack-size odds of a hope and the Mega Millions long shot of a wish—I moved to wishing.

I wished for the way he had been only hours ago. I wished I could wipe away the things that haunted him. I wished I weren't so weak. And for three slow breaths in and back out, I allowed a wish I had pushed away every time until this one: I wished I could wrap my hands around his neck and squeeze just . . . like . . . this.

My peripheral vision blackened, and I ignored the things living in those dark shadows, the monsters of sharp-toothed reality. I never stared those things straight-on—the things most likely to happen. His shoulders twitched, begging to end the tension with either a full-out, final squeeze, or a release. He wore his favorite baby-blue T-shirt, so tight it showed every taut muscle beneath the soft fabric. Hours ago, I'd pressed my cheek against that shirt, his cologne soft and welcoming, his arm draped across my back and hand tucked into my waistband. I'd felt safe, loved. I'd felt at home.

The reality monsters crawled out from their dark places and up the sides of the bed, whispering truths that for the first time I found I wanted to hear.

He sprang upright, jerking his hands apart and up like he had the sudden urge to do jumping jacks. The nape of my neck tingled where a few strands of my long, curly hair had jerked back with him, tangled in his watchband. For a moment, he hovered like Peter Pan's shadow, like no human could possibly be attached to the dark form with the thick shoulders beefed up during college ball. I'd been holding my breath, cutting off the air myself to keep some small scrap of control, and I was so light-headed the vessels over my ears pounded louder than his breathing. Fresh oxygen stung my lungs, and I was suddenly aware of the rest of my body, which had mysteriously vanished when the only thing that mattered was my access to another breath.

I wished for words, explanations, accusations, anything to put a name to what had gone wrong enough to spin an average day into a nightmare night. Vodka had played its part, it always did, but it was more than that. Lots of people had a little vodka without turning into a human claw machine, grabbing at their thin-necked wife amid the wrinkled, cardboard-colored sheets. Something was wrong inside his head. After all these years I'd figured that out, finally; I could see there was more wrong in his head for behaving this way than in mine for believing it could get better.

"The last straw," he said.

Which always made me picture an icy lemonade in a tall glass with slices of real lemon and an old-fashioned red and white paper straw poking out the top, stained with lipstick. "It was just the last straw." His hands went to the sides of his head, fingers twisted like they could tangle into his stubbly hair, and then pushed until his temples must have pounded like mine.

I was so happy for the interruption of his damned "Fi-fah" that I welcomed the inevitable appearance of the straw. Even though my mind screamed the question, I knew better than to ask, "What was the last straw? What, exactly?" Because he didn't know any more than I did. No one likes to face their own crazy, irrational anger—least of all a crazy, irrational person. I zipped my lips. Bit my tongue. Held my peace. I knew better than to apologize, agree, or make any move at all.

"Don't you cry, Cara. You attention hound. Don't play like a victim. Don't. You. Cry."

I hadn't cried in years, at least no more than an eye-dabbing tear over a poignant movie. But I started crying anyhow. Not because I was scared; of course I *was* scared, but that wasn't what made me cry. My neck hurt, too, but I'd been hurt a lot worse, and I rarely cried just because something hurt. I'd delivered babies with no medication and kept so eerily silent the doctors were afraid for me. No, these tears were for my old mantra, because it had finally failed. *Most of the time he's good. And I love him,* I had always told myself. *I love him enough to stay.*

But for the first time, I didn't love him. I didn't love him enough to stay. I didn't hate him, though I knew I would have if I'd been lucky enough to be born a pessimist; rather, I didn't feel anything for him at all. He had become a big, emotionless, black hole in my core. A hole that didn't even sting when I poked at it.

"Let's talk outside," I whispered, imagining that sparing the kids his yelling, his threats this one time was going to make them less damaged, less afraid. Imagining, too, that they wouldn't know tomorrow's turtleneck was out of necessity.

When we walked through the den, I angled my head just enough to check the balcony for little eyes peeking over, but saw none. Of course, the yelling hadn't started yet. They didn't know there was anything to be afraid of tonight. Why would they? Jada had sat on the rug during our movie, weaving a strand of yarn between Matt's toes and around his ankle until he looked like a web-footed, living dream catcher. She'd tucked her long blond hair behind her ears and giggled the mischievous, bubbly giggle of an eleven-year-old who thinks she is making someone a fool and getting away with it. Jada was my little elf girl.

We had eaten ice cream together, sharing spoonfuls until a spot dribbled onto his shirt. That's when he had changed into the baby-blue shirt, and I'd snuggled back in against it.

It was a wholly different man following me outside to talk about the nothingness that had happened to change everything. He saw me look up for the kids, and his breathing went through his teeth again.

The glass door rattled closed behind him, and I fell into a lounge chair before he had any new ideas of what to do with me. He stood statue-still and silent, either planning his next move or trying to remember, like I was, what we were doing outside in the middle of the night.

The Southern air smelled like school, or the way that always made me think of school in early September. I was from Wisconsin, and never completely comfortable with the food, manners, or habits just outside of Little Rock, Arkansas, even though I'd lived there longer than I'd lived in any other state.

Hershey, my chocolate Lab, flipped out through her doggy door and paced the porch perimeter from twenty feet out. It was cold, but I ignored the gooseflesh and imagined the chill sizzling against the heat inside his head.

That was my optimist showing, pretending cool air was a cure for madness. Some people think optimists and pessimists are created, but I've always known better. We're born into these political parties and die with an unchanged, slanted mind-set. The optimist party is erroneously considered superior, but we should have been weeded out Darwinian-style hundreds of years ago. No matter how repeatedly life draws out her doom-and-gloom conclusions for us, we find reason to stay, hoping and wishing when the more survival-equipped pessimist would make the wise decision to run. Run like hell.

"Look at your feet," he said, wrinkling his lip in distaste.

I bent my knees and rubbed my hands over my bare legs enough to look like I was warming them, but not enough to look like I was complaining about the cold; then I tucked my feet under the hem of my short nightshirt. His mother's feet were a dainty size six. She tried on the tiny display models at the shoe store while I dug through mountains of boxes looking for an eight, even though I really needed a nine to be comfortable. I didn't need to look at my feet to see how unpretty they were.

"You know how hard I work. And no one appreciates it. You know that, right?" His hands cupped the sides of his head again, pulling out and then pressing in, matching his breathing, pull on the inhale, push on the exhale. "You have to stop. You just have to stop making me so angry!" He waved out toward where my dog was still pacing, tail so low it almost dragged along the dry fall grass. I imagined it leaving a fire trail behind, and I couldn't remember what fairy tale the image came from. Had it been a fox? A tiger? A tiger by the tail.

He wasn't talking about the dog, though. She was invisible to him, exactly like she meant to be. He was talking about the ideas that made him as drunk as the vodka. They were Big. Always, big. He left the medium-size ideas and the small ideas for others to toy with. People like me.

"I understand how hard it is for you." I looked behind the sadness to the wildness deep in his dark eyes. I could practically see the anxious neurons zipping around and could almost understand why he drowned them with vodka every couple of months.

I stuck to the script. "Maybe you should change jobs. Get your mind on something new." I waved like he had, out at the nothingness of the field and the forest beyond, where the only things giving us a sideways look were the mosquitoes brave enough to look away from the diving bats.

"Dammit!" He threw his head back. "Dammmmm-it!" He stretched out the word, loud and long like a song to the stars. "A regular day job is not for me. Never was. Jobs like that were for my father."

He struck his index finger against my chest three times, and focused on it for several heartbeats, eyes narrowed. "You should try those pills again. Maybe the nausea was from something else. Have you seen Shane's wife? Her tits grew at least a cup." He held his hands inches in front of me, air-massaging imaginary breasts as though the proper fertilizer would make them sprout like healthy eggplants.

"I'll try again," I said, pretending I hadn't flushed the pink pills he'd ordered from Chest Success to save me from my chest fail. The package included a complimentary bottle of pheromone spray, boasting a woman who didn't need the breast pills or more than a quarter yard of fabric for any outfit in her closet. She was probably born with no body hair, and her feet were no doubt size six. "Why don't we get some sleep? I'm leading a software meeting in the morning. I have to be on top of my game." I stood, smiling even though he wasn't, then walked around him to the door with my hand out behind me, hoping, wishing, praying that he would take it and follow me inside.

He took the hand and used it as a pivot point, a handle, a lever, to swing me into the wall. It was siding here, just under the porch, and that was better than the brick on the rest of the house, I told myself, twisting so my hip would hit with the next swing. It was a habit I'd developed when I was pregnant. Whenever you're slammed into a wall, protect your belly, protect the baby. There was no baby now, and my belly would have bruised less than my hip would, but those habits, the old ones, they die hard.

− 3 −

Rise
Sticks and Stones

Mom called me determined, or a Taurus, but Grandma said straight up, "You mean as stubborn as a jackass." Even when I was three and pretending not to understand them, I knew exactly what they meant, and I knew they were right.

That stubborn streak remained strong with each bad relationship. I believed that I could fix it, that I could wait out the bad times and talk some sense into everyone. Of course, I also made secret plans to get away, saving money in my tampon box under the instructions for use, but the fact that my cash would fit unnoticed in my tampon box showed my level of dedication.

I stuck with most of these relationships a lot longer than I should have for a million small reasons that all felt big at the time. I'm stubborn enough to want to see something all the way through, and I believe hard work can fix things when they're broken. My mom's strong religious beliefs were another powerful reason I stayed even when it seemed unlikely I would come out alive. *Stay and pray,* she would say. Because divorce under the wrong circumstances was a sure path to damnation. Larger and more important than all of those reasons, I stayed because of a little old liar called fear.

My kids and I had spent years walking on our tiptoes, which was great for calf development but not so great for posture because of the way we had to duck our heads to avoid sharp, flying words. The bad moments had outweighed the good, but optimism had been pressing her heavy thumb hard on the scale. I would always be an optimist, but I had finally learned to recognize her in the mirror—the twelve-step process had begun. When I found myself alone and in a flattened, hopeless position that must be what addicts call the bottom, I finally believed that there was a top.

Matt and I divorced, and I believed that was a big enough step for the kids and me to rebuild our damaged family. But months later, Hope, the oldest at seventeen, still slept on the floor next to her door, listening. She had seen the most, and she felt the most protective of me and the younger kids. If anyone could prove the stereotype of an oldest child, it was Hope. Her long, dark hair and tiny nose made her a stunning beauty, model-perfect if she could add ten or twelve inches to her five-foot-two frame, but on the inside she had those extra inches and then some. Hope was an organized, calculating, determined force of nature. And somewhere along the line she had become a very angry force, too. Was that one of the twelve steps? Or maybe I was thinking of grief, not recovery. Then again, we were probably navigating the steps of a dozen different traumas at once, in which case, all emotions were justified. Even though Hope's anger threw out stinging words at times, I preferred them to silence.

Fifteen-year-old Drew carried a shotgun shell in his pocket and a chip on his shoulder, but lacked the confidence to use either one effectively. He was the silent one, so much like me it hurt. I could see the things boiling under his surface, though I knew that no one else could. He was almost six feet tall, thin, with loose brown curls that he had kept short until recently. He was devilishly handsome, but lacked the self-assurance to use that superpower. I thought of him as my Mini-Me, but the optimism was weaker in his blood. It was a worrisome combination, the silence without the little voice to cheer him up. I needed a way past his well-structured walls, and I didn't have much time to find it.

Jada and Roman were young enough to pretend they were unaffected, even though Jada's sixth-grade poetry notebook was too full of sunshine and rainbows, too optimistic, when the truth was muddy and shadowed. My elf girl might be the most difficult to heal. I'd passed optimism to her full force, like a congenital disease.

Roman was tiny, thin, and stressed in the honest way only an almost-two-year-old can be—he wanted to be endlessly held and cared for.

Those four green-eyed beauties were my everything. Too many times my determination to give them a perfect life had included giving them a father figure. But I had finally reached my own last straw. I had a good job as a senior computer programmer systems analyst, and I was working hard to grow my side income as a writer. Still, I couldn't afford the big house we were living in on my own, and more than one man had left me with his debt. Our finances were a mess, and the stash at the bottom of my tampon box wasn't going to take me far.

We would have to sell the house. I told myself that was for the best, even though the kids and I had sacrificed for years to have it built. It didn't feel much like a home anymore, and the older kids were afraid there, too. Maybe they had always been, and I had only imagined my silence protecting them. What a weighty little bitch optimism is.

Just after sunset on a cold November night, Hope whisper-yelled down from the balcony, "I swear I see him out there sometimes. Out back in the shadows or in the kitchen window at midnight."

"Who?" I asked, and Drew stomped up the stairs, slamming his bedroom door before I could apologize. After so many years of being a pretender, I had trouble remembering to be honest.

Hope rolled her eyes in that way all seventeen-year-old girls have perfected.

"Who's outside?" Jada asked, running behind Hope with eyes aglow and turban-wrapped hair dripping on her nightshirt, a holey Gumby shirt that I'd worn in junior high and she loved like a blankie.

I leveled a glare at Hope, and she threw her hands up. She hadn't realized Jada was out of the shower. "We were talking about the FedEx guy," I said, slipping comfortably back into my pretender skin.

Jada, the flightiest child I'd ever known, had already forgotten. She giggled, untangling Roman's right hand from Hershey's ear only to find his left hand with a firm grip. The commotion barely disturbed the Lab's nap. We let her sleep in the dining room now, all of us claiming it was to keep her safe from a prowling coyote we'd heard screaming in the forest.

We had been afraid of more than one man over the years. Matt had been the most violent, but he was sane enough to know I had found my courage and bought a gun. After all the late nights of terror with his hands around my throat, Matt had become a very small, pitiful man in my memory. The man Hope saw or imagined out the window was the man we'd left before Matt. His name was Adam. He haunted us because he wasn't sane enough to be afraid. He had been once. He had even been a genius. But there is truly a fine line between genius and insanity, and he had crossed over for good.

He was the weight that held us back from recovery steps. He kept us so tight in our own shells we couldn't reach out, not even to one another.

We lived in virtual silence that fall, waiting for the house to sell, waiting for a new life to start, waiting for our fear to dissipate.

Our nerves were so frazzled that none of us were sleeping. Roman had moved permanently into my bed after three straight nights of me lying on the floor beside the toddler bed, holding his hand. If we had a giant mattress that would hold us all, and we could lock it in a vault at night, maybe then we would sleep. In a cruel twist, having the danger-ous men out of sight, where we couldn't make believe we'd catch a sign of whatever set them off, we were stuck in a state of hypervigilance, waiting for one to appear. Waiting for the next strike, one we'd never see coming.

On the Tuesday before Thanksgiving break, I spent the day pack-ing for a secret getaway. Not only had I kept the idea a secret from the kids, I'd been careful not to write down the address of the cabin I'd rented a couple of hours north of us in the foothills of the Ozark Mountains. It would have been a prettier spot a few weeks ago, before the leaves dropped, but even stark landscapes would be an improve-ment over the view from my kitchen window.

"What happened?" Hope said when she walked through the door and saw the line of suitcases. Then she repeated it with a panicked squeal, "What happened?" The rattle in her voice made it sound raspy and old. "Did he do something? Did he come here?"

I ran down the stairs and nearly slid the last four when I saw how white she'd gone. "Nothing. It's okay." But I was flustered enough that she wasn't convinced. I held both palms up. A surrender. A promise. "We just need to get out of here for a couple days or we're going to lose our minds. No one came here. Nothing happened."

She nodded.

Drew kicked his duffel bag. To him, this would feel like running away, and he wouldn't like that. "Where?" he asked.

How long had it been since he'd put two words together? "I'll tell you in the car." I made a sweeping gesture with my hands. "You've got twenty minutes to grab entertainment for a quiet weekend. I packed your clothes and the basics."

More like forty minutes later and after we'd gone down the driveway and back up again for Jada's shoes—how a kid can get in the car and not notice they aren't wearing any shoes, I will never know—we finally drove north, away from our house that wasn't home. The kids sat straight in their seats, looking forward with their eyes and backward with their minds.

When had we forgotten how to take a road trip? When had we forgotten how to laugh?

Jada livened things up when she paired her phone with the radio and tortured us with a playlist of pop songs remixed by the Chipmunks. Nothing screams road trip like kids complaining about the tunes. It was a start, anyhow. I decided not to save my emergency mom-trick for later; it looked like we were one big catastrophe right from the start. "Cheese Doritos?" I asked, pulling the crinkly bag from the floorboard on the front passenger side, where Hope was tucked in with three bags that wouldn't fit in my Accord's trunk.

It was the closest to happy I'd seen them in a while. Doritos were a rare treat. Years ago, Adam had forbade them in the house because he couldn't stand the smell. Even after he had gone, I let the smell remind me of him. No more. We were letting go of stupid, imaginary boundaries. The car filled with cheesy corn-chip breath. I smiled.

When the kids were full of Doritos and empty of complaints, they started dozing off in the standard pattern of youngest to oldest. Drew was kind enough to kill Jada's music before he slipped into dreamland. It wasn't until Hope's head went slack against a pillow she'd jammed between her seat belt and her cheek that I realized I'd forgotten to tell them where we were going. It was beyond bizarre that none of them had remembered to ask. It made me smile for a second to feel their absolute trust, but then I realized something deeper and sadder was behind their silence. They hadn't asked because it didn't matter. We were going away from the life where bad things had happened, and as far as they were concerned the coordinates of the place we landed were irrelevant.

The road turned hilly and shadowed as we headed toward the mountains. The early sunset in fall and winter used to make me sad, eating away my productive daylight hours inch by inch. But I had become a creature of the night, a shadow who felt safest when no one could see. I crept around the house with the lights off, memorizing how many steps would take me to the staircase and dragging my hand along walls to stay oriented. I'd taken to reading under the covers, sometimes even pulling my laptop under with me to write in a warm bubble that smelled of melting ozone. It was a silly habit for a grown woman, but like it had when I was six, the blanket bubble felt like an impenetrable shield.

The sun was only peeking through on high spots by the time we reached Dover, Arkansas. I started seeing evidence of the tornado that had skipped through the hills in the spring. Oaks that had seen the Civil War were taking their final bow in groves of thinner, more pliable species that had weathered just fine. Small houses with mismatched roof patches and freshly installed storm shelters lined the beast's path. A fireplace that once warmed a family now towered alone at one end of a long concrete pad, swept clean enough for dancing.

Just around a sharp curve, at the top of a small hill, I spotted my dream home. It was two stories with warm brown bricks and dark chocolate shutters. Tall columns on the front porch made it look regal and very Southern. Large flower beds lined the sidewalk, with varying shades of green perennials that looked alive in every season.

I pulled into the drive, and let my mouth hang open. Odds were pretty good no one was home, since the tornado had peeled much of the roof away and the windows had only small, jagged bits of glass hanging stubbornly in the frames. I wondered if the pressure had blown them out or if the local teens and a case of Budweiser had done the job on a Saturday night.

In one of the upstairs windows, a red curtain hung outside, about a foot under the bottom sill, motionless despite the breeze. It was like something out of a postapocalyptic movie, or a stark black-and-white photo shoot where a single focal point had been colored in. The sun lit the edges of everything, blurring the details in the center and making the whole scene muted and surreal.

Nothing could have convinced me not to get out for a closer look. I felt suddenly very strong, bulletproof—even strawproof. The kids would carry on with their naps as long as I left the car running.

Around the west side, a wall had tumbled in an almost perfectly diagonal line from roof to foundation. The upstairs room with the red curtains was still covered enough that I couldn't see in. It didn't bother me, though. I already knew that room as well as I needed to. Behind it, upstairs on the back of the house, was a room fully decorated in pink— not the bright modern pink of plastic toys, but the old-fashioned, pale pink of yesterday. The bed had a lace canopy, and I imagined dolls piled on it. I imagined, too, that it contained a dollhouse made to look exactly like the big house. A tiny replica of a dream. It made me smile.

The last rays of sunset made the master bedroom on the lower floor look alive enough that I looked away, feeling like a Peeping Tom staring into such an intimate space. I couldn't help myself, though: I moved back in for a closer look. Bricks littered the floor and bed like favorite shoes ready to be packed for a trip to Aruba. A dusty red robe hung behind the door, and that more than anything made it feel like a home, like a place where people had not only been alive, but lived. I wished I could meet the woman who had hung red curtains and worn the red robe.

No, that wasn't it at all. I wished I could *be* that woman. She was strong and courageous. She never would have let things get so bad or settled for living so small, so far away from her dreams. She would have stood up and taken charge. Her house belonged to her all the way through. It was a home. Even with the holes, it felt safer than my own.

Broken two-by-fours hung from the upper floor like teeth, but I had the idea they were yawning lazily rather than flexing to clamp down like a guillotine. A long nail hung off the end of a splintery board, as shiny as a freshly minted coin. It fell into my hand almost before I touched it, sun-warmed and filled with potential. I put it in my pocket and pushed my index finger into a cookie-dough-soft piece of Sheet-rock, taking note of how insubstantial it was. A wall, even one that hadn't been pulverized by tornado and rains, was barely stronger than my blanket tent.

I leaned in to see a family photo hanging firm and straight even while the wall disintegrated around it. Dirt clung so heavy on the glass that the people were only silhouettes, but I could see them clearly in my mind's eye. Man, woman, two kids, and a dog. And the woman wore a deep-cut, V-neck shirt. No turtlenecks for her. Caroline, that was her name, or that was what I called her, anyhow. It was a strong name with a lot of history. Someone named Caroline would cross in a wagon train to the west. She would continue with the kids and oxen even after her husband died of pneumonia during a winter storm. She would build her own damn cabin and plant a garden to feed her kids. Someone named Caroline would live.

This someone named Cara had every intention of living, too, even if she was slower to find her strength than Caroline would have been.

A glimmer in the leaves and rubble near the toppled nightstand caught my eye. Jewelry, I thought, maybe something meaningful. Maybe something of Caroline's. Using a long piece of mint-colored crown molding, I swatted away a chunk of plaster. It was a watch.

Tick-tock. Fi-fah.

Had I heard it ticking even before I picked it up? No, this watch was silent. The tick I heard now wasn't ten feet away, but right in my ear, as though the hand wearing it were around my throat. It didn't belong in the peaceful, sleeping house. I didn't want it there. With a slide, swivel, flip of my excavating stick, I hooked a small, bent nail through the band and pulled the watch to me like a dangerous but familiar fish. The crystal had been smashed, stopping the hands both straight up. Midnight. Was that when the tornado hit? I couldn't remember for sure.

Without touching it, I dropped it in a muddy pool and pushed it deep into the soft earth with my stick. Then I lowered a brick on it and piled three more on top of that. A monument, a tombstone, the death of an era.

Feeling light and noble, as though I had done the lonely house a great service, I went back to my wall and leaned inside. Silence. Beautiful, and complete. The nail in my pocket still felt warm against my palm, and I was fully aware that my thoughts and actions were half crazy. But I'd been holding my sanity together in the midst of craziness for so long. Could anyone deny me a small slip when no one was looking, when I was fully and totally alone for the first time in God knows how long?

The room felt like coming home. I had an almost overwhelming urge to step inside and sweep away the flotsam and jetsam. While I had never done major home repairs, I knew how to use a hammer well enough that I figured I could put the wall back up if I set my mind to it. The frame looked simple, with Sheetrock on the inside and a flat board under the brick outside. In fact, the kids and I could fix the entire place, make it a home again, hang a bird feeder over the dining-room window and build a matching house for Hershey under the big hickory tree.

It was ridiculous, of course it was, but I couldn't shake the idea. I'd fallen instantly in love with everything about the place, even though nothing about it was practical. It was hours away from the kids' schools and my programming job and freelance work with the newspaper in Little Rock. But what if I found another place like this, somewhere closer, somewhere perfect?

I turned and walked slowly back to the car, smiling, energized. What if we didn't find a tornado-ravaged house, but a small spot of land, and just built the whole thing exactly how we wanted it? I looked back. Exactly like this would do.

I'd grown up in Wisconsin and learned early to use a hatchet to knock small limbs off trees Dad felled for firewood. I had made a built-in bookcase in the first house I bought, and used a jigsaw to make a plywood beanbag toss for the kids. Building a house was just a repetition of those skills: measure, cut, nail. Why couldn't I build a house?

I'd hang red drapes in that second-floor bedroom, up high and safe from Peeping Toms, and make it mine. The supplies weren't the expensive part of building a house, it was the labor.

Even though I laughed over the image of the kids and me as a construction team, I liked the idea a lot. Sure, it was a little nuts, but it was the first workable plan I'd come up with that fit our limited finances. We could do it. I knew we could. Building a house would prove we were strong. It would prove that despite my stupidity in staying with idiots for so long, I was still intelligent. It would prove so many things—most of all that we were alive.

The kids slept away the final hour to the cabin while I dreamed up things that feel possible only when you are physically and emotionally exhausted on a road trip. The hypnotic white lines flashing subliminal messages that you are a superhero, that anything is possible, that you are good, that you are worthy.

"We're here!" I sang out when I'd backed as close as I could to the path leading away from a quaint board carved with the name Hickory Haven. I'd had to fight the urge to say, *We're home*. My new habit seemed to be feeling more at home in every shelter but the place we lived.

"Camping?" Drew yawned.

"God, it better not be," Hope said, nose pressed against the window.

"Camping!" Jada squealed, making Roman giggle and kick his feet.

"Marshmallows!" he chimed.

"Not the rustic sort. I don't have the energy. See that light?" I pointed down the dark path. "Our cabin away from home. Our weekend retreat."

My kids weren't often complainers. In the way some play the "so many people have it worse than us" game to lift their spirits, my kids lived with a constant mind-set of "we know how bad it can get, and this is nothing." We didn't need games to quiet our grievances.

Drew hauled the cooler while the girls and I toted backpacks and duffels. Roman ran along beside us down the path. "Who! Who! Who!" he chanted, as wide-eyed as the owl he mimicked while fear and excitement battled for command of his mind. He'd never been in a forest at night. Every new noise made him toddle a little faster, but he was growing independent enough to resist clinging to my legs.

When he veered close, index finger in his mouth and lip quivering over a ghostly scream that had sent a shiver down my spine, too, I gave him an ultimatum: "It's you or the bag of cupcakes, kid. And I'm hungry enough to make it a real dilemma." The cabin was in sight by then, and he pumped his legs faster to catch up with Jada and Drew. Hope, my girly-girl, was bringing up the rear. She was a city mouse. But her hesitation was more than an aversion to forest things. She knew the most dangerous part of hiding was that we'd have to go back again.

We ate, read, ate, slept, and then woke up to eat more before taking a morning nap. When had basic functions like changing clothes become such an effort? The Ozark mountain cabin was the perfect, quiet getaway to spend hours looking out over the mountains contemplating my future. Who am I kidding? That's what it *would* have been, without four restless kids.

I was sitting at the table, arranging silverware into a house plan while Jada and Hope started their tenth snippy argument of the morning. When I started fantasizing about running down the side of the mountain to hide behind a tree until the vacation was over, I jumped up and yelled loud enough to make Drew jump, "Treasure hunt! It'll blow some stink off you," giving them the mom-glare that said it wasn't optional.

I grabbed a handful of plastic shopping bags. "Best find gets a prize." Having treasure hunts instead of walks was a habit my mom had started when I was a little girl. Obviously, she had been born an optimist, too. She was in Wisconsin that fall, visiting her siblings. My mom was my best friend—my only friend—but even she didn't know everything that had happened with Matt and Adam. Shame is the best secret keeper.

Jada ran ahead, with Drew keeping an eye on her so he wouldn't have to make small talk with me. Hope helped me with Roman, herding him along the path and pulling him away from a fuzzy blob of fungus and then a pile of scat, all the while planning an elaborate Christmas party aloud. Parties were her thing.

By the time Jada ran back, crying over a scraped knee, I discovered that my plastic bag was filled to the top while everyone else's were empty balls in their fists. Roman bawled a sympathy wail for Jada's knee, so obviously fake I was confident he wouldn't make his million in Hollywood.

"Firewood?" Drew asked, his left eyebrow angled up like he'd only just noticed his mother was slap-ass nuts.

"No. I don't . . . I'm not sure . . ." But then I looked down at the bag full of sticks and knew exactly what I intended to do with them. And I also remembered that—especially with Drew—the time for tall tales had ended. "I was thinking of making my dream house. Like your old Lincoln logs. Remember the elaborate houses we used to make?"

I found a Band-Aid in my mini backpack and stretched it across Jada's knee. She ran off down the path without pausing to wipe her tears or pull her pant leg back down to her ankle.

Drew stretched his stride to put himself halfway between Jada and me, just far enough that conversation wasn't comfortable. But then he leaned down and picked up a stick, took a few steps, snagged another, and then one more. Hope must have finished her Christmas plan and had moved on to her ideal Christmas wedding venue—never mind that she didn't have a boyfriend—complete with wine-colored roses and invitations printed on vintage wrapping paper. All the while, Drew filled his bag with sticks. Out of the corner of my eye, I caught Hope gathering them, too. Stop the world and let me off: Hope had touched nature.

"Pee-pee," Roman said, tucking his hand between his legs and doing a little dance.

"You get to pee-pee on your first tree!" I announced, helping him drop gray fleece pants and Spider-Man underwear to his knees. I worried for a split second that he wouldn't go outside and I'd have to carry a soggy boy all the way back to the cabin. But peeing outdoors is a universal pleasure for human males, and he joined his band of brothers with a deep laugh, chin pressed against his chest.

By the time our noses and fingers were red and tingly from the cold and Roman had marked his territory on three trees, we headed back to Hickory Haven carrying five bags of sticks, one storm-damaged bird nest, and a handful of the most beautiful rocks Jada had ever seen, which appeared as unique as street gravel.

"Was the clock right when we left?" Hope asked, adjusting the time on the microwave to match her cell.

"We're on vacation," I answered. "There is no such thing as a clock." But her forehead had gone all bunchy and she was eyeing the clock on the fireplace mantel, which was off by several hours. So I wasn't the only one who worried about someone coming in and changing things, moving them around to send us messages. That shouldn't surprise me. Thankfully she was only worried about the change, though, not reminded of the sound a watch makes right up close to your ear through adrenaline-flooded eardrums.

"Ours used to change." She waved at the clocks. "A long time ago. Someone used to come in and change the clocks to all different times."

I hadn't known that, and it bothered me that she hadn't told me she set them all right. It also made me wonder what else Adam had done that I didn't know about from all the long years when I wasn't the only one keeping secrets.

"People could come in from different time zones and set the clocks to their own times. I've done that in hotels to avoid jet lag." I held her gaze. "No one knows where we are. No one was in here."

I believed I was telling the truth, and she could see that, but she was still afraid.

Oblivious to the fungus and a few tiny spiders, Drew dumped his treasure bag onto the small kitchen table. We each took a chair, as orchestrated as though we did this every day of the week, and began stacking the sticks into a floor plan.

Roman sat at my feet with three inverted pots and a Tupperware bowl, whacking a rhythm with two thin sticks like he'd been born to thump skins in a garage band. Speaking of garages, my three-car stick addition was coming together nicely, but it wasn't staying together. When anyone breathed wrong, or bumped the table with an elbow, the sticks shifted into an abstract art form. Drew bit his lower lip, inhaled dramatically, and then went back to carefully placing sticks, glaring like his willpower alone would keep them in place.

"Where's the closest grocery? We should have Thanksgiving tomorrow," Hope said from the refrigerator where she was pulling out cold cuts for supper.

"That's right. Tomorrow is Thanksgiving. The whole trip was last-minute. I was just thinking sandwiches would be simple." I felt bad. Tradition was important, especially when everything had gone so topsy-turvy. "I should've at least grabbed smoked turkey at the deli instead of maple ham."

"Jada and I will do it," Hope said, leveling a glare over my shoulder at Jada, making it clear that despite Jada's lack of interest in planning or preparing Thanksgiving dinner, she was damn well going to do it.

I hid a smile. It would be good for the girls to do something together. As the oldest child and a junior in high school, Hope loved taking charge, which never went over well with free-spirited Jada. She was in the sixth grade and exercising her preteen rebellion whenever a task looked too much like work. "There's a small market about five miles back. It won't have a great selection, but I'll bet you guys can come up with something. It'll be fun."

Hope and Jada disappeared up to the loft with a notebook and a pencil to plan our feast. If they made it back down without bloodshed, it would be a miracle.

"There's a sewing kit out in the trunk," I told Drew. "Think we could tie these corners together so we don't have to build the same thing over and over again?"

He shrugged and went out with the car keys. When he didn't come right back in, I decided not to go looking. I hadn't worked out how to help my man-child through the anger and guilt of the past, let alone how to build a future. We were sitting side by side building a stick house together, like the three little pigs, and maybe right now that was enough.

I twirled my magic nail—that's how I started thinking of it, like a magic bean that might sprout a house—between my fingers until Roman noticed and grunted at it.

"Mine," he said.

"Yours," I agreed, pulling a bait and switch with a cookie.

"Om-nom-nom." He rocked sideways while he walked across the room like Godzilla taking Tokyo. "Cookie Monster. Om-nom-nom."

Drew pushed through the door with the sewing kit under his arm and a fistful of two-foot-long sticks.

Roman ran at him, squealing. "Cookie Monster!"

Since Drew had been the one to make up the game, he gave chase, stomping and roaring while Roman giggled himself into a case of the hiccups.

I doodled a floor plan on a three-by-five notepad next to the phone. Drew flopped into his chair and stared at the plan before taking the pencil and pad to draw his version on the next page.

Hope and Jada stomped down the stairs, louder than a herd of elephants. No blood had been shed that I could see, but Jada's nose was red and her eyes were puffy. I wanted to hug her, but she didn't ask and I let her keep her dignity. "We won't be gone long," Hope said, grabbing the keys from the table and shaking a paper. "We have a list."

No one could plan a meal or a party like Hope, but I worried about what would happen when she got to the miniature grocery store and found them lacking most of her essentials.

"Be flexible," I told her, thumping my foot against Drew's shin when he smirked. "It's not a Kroger. It's more for emergency camping supplies than holiday feasts."

Drew tossed the drawing pad back to me. In his version, he'd labeled the bedrooms with our initials and wrote "Harry Potter Cupboard" next to the staircase, which made me smile. Even after everything he'd been through, he still believed in magic. I flipped to the next page, started with his basic plan, made a few changes, and Frisbeed it back to him. I'd added a room labeled "Future Library," which could be a bedroom until a kid or two went to college.

He pursed his lips to one side, biting the inside of his cheek, a habit I'd tried to break him of since his first molars broke through. He nodded and released his cheek without me having to tap it and remind him. On the next page he sketched the front of the house, placing the windows and door so they would match up with what we had wordlessly agreed on for the interior.

It was nothing complex, just a two-story rectangle with the bedrooms upstairs and the den, kitchen, dining room, and library downstairs. I added shutters to the windows, labeled them "chocolate brown," and sketched a porch with tall columns. Drew raised his eyebrows and nodded.

He took the pencil and added a shop. I added a tree house, so he put in a zip line and a rock wall. "Diamond Mine," I wrote in a circle in the back lawn near the tree house. He added a portal to an alternate reality, but then flipped back to the interior drawing of the upstairs and penciled in toilets and showers while I rolled a ball to Roman.

What was I thinking? Giving these kids false hope, letting them plan for a future house that was as impossibly beyond our reach as the portal to another dimension. I pulled the nail out, twirling it between my fingers while Roman played basketball in a laundry basket. Then he climbed in and said, "I'm a boat. Whee!"

He jumped, knocking his boat over when the door flew open. He caught himself on his hands but whimpered anyhow. The blood rushed in my ears like a storm. Jada and Hope looked like pack mules, loaded down with shopping bags and pink-cheeked from the walk in the cold. But something was very wrong. Hope's face was drawn and pale, and I could hear her breath rattling in and out from across the room. Drew stood up so fast his chair spilled over like Roman's basket boat.

"Thump," Roman said, whacking his palms against the worn wood floor. "Thump. Thump. Thump."

Drew was behind Hope, locking the dead bolt and stringing the chain in place before I had made it to my feet.

"What?" I asked in a breathy whisper. "What happened?"

Hope cut her eyes at Jada. But I waved my hand. "We aren't pretending anymore. We aren't covering things up for anyone. We can say things that are true." I wanted to mean it, to really, fully mean it, but I was still as afraid to speak some things aloud as I was to hear them.

"I think a car followed us out of the parking lot and all the way until I turned on the gravel drive." She swallowed hard, hugging the shopping bags hard enough that bread or eggs would have to be salvaged as French toast. "I should have gone another way. I should have tried to lose him."

Drew leaned forward, arms waving. "Don't you ever drive around like a maniac trying to lose someone. You did the right thing. Stay inside. We're calling the police."

Jada let go of her bags and ran upstairs. It was time for me to talk to her. Tell her some hard truths. Not everything. The big kids didn't know everything, or even half of everything, but enough that she would stay alert. She had been a toddler when I'd married Adam and his mind was attacked by schizophrenia months later. He had turned into someone so terrifying that years after the divorce we still viewed the world through peepholes and rearview mirrors.

I hooked my arms through Hope's shopping bags. "We're fine. No one can possibly know where we are."

"You can't know that!" she yelled.

"I made the reservation from a coffee shop and paid by check with a new account. We didn't pack a thing until the day we left, and I didn't even tell you guys where we were going. You didn't know until we pulled up and unloaded the car. I stopped several times along the way in remote locations where I would have seen anyone following." Instantly, I regretted telling them so much. "We're safe." They were wide-eyed and still, processing what it all meant. Calculating our level of danger. Code red. Severe.

Roman tugged at my pant leg and I hoisted him onto my hip.

As much as I wanted to believe he was immune, he could sense the fear and anger flowing thick enough around our ankles to float his little boat.

By trying to reassure them, I had let them know that we really could be in danger and, more important, had made hiding feel necessary. Was there such a thing as too much truth? I believed there was, and I had just crossed a dangerous line. Then again, if they didn't know about the danger, they wouldn't be on guard. Life had gotten too complicated, too gray. I missed the good old days when I was young, I knew every-thing, and the world was drawn in stark lines of black and white.

Drew and I carried the groceries to the kitchen and loaded the fridge.

"I bought ice cream," Hope said, "and a brownie mix. Let's pig out tonight and drown the fat in holiday food tomorrow."

"I'm dying for ice cream," Roman said with a dramatic hand to his forehead. The surface tension broke with our laughter even if the wires underneath were still tight with fear.

I went up to talk with Jada while they finished stowing the grocer-ies and started baking the brownies. When we came down, with Jada more quiet and subdued than any free-minded hippie child should ever be, I noticed that all the shades and curtains were closed. The kitchen window was covered with a sheet of newspaper.

I wanted to scream and rip it all down. My kids shouldn't have to be afraid. They shouldn't have to hide like criminals. They deserved to feel safe in a Thanksgiving cabin in the woods. They deserved to feel safe at home. I squeezed the nail in my pocket until it dug a hole in my palm. Next I'd be fashioning a crown of thorny sticks. I didn't want the nail to turn me into a sacrifice, a victim; I wanted its magic to save us. But what if there wasn't enough magic in the world to keep us safe?

Four bottles of white school glue lined the edge of the table by our model house. Jada sat down and piled tiny twigs into a stick figure. I ripped a napkin into the shape of a dress. She took it without meeting my eyes. If her tiny people had faces, they would be weeping.

Drew sat next to her, his eyes alight, anxious to try out the glue. Instead, he flipped to the upstairs page of our mutely drawn house plans, pointing out Jada's initials on a bedroom. He sketched a tiny bed in one corner, then sketched a huge circle next to it and wrote, "Hot Tub." She nodded, and stretched her lips sideways in what she may have thought approximated a smile, and then went back to her stick figures.

I ripped out a piece of Hope's notebook paper and handed it to Jada with a bottle of glue. "We'll have to clear this away for our feast tomorrow. Anything you want to keep will have to be glued to something mobile," I said.

She nodded, silent and no doubt imagining scenes I didn't want to see. She made globby white lines and began moving her stick person to the paper. I found scissors in the kitchen and gave them to her with a floral paper towel that would make more fashionable dresses than the plain white napkin I'd started her out with.

Drew began gluing the stick house together in an exact replica of our plan while I stacked firewood into a crude newspaper-filled pyramid in the fireplace and lit it. I had the impression we were in for a long, sleepless night. The fact that we were about to load up on peanut-butter ice cream and brownies with fudge swirls would barely contribute to the insomnia, but we would all blame it on that in the morning.

Honesty was a skill we'd all have to work to master. It was as big a challenge as banishing the ghosts.

– 4 –

Fall
What I Learned in First Grade

It takes years to build a mind-set of defeat. Girls are at a higher risk with lower pay, lesser jobs, and even many gods declaring them a step or two lower than their male counterparts. But if you toss a few bullies in the mix, anyone can declare themselves powerless.

My brother and I grew up swinging wildly from the branches of young pines on forty acres in rural Wisconsin. John was three years older than me, so he was allowed to do more things. But he was never a match for kids his own age, always a step or two behind in strength, lessons, and social behavior.

None of that mattered to me before I joined him at elementary school, though. We were Tarzan and Jane with our black poodle mix, Snoopy, running along the forest floor beneath us. Forty acres was Mom and Dad's claim, but—land titles be damned—John and I staked out hundreds of country acres as our personal playground.

For practical and survival reasons, our most prized possessions were matching pocketknives. Dad had melted our names into the fake bone handles in crooked cursive. With these sharp little marvels we whittled spear tips, sawed ropes, and dug animal traps. And when the blades bent sideways, we hammered them flat on the anvil behind the garage. Occasionally, when our adventure demanded a larger blade, John snuck a rusty hatchet into our afternoon picnic satchel.

On the surface, it was an idyllic life start. But like passengers on the *Titanic,* I learned that the surface view can be a bitch of a liar.

The year I turned six I stole a book titled *Make It Yourself* from Mom's book-club mailing. I expected my pocketknife to be the only tool needed to make the sweaters and turquoise afghan on the cover, so I was disappointed to learn about knitting needles and crochet hooks. I found a ball of white cotton string Dad used to mark vegetable rows in the garden. Then I eventually created makeshift knitting needles out of long, skinny paintbrushes and hid in the basement with them, terrified that I'd be caught while I followed the step-by-step pictures. I'd never seen a six-year-old knitting. I'd never seen anyone knitting. But in cartoons it was for wise old women in rocking chairs. Like staying up late to watch horror movies or drinking beer, knitting was not for children.

John caught me knitting and told Mom, who immediately bought me a set of emerald-green knitting needles and gave me a ball of orange yarn that had been her mother's. A skinny child with knitting needles turns invisible in the shadowed corners of a room, so I spent a lot of time listening and thinking that fall of my first-grade year.

My grandma Laura, Mom's mama, had just died, and our family dynamics had shifted. Mom was sad in an aching sort of way that I could see even when her back was to me. Her head was lower, curtaining her brown eyes with her long dark hair, and her shoulders slumped; but it was more than that, more than just the heaviness of grief pushing down. As she canned tomatoes that autumn over the old gas stove, every lift of her arm, every step from the stove to the sink was lighter, as though she were growing transparent and would soon float away to wherever her mama had gone.

From the dining-room table I kept watch through my clicking emerald needles, careful not to drop a stitch. The way the string looped, tied, and held everything together was soothing. I believed that if I could tie enough knots it would hold us all together.

First grade had put me in the same school as my brother, and that changed everything. It taught me to hide, to stay quiet, and it taught me to hate. Not the gentle you're-not-my-friend hate of finicky first graders, but the real, vehement thing, ugly, dark, and lasting. The fullness of hate took me by surprise, since my mom was a fanatically religious woman who drove me to church three times a week and carried her Bible into the grocery store and on walks down deserted country roads. "You have to forgive no matter what," she told me, "or you'll burn in hell."

Burning in hell sounded a lot less pleasant than snuggling up in front of our fireplace, but I couldn't fully subscribe to the idea that my hate was wrong. Mom said even if the truck that had hit my brother and almost killed him that year would have actually taken him from us, she would have forgiven the man who was driving. God commanded that. I tried to be as light and good as she was and believe that suffering was all for a bigger purpose, for some plan, but I wanted a more immediate answer.

As luck would have it, Dad was an atheist. This was really convenient whenever I wanted to subscribe to an alternative view, but less than pleasant for the enormous weight of tension and disagreement between my polar-opposite parents. My childhood self most resembled a tightrope walker dodging projectiles. Every spoken word was up for debate, every activity; even my thoughts had to be weighed and weeded to a middle ground that I hoped might be acceptable to both. The atmosphere turned me into a listener, a thinker, and a careful negotiator.

But most of all, I became a dreamer, creating magical realms of Wisconsin winter igloos or summer forts that gave me an escape. And if I wasn't able to sneak away to one of my hideouts, I availed myself of books. I read about aliens, elves, and unicorns; I spent several years believing I could develop telepathy followed by several more pretending I lived in Middle Earth. In the realms of my books, people understood one another at the end. Everyone compromised. Every problem was wrapped up nice and neat.

The endless conflict and my adopted role as negotiator had little to do with my discovery of hatred, though. I found that on the school bus and in the halls of Lemonweir Elementary School. Antibullying wasn't a thing then. In fact, even teachers and bus drivers were bullies, and no one ever called them out for it. Maybe they had the idea that it was a way to toughen the weak, but I doubt it was anything so noble. Humans have traditionally picked on the weak to make themselves feel powerful, and there is nothing noble about that. In my mind, there is nothing forgivable about it either.

My brother was weak. He was small and his head was misshapen from a premature birth and a host of problems that went undiagnosed in those days. Getting hit by a truck while we played in a flooded, closed street had set him back even further, with a limp and less confidence. The poor kid never had a chance.

As we stepped on the bus every morning he was tripped, smacked in the head, spit at, and slammed against seats and windows. It was a ten-mile ride into school on gravel country roads. Ten miles turns out to be just the distance needed to destroy a small boy for good and take a decent chunk of his little sister along with him. The bus driver vacillated between ignoring the bullies and essentially joining them by punishing my puny brother for the disturbances. At one point she had a seat belt installed at the front of the bus to keep him safely seated; unfortunately it also served to hold him still for the poundings. There was no escape.

School was more of the same. I watched my brother's face crack against the porcelain water fountain when he leaned in for a drink. I saw the torture on the playground and his fear of going into the bathroom, where anyone might be waiting. His glasses were continually broken by fists, feet, and flying books. He was sent to the office for punishment. He was a tiny, quiet problem.

And when we got home, the punishment continued, because his glasses were broken, because the school called again, because he might get kicked off the bus, or because he stole twenty dollars from my mom's purse to try buying a friend for just one day of peace.

Mom was powerless, not allowed to own a car because it would take her to more religious activities. I was the smallest, skinniest kid in my class, too shy to speak, too weak to fight, a failure at the telekinetic powers I needed to attack the bullies.

The most important lessons I learned in school were how to be powerless, how to take a punch, and how to hate in silence. I learned that being a tattletale makes the bullies hit harder, and no one, not even your family, can save you.

Truth Tellers

Since sleep wasn't on our menu at the Thanksgiving cabin, but an enormous meal was, we spent the night alternating between the stick-house design and helping Hope prepare green-bean casserole, a swanky eight-cheese macaroni dish, and a pie. For our feast the next day we would just sit back and smell it baking alongside the peppered ham. We had a lot to be thankful for.

Drew and I worked out the lower level of the house, spreading extra glue on the structural pieces and spending an inordinate amount of time getting the staircase right. I made doors with pieces of cardboard, and hinged them in place with loops of thread from the sewing kit. My library had French doors with glass panels made out of plastic wrap from a block of cheese.

Roman handed Drew a chunk of bark the size of a domino. "Swing."

"I'll put it right here," Drew said, "so Mommy can watch you from her library window."

"No. Here." Roman moved the bark swing deliberately to the side of the house, sounding exasperated, like Drew should know where the swing belonged.

When the first floor was mostly complete, we carefully slid the structure onto a cereal box that had been cut at the seams and spread flat. I moved it to the hearth, where the fire would dry it quickly. Roman had fallen asleep by then, so it was safe from his drummer hands.

We started on the second floor while Hope and Jada made furniture out of sticks, cardboard, and anything else they could think of. A milk top made the coffee table, and water-bottle pieces had been turned into bathtubs and television screens. When I stood up to stretch at one A.M., I went for a glass of juice. I laughed at the state of the refrigerator. Foil casseroles filled with Thanksgiving treats filled the bottom two layers, which was normal enough. But on the other shelves and in the door, every container was missing bits and pieces that had been cut away and turned into furniture or decoration. The covers were gone from the mini tub of butter, the milk, and the juice. Labels were peeled away from the mustard and mayonnaise, and the entire top of the egg carton was gone. If this went on much longer they would be carving lounge chairs from blocks of cheddar.

Crafts and projects had always been part of our lives, but never like this, never so focused and certainly not with a purpose that captured the girls and Drew with equal and united energy.

I sat across from Drew and straightened a bedroom wall, but my energy was sapped and no amount of juice revived me. Jada had crashed more than an hour ago, one arm and one leg draped off the sofa. She was the only morning person in the family, so she was always the first to fall asleep, sometimes even before Roman. "I'm fading, guys. Roman will be up in a couple hours so I'm going to sleep awhile." Drew and Hope made distant "Umm-hmm" noises without looking up. The design and division of labor were remarkably organized even though we rarely said a word aloud. We were united with a single, cohesive vision and purpose.

I climbed in the bed next to Roman, expecting to crash fast. But the night noises in the middle of the forest were foreign. Every scrape and scurry made me wonder if Hope had been right, if maybe someone had followed us after all. Recurring nightmares pulled me into a state of semirest with an unwelcome familiarity. The location and small details changed, but I was always inside a house, trying to lock a door that wouldn't lock. Either the lock would be broken or it would spin back around and unlock itself. With slow, methodical steps, the danger crept closer to my unlockable door. I woke at sunrise in a cold sweat with an irrational level of terror.

I slipped my shoes and coat on and grabbed my car keys and cell. The covered windows and locked doors were making me more afraid, not less. I needed out, even if it was just for a few minutes. Using the residual nightmare adrenaline, I ran full speed up the path, tugged open the driver's-side door, and sat, tucking my hands under my arms in the cold morning air. Then, to keep from crying, because I hated crying, I started straightening things in the car. Dorito crumbs, napkins, earbuds, I worked over anything out of place—and there was plenty of it to keep me busy.

I ran across the stack of mail I'd grabbed on our way out of town, and the ordinariness of the gas bill and preapproved credit-card applications first calmed and then angered me. I didn't want same-old, same-old. We needed something new. Something big. Something that changed the way we saw ourselves. We needed to replace the victims we'd become with heroes. No matter how hard I tried to see that possibility as the truth, it felt like make-believe, like another lie I would start and the kids would dutifully repeat.

I threw open the car door and jumped out, snowing bits of napkin and Doritos onto the leaves and gravel. Slowly, I walked back to the cabin. By the time I reached the porch, the idea had grown larger. *We're free. We can do anything.*

But before I went inside, I still checked the window to see if I could see in around the shade. It was sealed tight, and I left it that way. The door was unlocked, which reminded me of my nightmare even though I knew I was the one who had left it unlocked. Okay, so we were on our way to being free, but we weren't there yet.

Jada was awake. I could hear her cards slapping the coffee table in a game of solitaire. She would cheat and win every game, and Hope would be shocked every time. I joined her, happy that Roman was sleeping in. We worked together, tossing cards in place like it was a timed, world-record-setting event. "Hope is afraid," she said, illegally sliding an upside-down card out from under a king.

"When we don't understand what someone is thinking, it can scare us," I said, hating my pretending after vowing that I wouldn't cover up for anyone anymore. But what could I do? You can't ever unlearn a thing. I was still pretending that it wasn't too late, that I could protect her. It was one of the last big lies I ever told myself.

"What are you thinking, Mommy?"

"I'm thinking after breakfast we should go for another treasure hunt while Thanksgiving is in the oven."

"I want cookies," Roman said, scooting backward down the stairs and stopping every other step to push Peek-a-boo, his ratty, one-eyed, stuffed cat, down ahead of him.

"We're having pancake cookies," I said, holding my arms out. He climbed into my lap and melted against me in the way only sleepy two-year-olds have mastered.

The blueberry pancakes woke the teenagers—or maybe that was the bacon—and they made adjustments and repairs to the stick house while they crammed maple-syrup lumps in their mouths so fast they had to be swallowing them whole.

For the next two days, we ate, built, walked, and then started the cycle over on repeat. We scrapped our plans to go hiking along the Buffalo River. Everyone was content to stay in with the project and go on occasional forest excursions for more twigs, nuts, and forest scraps. It was the most thankful Thanksgiving I could remember.

Saturday night, our last at the cabin, we packed most of our things, pretending all the while that it didn't really mean we were going back to our house. I climbed into bed feeling completely safe for the first time in years. The curtains and shades were all tucked down tight, the door was triple-locked, and the newspaper was still taped over the kitchen window. But hey, whatever it takes.

I sank into the too-soft mattress with a smile while the idea of being all the way safe wrapped around me. In the morning I wouldn't have to tiptoe around any man, or test his mood. I no longer had to weigh each word or send warning looks to the kids: Careful, it's one of those days. Stay clear. Don't rock the boat. I could sleep straight through until morning. No one would wake me with telltale breathing, wild yelling, or frantic whispers about the corporations pursuing his patents. No hands around my neck.

I rolled onto my side, covering my ear with the blanket like my mom had when I was little. She had tucked her dad's wool army blanket between two thinner, softer ones, telling me that wool was not only the warmest sort of blanket but the only sort that made people dream brighter dreams. I still slept under a wool comforter in the winter, and now more than ever, I believed in dreams.

Only a few experiences in my life felt so profound while they were happening that I consciously tucked them away as a permanent memory. This was one of those moments, feeling safe in my bed for the first time in . . . Geez, how long was it? Eleven years? More? For the rest of my life, I would pull out this moment every single night when I climbed into bed. I would smile and remember that I was safe, that I could sleep straight until sunrise without fear, and I would also remember the thousands of women and children who hadn't made it that far yet.

I would remember that I was a very fortunate girl.

Sunday morning started with the last of the peppered ham and pancakes—or pancake cookies if you were two and a picky eater. We had learned to call all meat chicken and tack the word cookie on to just about every other food. As every ad exec and mom knows, it's all in the packaging. But no amount of catchy packaging was going to smooth the scowls away from the older kids. The three of them looked like they were eating sand cakes, and calling them sand cookies wasn't going to do the trick.

I pretended that a couple of happy nights knowing I was safe would hold me for a long time, but in reality it was just enough to tease me into wanting that sort of thing full-time. *Don't be greedy,* I told myself. *Be patient.* But I wanted to dropkick that patronizing voice into next week. I was sick and damn tired of being patient. If wanting to sleep without fear was greedy then I was damn well ready to accept the label. I smiled and squeezed the nail in my pocket. Already I felt more like the woman who had hung the red curtains, my imagined Caroline, than I had a few days ago.

Drew practically growled when he caught me smiling. He had been wrapping our stick house with pages torn from the yellow pages. I hadn't yelled at him for destroying the phone book. Not many people bothered with yellow pages anymore, and our house—our dream—had to be protected.

"We'll get it home safe," I told him, "even if we have to leave one of your siblings behind."

"Not me!" Jada yelled, poking a broom under the sofa to scoop out her socks.

"Me!" Roman yelled. "Pick me!"

I scooped him up and buried my face in his tummy, blowing

raspberries. "I'll pick you for the tickle-monster attack. That's what I'll do!" When he'd giggled himself into the hiccups, I put him down and he ran down the path three steps ahead of me. The first load to the car was the heaviest. The kids followed, slow and quiet.

Despite the fact that we'd eaten most of the food we'd brought, and the food the girls picked up for our feast, it looked like we were taking back more than we had brought.

The stick house fit in the trunk as long as three shopping bags of laundry rode on the floorboards around the kids' feet. With a final walk-through to collect all the things Jada had left behind, we said a sad good-bye to Hickory Haven.

Per usual, the kids conked out quickly, or at least I thought they did. When we were about a mile from my tornado house, I got a better look at Drew in the passenger seat and realized he had probably been faking it for the whole hour. "I'd like to show you a house," I whispered.

He sat up, eyes open behind his sunglasses, not even bothering to fake a yawn or stretch. His left earbud dropped to his shoulder.

Come out, come out, wherever you are! I wanted to sing. It had worked when he was Roman's age and hiding from something he was afraid to look in the eye.

When I pulled into the drive, I could see it was like coming home for him, too. He wasn't a little boy anymore. He was a teenager who had seen more of the harsh realities of life than a lot of grown men. Before I had the car at a complete stop, he opened his door and his right foot skimmed over the leaf-cluttered driveway.

I stayed in my seat, twirling the nail between my fingers. The house had already given me what I needed, even though I couldn't put that thing into words. Courage, that was part of it, but also vision. Hope?

Drew rounded the side of the house opposite the master bedroom. I had no idea what he would find, but I was sure it would be exactly what he needed. The girls needed things, too, but I didn't think they were going to find them here at the edge of the storm damage. Their healing would take more time. They would need to travel a lot closer to the eye of the storm. I was afraid for them. But we had lived under a dark cloud for so long that I wasn't as frightened as I should have been. I was desensitized in the same way as a child who grows up next to an artillery range and doesn't go inside when he hears thunder, dismissing every warning boom as just another background explosion.

A shadow moved past the dining-room window and I jumped, almost dropped my nail. Not only because I worried for a second that Drew had gone inside, but because there was no way I could know that window was the dining room. I knew it, though, as definitely as I knew that Drew hadn't gone in, that whatever shadow I'd seen had come from inside of me. I'd spent weeks, even years, trying to piece together Matt's and Adam's truths, and now I was the one left fractured and wandering empty houses like a lost spirit. I clung to Caroline's nail, needing her strength until I could believe in my own and stitch my shadow back in place. The red curtains snapped in the wind and I shivered.

Inch by inch, I compared the layout of the house to the one Drew and I had drawn and then made out of sticks. We had worked it out together, one room at a time, vetoing one another's ideas along the way, the whole thing accomplished without a word. Yet I knew beyond any shadow of a doubt that our stick house would match this one, probably to exact scale, room for room, inch for inch. My library was where the master bedroom was here, though, because I was planning to sleep upstairs, closer to the clouds than the earth.

A tiny bird landed near the chocolate-colored front door. I looked back at the girls and Roman, confirming that they were asleep for real. I could see the blue milk-lid coffee table in our stick house and had the idea that even the girls' furniture and decorations would match those in the house in front of us. I hadn't noticed a swing in the backyard, but I knew that Roman's swing was there, too, exactly where he told Drew to put it.

The next handful of breaths came so fast and loud that I worried I'd wake them all. Had I lost my mind? Had I been possessed? Had we all?

The nail kept spinning between my fingers, warm and almost alive. I blew out a breath. *Calm the hell down before you throw the baby out with the bathwater.* I wasn't even sure what that meant, but it made me think of my grandmother, and her memory calmed me. I stared at the house, trying to see it through someone else's eyes. It wasn't the most beautiful house I'd ever seen, just a big, plain box. But it was something . . . something to me. I didn't want to know the rest of the house's story. That was the past, and I was never looking to the past again. From now on, the kids and I were all about the future. A good future filled with good fortune.

Drew came back around the same side of the house where he had disappeared, right hand in his pocket. I wouldn't ask him what he had found, or more likely what had found him. Like the nail, warm and promising in my palm, it would be just the thing he needed.

He was smiling when he sat down. It wasn't a full-out foolish grin or anything; in fact, it looked more like the frown he'd maintained the past couple of years had relaxed into a neutral expression, but that was closer to a smile than we'd had in a long time. The earbuds hung loose from his back pocket and he left them there. If I'd learned that they hadn't worked for six months, it wouldn't have surprised me. They were a mask he no longer needed.

When I looped my arm around his seat and turned to back the car out, a little "Oouu" escaped. The girls and Roman were wide awake and staring at the house, riveted. I smiled a little and waited, just in case I'd been wrong and one of them did need to get out and look around. But where this house was concerned, I was dead right every time. I eased the car sideways off the driveway, slower than I needed to, and paused there, angled so they could get a good look out the side windows.

They didn't say anything; none of us did. None of us needed to. In fact, we never spoke out loud about that home, not once.

We were thirty minutes from our house when Roman groaned in the frustrated way that meant his back was tired of the car seat and he was arching, straining against the chest guard I called his car armor. "Almost home!" I sang, feeling like a liar. The place we were going wasn't our home, and we were all afraid of what we might find there. "Do you want your juice?"

"I want cookies," Roman said, his mood lifting with the request. "Cookies with baby kisses."

"We'll make some tonight," Hope said, "for our lunch snack." She liked planning their bag lunches for school, and even though I hadn't told them how limited our income was, she saved by making home-baked treats.

"Cookies for lunch!" Roman sang.

"You want to make a tent tonight, Roman?" Drew asked. "We can camp out in the den."

"In the cabin?" he asked, eyebrows high, nodding rapidly.

"Not the cabin. I'll show you. We're almost there. See the car crash?" Drew pointed to Roman's favorite billboard, a local attorney's personal-injury ad with the back half of a real compact car crashed through the sign. "We're almost . . . there."

Roman idolized his big brother, but they rarely played together. It was the first of many new things. If only all of them could be good.

The house, the non-home, was still standing. Despite a few dark moments and wicked thoughts, I knew that that was a good thing. I rolled my window down and opened the crammed-full mailbox. A good citizen would have remembered to have the mail held for the extra days away.

I pulled into the garage a bit too fast and had to stop hard to keep from hitting the shelf lined with oil, nails, butterfly nets, and basketballs. "Wait, I meant to back in. Easier to unload." I managed to get the car out and back in again in reverse, but I was shaky, and the kids didn't get out of the car even after I got out and opened the trunk. Roman's window-muffled voice called out for cookies, but no one moved.

Arms loaded with luggage and supplies, I thumped my elbow on the window until Jada opened her door. "Take Roman over to Mrs. Lenz's to get Hershey."

"Hershey!" Roman yelled, his cookies temporarily forgotten.

Drew got out and grabbed bags and stray shoes while I pushed into the dining room. He somehow managed to get beside me, his anger redirected into a fierce desire to protect. I dropped the bags in the kitchen. Hope was right behind us. She went to the microwave and reset the clock, then started working on the oven clock, which was a pain to change using the temperature up and down arrows. They hadn't been intentionally changed, only flashing zeros because of an electrical flicker, but it was an ugly reminder of uglier days.

"Grilled cheese and hot dogs for lunch," Hope said, unloading the cooler.

"And carrots," I added. Flickering clocks wasn't going to scare me out of feeding the kids their veggies. I wasn't that far gone.

"Raw," she said, which applied equally to the carrots and our emotional state.

Holding my nail in my right fist like Dumbo's feather, I did a quick walk-through of the downstairs and could hear Drew doing the same upstairs.

The kids and the dog ran in through the garage door. Hershey's nails clicked on the tile floor, reminding me of a speed-typist at a keyboard. The happy Lab nearly bowled me over, let me rub her ears and pat her ribs, then set off smelling a trail through the house to see if Roman had left fresh crumbs while she was away.

"Mommy?" Drew called from upstairs. I smiled even though I knew that whatever he was calling me for wouldn't be anything to smile about. I loved that all the kids still called me Mommy. It made me feel like I should win a parenting prize.

"Roman, help Jada get Hershey's food and water bowls filled. And can you find his ball?"

"Fetch, Hershey!" he yelled, dropping to his belly to peer under the sofa for a tennis ball. No doubt he'd find a dozen under there and toss them all out. It was a wonder no one had broken a hip tripping over them yet.

I took the stairs two at a time and pretended that was why my heart was so loud in my ears when I got to the top. Drew was in Roman's room.

"This how it looked when we left?" he asked.

Heaps of clothes surrounded the dresser, and toys were scattered everywhere. "I was packing away the summer clothes and sorting for winter while Roman looked for toys he'd outgrown. Neither of us finished." I shrugged. I could definitely see why he might think the room had been ransacked.

Drew's hand went into his right pocket and stayed there. He had his own feather. If he could deal with this, so could I. "Anything else?" I asked, proud that my voice cracked only a little.

Roman's hands were slapping the stairs, followed by his knees. "Sissy's makin' cookies!" he said, arms up in the air like he was measuring an enormous cookie pile.

"First she's making cheese and bread. Then cookies," Drew said, giving me time to absorb that everything was okay, and that we shouldn't have to worry so much that it might not be.

We didn't find anything wrong in the house, though we would wonder through the day if small things had been moved. Nothing had been damaged or taken, unless a sense of security counted, but that had been so thoroughly destroyed years ago it would be hard to argue that a new invasion could mar whatever remained.

"Food's on!" Hope called. We raced to the table. She didn't like cold food and expected subsecond response time. If she was willing to do most of the cooking, none of us dared object to her rules.

Roman and Jada ate their grilled cheese with hot dogs sliced in half the long way inside the sandwich. Then they dipped the salty, gooey, grilled mess in ketchup. Roman dipped his carrots in the ketchup, too. Whatever it took to get them down. My rule making had definitely gone lax. Pick your battle, my mom always said, and the silent battle in my head was sapping my energy.

Unlike the final meals at the cabin, where we laughed and talked over each other with three conversations at once, this meal was silent except for carrots crunching, ketchup splatting, and juice cups clicking.

"We're building it for real, right?" Jada blew the question out like it had been bottled and corked for years.

We all stared at her, chewing paused, eyes wide. Then we blinked in unison and unfroze. I was relieved for a half second until they all turned their eyes to me, waiting for the answer. Needing it to be yes.

When my mouth opened, I meant to ask, *What? Build what? Cookies?* But we were truth tellers now. No more liar, liar, pants on fire for our family.

"Yes," I said. "We are building it."

And that was that. The older kids had already cast their vote. And since Roman was at a stage when he preferred dirt, sticks, and rocks to anything Fisher-Price had to offer, we assumed that he gave the project a couple of mud-stained thumbs up.

We ate. We unpacked and did laundry. And for the first time in what, months? Years? A decade? I had a crazy goal, an impossible dream that made me smile and gave me hope. The kids were transformed, unrecognizable from the nervous beings who had left for a mystery vacation only days ago.

Thanksgiving.

Yes, it was a time for that.

— 6 —

Coffee with *Fall* Cream

The oldest three kids were in elementary and middle school and Roman wasn't even thought of yet. My second husband, Adam, stood in front of our French doors, staring across our backyard and into the neighbor's. His Yugoslavian features were distinct and handsome. His dark hair, long on top and parted straight down the middle, hung just under his eyes. If his hands were free just then, he would have pushed it back in a way that had once made my knees weak and my tummy flutter. His left eye was always closed a bit more than the right, just on the edge of a wink.

I was cleaning my fifty-gallon fish tank, more because it was a good place to keep an eye on him than because it needed cleaning. Something important was happening; he never stood in front of windows without a good reason. Every thirty seconds—timed so precisely that I knew he was counting it out—he lifted his index finger to the window and drew a letter. Someone was out there watching. He had me as sure of it as he was.

He really was smart, genius-level smart. My own Da Vinci–minded inventor. He held patents on a handful of creative devices that could actually make the world a better place. Always thinking. Always a step ahead of the average guy.

I had seen a few letters from companies interested in his ideas. They were real. And he told me he was negotiating with major people who wanted a piece of his latest patent. It was big, he said, a revolution for the construction industry, bigger than the cut iron nail. And a dark car had been following him, putting on the pressure to sell for pennies on the dollar.

Technical drawings and disassembled devices covered every inch of his cluttered office. Dozens of clocks and watches, a telegraph printer that had worked when he bought it, bizarre medical tools, tubes, mechanisms from the Victorian era, and boxes of modern electronics all gave the space a surreal, science-fiction look. He never built anything new or put the ancient things back together, just placed the screws, gears, diodes, and microchips in neat lines on his worktable, each screw and component meticulously labeled.

The kids had to be kept away from these important experiments, and I wasn't allowed to touch them either. Jada was just a toddler, grabbing with damp fists at the metal pieces whenever she tottered close. But she was easier to keep clear of the parts than Drew, who was early in his elementary-school years and already building perpetual-motion machines and robots. They were learning, though, that touching the forbidden projects was not worth Adam's belt.

Someone always wanted the ideas blossoming in his head, the things he put on paper only after they had bent and tortured him—and me—for months. In a single hour he might sketch ideas for bubble-bath containers, children's socks, and complex laser scanners. But he had never actually sold a patent. Not one. And while I'd seen them come in the mail with a gold seal and a red ribbon to prove their status with the U.S. Patent and Trademark Office, I had no idea where he hid them after holding them up in victory and promising big things.

I had never seen the cars following him, or noticed anyone sitting in the red truck in the neighbor's backyard. That's what he was staring at, writing a secret message on the window to someone hidden in that truck.

"Why isn't it a black truck," I asked. "I thought you said a black truck was following you."

"That's part of the message. They want to make sure I see it. A red flag." He pointed up at the air-conditioning vent over his head and then pressed an index finger over his lips to let me know they were listening. They were always listening. And then, as though he'd still been counting off the seconds while answering me, he broke off to drag his index finger slowly across the glass to form a letter "G."

I tossed a small handful of rock salt into the aquarium and sprinkled fish flakes on the waving surface. He wasn't going to tell me anything more and I wasn't in the mood to be reminded that I wasn't smart enough to understand the intricate details of high-power negotiating.

When I looked up, he had formed his index finger and thumb into the shape of a handgun, the way my brother and I had when we were barefooted Indians fighting cowboys around jack pines in Wisconsin. He jerked the hand back and then settled the fingertip against the glass again and again.

Bang. Bang. Bang.

The phone rang, but he didn't seem to notice. I went to the den and closed the door before I answered.

"This is Mr. Travis from the Peabody. I'm calling about an outstanding balance, three months overdue."

It was hard to concentrate. Images of Adam shooting out the back door at the red pickup truck were circling, looking for an explanation before they settled on a perch. "We've never stayed at the Peabody," I finally said. "There must be a mistake."

"No mistake. I've got the invoice in front of me for a boardroom rental totaling twelve hundred dollars." He continued with the date and time, but they meant nothing to me. I got a kick out of how hard he tried to sound stuffy, failing miserably with his extreme Southern accent. ". . . the Furton boardroom for six hours. The bill is nonnegotiable." I heard something tapping, like a pen on a desk, and reminded myself it was not Adam's finger against the door glass.

I had little fight left in me, but we didn't have enough in our bank account to cover the bill. Adam had been taking a lot of time off to work on the patents. We'd have all the money we ever needed after just one big sale, he promised. I blew out a breath and realized I was still holding the phone. Rustling and whispering on the other end surprised me. Mr. Travis should know that whispering wasn't the least bit stuffy or dignified.

"Miss Kimmy helped your husband prepare the room and has some insight if it would help."

"Yes, plea—" But he had already handed the phone over and I could hear the rapid, nervous breathing of a young woman.

"I was, like, the one to help set up the boardroom that day. He was two hours early, and he talked half the staff into helping him." She breathed out a laugh, but not a happy one. "He kept, like, winking at the women and patting Jeff and Tyrone on the shoulder like he'd known them his whole life." Her voice dropped to a whisper. "I talked the kitchen into giving him enough coffee for his guests even though he didn't pay for it. He said it was a big event—real important, like." She was talking in a normal volume again.

My hair stood on end. Of course it was a big event. All Adam's events were big. And it was no surprise that he'd charmed everyone into serving him; he had that way about him. He was likable, believable, and the nicest guy in the world . . . until he wasn't.

She wasn't done, though. "He named a bunch of super important guys from Apple and Google and stuff like that. Big people. There were execs coming in from all over the country, or maybe he said all over the world, I don't remember exactly. And he had a patent—even showed it to me when no one else was looking—that all these companies wanted to buy. It looked real. And he didn't seem like he was crazy or anything. Not at first."

Oh, Kimmy, they never do. They never seem crazy until you get up real close. Then you see crazy like you never imagined.'

All at once I was furious. He had really done it. He had made a big deal and sold one of his patents and then hid it from me. After all the years I had tiptoed around and tried to make his life happy, he had cut me out at the end. I was speechless, and it seemed little Miss Kimmy was, too. But then she started again in a whisper I could barely hear through the angry blood pounding across my eardrums.

"He announced the meeting was starting with this crooked little smile, that cat-who-ate-the-canary smile, you know?"

Yes. I knew.

"And then he closed the double doors with a little bow to us—to me and Tyrone."

Her breathing went funny again and she was quiet for too long. "Did something happen?" I asked. "Did he throw them out or something?"

"Yes. Well, no, he didn't throw them out, but something did happen. Or, didn't happen." She groaned a little. "Oh fudge. I'll just say it. There was no one there. No one had gone in the room before he closed the doors. The folders were in front of each chair—I'd helped him make copies and they had all sorts of figures and sales lists in them—and the coffee mugs were full. We could hear him talking. Presenting. But there weren't any people."

"Videoconference?" I asked, even though it made no sense.

"The Furton Room doesn't have equipment. Not even a telephone. And he didn't have anything with him. And besides, the coffee . . ."

"Yeah. The coffee. And the papers." I had shredded three tissues into confetti in my lap.

"When he opened the doors, Tyrone asked him how things went and he said, Oh, they went just perfect. He had them right where he wanted them. It was all even bigger than he thought. That's what he said, it was bigger than he thought. And then he left. He didn't take any of the papers with him and all that coffee was just sitting there cold. Some mugs were half empty. Some of them had used sugar and cream." She laughed. "I mean—"

"I get it. He was alone in the room the entire time. There were no other doors in or out?"

"No. Just the main entry and a table down the middle that seats twenty-two. Sometimes we put chairs along one wall, there's room, but he didn't ask for extra chairs."

"No," I said. "I guess he wouldn't need extra chairs, would he." I wasn't really listening to her anymore. I couldn't wrap my head around it. "Listen, I'll talk to Adam about the bill and see what's going on."

"Oh my God! I shouldn't have said so much. It was just so weird. Did I break some confidentiality thing?"

"No, no. You're fine. We'll get the bill straightened out. Thank you so much for explaining." I hung up before she could say anything else, before she could hear the scream in my head.

He hadn't sold a patent. He hadn't sold anything. Why hadn't they shown up, these people he invited? It didn't make sense. Had he given them the wrong date? The wrong address? Anything was possible, anything at all. Until you thought for just one second about the coffee. Then everything unraveled into the explanation I'd been hiding from for too long.

Adam's behavior had slipped beyond eccentric long ago. He had bridged over into insanity.

− 7 −

Rise
Plan B Is for Sissies

Every night after the kids went to bed, I worked on a book I'd been trying to write for too long. I had sold a couple of middle-grade novels, but I wanted to break into the adult mystery market. The goal gave me hope for a completely new future.

I was exhausted after doing the laundry and unpacking from our Thanksgiving trip and decided the book could rest for another night. I stacked my hoard of mystery novels on the other side of the bed just under the pillow, where I was pleased to know they would remain undisturbed. It was now the empty side of the bed, not someone else's side, and that reminded me to breathe easy. I climbed in with a notebook, a pen, and a remnant of the smile I'd taken to bed in the cabin.

I started making a short to-do list of errands to complete before we built a life-size version of our stick house. I really meant to do this, and it felt good. It felt big and loud and real. It felt alive.

The list filled the first page, then the second, and was well on the way to flooding the third when I dozed off. Even though it was already apparent that we were in over our heads, I had no intention of backing down. A woman stubborn enough to stay with an abusive man is not a woman who gives up easily. We would do this. We'd dive in and keep working, eyes straight ahead.

At the top of page four, I wrote, "Plan B." I stared at the blank page, imagining the depressing alternatives. We could buy a tiny house and stack bunk beds in the corners. I could write in a closet or just give it up and keep programming. The kids would go off to college feeling as low, afraid, and small as they did today. I ripped the page out, crumpled it, and threw it on the floor.

Backup plans were for quitters. They were for people who were scared. They were not for people brave enough to hang red curtains and wear V-neck shirts. I told myself we had faced our worst fears and had nothing more to be afraid of. I pretended I believed it. "It's do-or-die time," I whispered. "Do or die." And then softer, moving my lips with nothing more than a hiss coming out to warn away the nightmares that turned out to be inevitable whether I whispered or shouted, "It's a figure of speech. Do or die. It's figurative, not literal."

The next week was crazy busy, and I wasn't one to use the "c" word lightly. I spent Monday and Tuesday patrolling a thirty-mile radius from our house, looking for land. Several promising properties were eliminated by the cost, one by a den of snakes, and several more by the strict neighborhood rules that required I use an approved, licensed contractor. I had already checked with the city and learned I could pull my own building and plumbing permits, and act as my own contractor. But that didn't mean neighborhoods had to approve me as a builder.

At sunset on Tuesday, a flood of texts came in from Drew while Roman and I were half lost and scanning ditches for realtor signs.

Drawing house plans? Drew asked. *Where's the oversize paper? Drafting ruler? Mechanical pencil? Where are you?*

"Time to go home," I told Roman, who had fallen into a sleepy trance. I stopped on the narrow side street I had wandered down and started a three-point turn that doubled to a six-point turn. When I shifted back into drive the final time, I spotted a handmade sign on a tree. Sloppy cursive writing announced one acre, with a barely legible phone number at the bottom. The acre looked like a park, with beautiful hardwoods trimmed high. It was on a hill with a pond on one side and a dense forest behind it. I pulled the passenger-side tires into the grass and got out, half expecting something terrible to appear—another snake den, skunks, vampires. But the land couldn't be more perfect.

I let Roman climb out, and I called the number while we hiked through the tall grass. "The number you have reached is not in service. Please check—" I redialed, changing the uncertain 0 into an 8.

"We just posted the sign this afternoon," a woman said, her Southern accent strong enough for a country song. "My daddy gave me that land when I turned eighteen, even though I said I wouldn't never live next to him. That was thirty years ago now. I decided on a whim to sell."

I made an offer on the acre over the phone. It was ten thousand less than they were asking but still ten thousand more than I had. Less than an hour later, we signed a basic, handwritten agreement on the hood of my car. When I flipped the paper over at a stop sign, I discovered that it was their receipt for four new truck tires and an alignment at Tire Town. I giggled until a few tears flowed. The entire thing was absurd. Maybe I really had traveled through Drew's portal to an alternate reality. I wasn't the sort of girl to buy an acre of land on a tire receipt. Roman laughed with me from the backseat, and I wiped away the tears, sobering. Today, I was exactly that sort of girl. The spontaneous girl in the rearview mirror was me after all.

Drew and I sketched preliminary plans at the dining-room table on giant sheets of paper, glancing over at the stick model for inspiration when things got tedious. We kept our pencils sharp and our lines straight, working into the early-morning hours to make sure the stair-case width met code and the landing had enough room to swing around a king-size mattress. Roman slipped by in stealth mode, stealing our erasers and hiding under the table to gnaw on them like a teething puppy. The tenth time I pulled a fat pink eraser from his slobbery fist, I lifted him up to see the stick house. "This is what we're drawing. We're going to build a big house like this. One we can live in."

"Yup," he said, nodding his head until his eyes jiggled. His feet were running before they hit the floor. He skidded into my mostly empty office, where Hope and Jada were googling energy-efficient building ideas from the PC propped on my great-grandmother's trunk. When they came up with something good, they shouted it out for us to incorporate. I could have moved the computer to the table, but the chaos of their conversations swinging from excitement to bickering and in-sults would have driven Drew and me nuts while we struggled to play amateur architect.

We had already named the imagined house Inkwell Manor. It would be the place where my dream of writing for a living came true. I stared down at the model house, imagining Roman crawling up the staircase. A tiny bag of colorful beads hung at the top of the stairs. One of the girls must have added it, but I had no idea why. Another bead bag hung over Hope's bedroom door, and one over the back door. It was a bizarre way to decorate. Then I spotted a series of sharp screws sticking through a wall in the garage and more by the front door. A mini skateboard blocked the dining-room door. "What on earth?" I mumbled, pricking my index finger against one of the screws.

Drew looked up, wearing a half smile that made him look all grown up. "You found the improvements. What do you think?"

"What are . . ." Then I saw the slivered edge of a CD along the back door and knew immediately what they had done. "Booby traps."

"*Home Alone*–style. Jada did the beads. Hope came up with some ideas that were seriously scary." He shook his head, but didn't lose the smile. "It's what you get, raising kids around your mystery novels."

"Are these cameras?" I pointed to the acorn hats on every corner of the house's exterior, and he nodded. Wouldn't it be nice if they really had made the modifications because I was a mystery writer? Wouldn't it be nice if imagination were the only thing they had to be afraid of?

I sat back down and sketched as quickly as I could. It was long past time to get out of this house.

On Friday morning I took the plans to a copy shop, painfully aware that even after I had the printer darken the ink they looked like exactly what they were, pencil-drawn renderings done by amateurs. I took them to my bank, shoulders back and confident that my great credit would put me on the fast track to borrow everything I needed. The balding loan officer whose heavy glasses slid to the tip of his nose twice a minute declined my request, and not without a smirk. "We only loan to licensed contractors. Experienced contractors." Down and back up went the glasses. "I can recommend a couple, hon. They'll take good care of you."

I tried two more banks, feeling so defeated at the last that my request sounded more like a squeaky apology. We could do this. I knew it with everything in me. But of course we couldn't do it without the money to buy supplies. And if the bank made us hire a contractor to oversee the work, we couldn't afford to do it at all.

Over the weekend I downplayed the rejections to the kids, playing it off like we had tons more options when I hadn't thought of a single new possibility.

After Roman dropped off to sleep on Sunday night, I remembered something that Jag Fischer, my old boss and the wealthy owner of three magazines, had once told me. He was a small man with wide eyes, perfectly gelled gray hair, and a perfectly full money clip in his front left pocket.

"Banks are easy," he had insisted. "Do two things and a bank will give you anything you want. First, you give them papers. Bury them with papers. Papers with dollar signs all over them mean you're important. Doesn't even matter if the dollar signs have little minus marks in front. To a bank, all dollar signs are golden." He dropped his hand over his pocket, unconsciously patting his own dollar signs, something he did dozens of times a day. He was right; the dollars made him seem large and in charge. "Second, and this is most important, give the stuffy bastards a deadline. Time is money and you don't want their old bank wasting yours. You need everything in two days—no more. Be eager and in charge. You make the rules, not them." He had laughed, shaking his head and no doubt remembering a loan officer pushing his heavy glasses up and sweating over papers while Jag clapped and said, "Chop, chop! I don't have all day. Gotta keep this money clip full."

So I stayed up past bedtime gathering three years of tax returns, statements of intent, bills, royalty statements from a couple of small novels and newspapers, documents for energy-efficient roof decking, and a few manuscript pages from my latest mystery novel. It was an impressive stack, all neatly labeled in envelopes and folders. I added a completed loan application for an impressive-looking bank downtown where I had never had any type of account. I may have parked in their lot one time to dash into a nearby bookstore, but that was the closest thing to an affiliation I had with them.

Bright and early, I put on a gray skirt suit, one that had been a little tight until divorce stress claimed the last postbaby pounds. I wore a red shirt underneath, because red meant power, and also because red meant Caroline. After touching up my makeup, I added a simple pearl necklace and earrings. They were department-store pearls, not the sort you passed on to your daughters, but they looked real, and this was a day for appearances, not reality.

As soon as the kids left for school, I dropped Roman off at a day care. I stopped at a shipping store and bought a white cardboard tube to hold my plans, and then sat in the car for a half dozen deep breaths, wishing I could get my head between my knees in the cramped front seat. "Do or die, Cara."

The car door stuck, but a solid shoulder whack knocked it open. I walked into the high-ceilinged bank lobby like I owned the place, my eyes straight ahead even when I sensed heads turning my way. If my skirt had a pocket, I would have patted it like it was filled with rolls of Benjamins. The loan officer at the floor desk shifted uncomfortably when he saw that I was headed for him. Before I said a word, he looked over his shoulder and waved me back to the head moneylender with the windowed office and heavy cherry door.

"Rothschild," he said, shaking my hand without getting fully to his feet. "What can we do for you today?" His eyes drifted to his paperwork, so I placed my long cardboard tube on the desk, diagonally across whatever he had found slightly more interesting than me.

"I'm building a house, and I need you to help me cover some of the materials. The labor is taken care of and the land is free and clear. I'll be the contractor."

He tipped back in his chair, not exactly propping his feet on his desk but his posture saying that he would have if my cardboard tube weren't in his way. "You can fill out an application and leave it with my assistant." And there it was, that smirk they must teach in loan-officer school.

I handed him the completed application. Before he had time to scan much of it, I slid a thin stack of his papers over and dropped three neat folders with labeled tags protruding. "Three years of tax returns," I said, then lifted the next folder, "and here's an asset breakdown. The copy of my blueprint," I tapped my fingertips on the tube, "is yours. I understand you'll need it for the inspections." I'd learned that at the last bank, the one that had turned me down before my seat was warm.

"And you're a licensed contractor?" he asked, leaning forward in his chair, head down while he thumbed through my papers, eyes pausing on the dollar signs.

"I've pulled the permits. And while I'm not licensed, I have a lot of experience researching energy-efficient building models." I added a folder of passive-solar designs to the stack, pretending that I had read as much of it as eleven-year-old Jada had.

But he was tilting back, stalled on the licensed-contractor nonsense. That quick, I'd lost him. The big fish was slipping right back into the pond.

So close. I had been so close.

"It's vital that I have this by Wednesday—Thursday at the absolute latest. I'm ready to break ground immediately." I raised my eyebrows, nodding my head. "You can do that for me, right? I was told you could— by Wednesday."

Who was this damn cheeky girl? She was not me. She was not the Cara who listened in terror to the fi-fah of her husband's breath while his thumbs pressed blue temporary tattoos on her skin. I had the irresistible urge to rub my neck, but redirected my hand to my clutch, a narrow leather bag that would have been more at home at a cocktail party. It had been that or my large bag filled with Cheerios remnants and tiny notebooks where I jotted down clever dialogue in the grocery line. I pulled out a tiny tin of mints, held it out. "Mr. Rothschild?"

He shook his head, leaning back over the papers and flipping through too fast to be doing anything more than a magician's trick of distracting me while the number ticker in his head weighed the risk of taking me on.

I dropped a mint on my tongue even though I hadn't wanted one and was afraid I would either choke on it or start drooling when the menthol hit my sinuses. He held up one of the papers and turned sideways to his computer. I smiled a bit, probably a mirror of the loan-officer smirk, when he slipped a pair of wire reading glasses on his nose before typing in a few numbers. He had barely been able to see my papers, let alone evaluate them with any real accounting math. He was as fake as my pearls.

"No accounts with us?" he asked, looking at the computer screen instead of me.

"This will be my first."

He scrolled a few pages, probably reading them, or at least the important parts. I was fairly certain it was my credit score he was looking at, and thankfully it was in remarkably good shape. I'd never liked debt and paid everything off in record time. But more than one man in my past had gone on spending sprees that gave me plenty to pay off.

"And you'll be able to do this immediately? By Wednesday?" I repeated, hoping he was distracted enough not to notice that my confidence, which had been unprecedentedly high to this point, was waning. My voice hadn't squeaked, but it had been a touch too high, too plaintive. I pushed my shoulders back and dropped my chin, willing my voice to drop, too. "I'll finish the foundation work before Christmas. Ice makes everything more complicated."

He sat back, his chair spinning slowly back toward me, seemingly on its own. His eyes focused on the edge of his desk, which I could see had been nicked, probably by the arms of this chair. Little imperfections like that would irritate a perfectionist, an accountant. As the silence stretched between us, the wall clock above his desk seemed to grow louder. The second hand jerked unsteadily through the uphill side of each minute with two steps forward and one step back.

An image of him jumping up and throwing his computer monitor across the room made me wince. That was the last straw! I imagined him yelling, his glasses dropping to the floor and his hands coming for my throat. *What were you thinking? You are too weak for this, Cara!* But his hands were actually steepled at his chin, another thing they must teach in business school, the contemplative pose, similar to Rodin's *Thinker* but with interlaced fingers to symbolize unity. We're in this together.

"I think," he said, slow and deliberate, bouncing his finger steeple off his chin. "I think we're going to be able to get this to you."

"By Wednesday?" I asked, fully aware I was pushing my luck.

He stood, and stuck out his hand. Somehow I managed to prop myself on my own shaky legs to return his firm handshake while his closemouthed smile signaled that we were now partners but would never be friends. "By Thursday," he said, letting me know that no matter how I'd entered the building, I did not own it after all. "Sit tight. I'll get your paperwork."

I walked out the front door, chin high, and with a construction loan for nearly a third more than I'd asked for. Sweat dripped between my shoulder blades and down the back of my knees in endless rivers.

"We did it! We have the money for everything we need and then some!" I shouted the minute the kids walked through the door. I had already told Roman, but the only part of celebrating he was interested in was the part that came with dessert.

The older kids were happy, but I detected a tiny bit of hesitation. We were celebrating our own enslavement. This project would chain us to a job site, and the work wasn't going to be easy.

"It's going to be a busy year!" Drew rubbed his hands together.

I shrugged, narrowing my eyes. "Actually, a busy nine months. Turns out a standard construction loan is not a full year."

"Nine months, then," Drew said, his eyebrows lifting under a couple of stray curls. The kids would be in school all day and I would have to keep my freelance jobs to pay the bills, which meant I'd be working full-time as a programmer and writing three to four hours a day. Nine months was possible . . . for an experienced crew. But for four kids and a woman who had struggled for more than an hour to get the light covers off the fluorescents in the garage last week, nine months was a heck of a stretch.

I closed my eyes and saw the tall glass of lemonade with the red and white paper straw, the last straw. It didn't scare me like it used to.

I licked my lips and went to the pantry for a jug of lemonade. "It's Cancún night!" I announced, the way I always did when we were having Mexican food. Once upon a time, Adam and I had spent a lot of time scuba diving, and Cancún had been a favorite spot.

"Everybody chops!" Hope said, waving her siblings toward cutting boards. Together, we made an enormous fajita dinner, talking and laughing with salsa music turned up loud. I couldn't help wondering if it was a last-meal celebration. We wouldn't have much time for hot meals in the next nine months. The three oldest did homework while I did cleanup, and then we herded into the car to drive the seven miles to our land, which was now officially our job site.

I'd brought four stakes—actually two old broom handles cut in half—a ball of neon-pink string, and a hundred-foot tape measure. The sun was setting but we could see well enough to pick the general location of the house on the upper section of our sloping acre. We pushed the stakes into the soggy earth with as much pride as Neil Armstrong claiming the moon. I had the distant thought that survey equipment was probably supposed to be brought in at this stage to align the front of the house with the road, some three hundred feet in front of it.

"Should we measure from the street back to this spot?" I asked, stomping next to the first stake.

"Just eyeball it," Drew said, and we did.

The rectangle of our neon-pink string looped around the broom stakes looked far too small to hold all the rooms we'd painstakingly designed, far too small to hold a life. I'd read that that would be the case, that during early phases the house would look too small and other times it would feel far too big. We had measured rooms and furniture, so I knew it wasn't as small as it looked. I stood in the muddy corner where my library would sprout and looked out an imaginary window. "It's perfect," I said.

"It's home," Hope added.

Then Roman threw up his fajitas and we loaded back in the car, all marveling over how fast his fever had come on and hoping he could make the seven miles back to the house without any more reappearing fajitas or surprises.

The rest of the fajitas stayed down, but the surprises did not.

The week before Christmas had visions of power tools dancing in our heads. I found a guy with a backhoe to dig the footer, a process we had only seen on YouTube videos but felt like we understood fairly well. We did our best to square up the broom handles by running lines diagonally across the rectangle in a giant X. Theoretically, according to a fiftyish guy in Utah who went by geo39th, if the lines of the X were the same length, and each of our parallel edges were equal lengths, the house would be perfectly square. Since this seemed like an important starting point, we hoped he was right.

I showed up thirty minutes early the morning Jimmy and his backhoe had agreed to be there, but he had still beat me by another thirty. I shouldn't have stopped for Christmas baking supplies.

"Wanted to beat the traffic," Jimmy said, or something like it. His Southern accent was so dramatically skewed by the thick plug of tobacco under his gray lip that I had spent the first five minutes of our phone conversation trying to translate his words from Spanish before I realized he was speaking some form of English. I nodded. Any miscommunication could be blamed on tractor noise. He stared at me, a loan-officer smirk on his face. Nothing wrong with being early, but it surprised me that he hadn't started digging. His tractor was burning fuel by the bathtub.

"Chalk?" he asked.

I shrugged, as lost as if he'd asked what I thought about dem Yanks or whatever sport was in season.

"Gotta mark it."

"Yes." I nudged a broomstick with my toe. How could he possibly miss my neon-pink string?

He raised his eyebrows, eyes shining with a gleam of amusement I was going to have to get used to seeing. "Bucket'll tangle in yo pretty string."

I'd bought the string at the lumberyard. They'd had orange and pink. I'd picked pink not because I was a girl, but because it looked especially visible and didn't look like hunting gear. Okay, and maybe partly because I was a girl. At any rate, it was construction string and I thought we had used it the right way. This was how geo39th marked his Utah foundation. I'd watched him run his strings more than a dozen times. But I looked at the gaping teeth on the backhoe's orange bucket and could see he was right. We had missed a step—apparently an important one. "Chalk?"

"Or top-side-down sprayin' paint."

"Chalk?" I asked again, imagining an extralarge chunk of Roman's sidewalk chalk and trying for a visual of how that could possibly help me mark a footing.

"Comes in a bag." He wiped thick, tanned fingers down his face and checked his watch.

"Bag of chalk. Hold on!" I ran to my car, sinking ankle-deep in a mud pocket along the way and carefully ignoring the cold goo seeping through my sock. Contractors don't shake off the mud; they wear it like a badge. I opened my trunk and grabbed a five-pound bag of flour. It had turned out to be a good thing that Roman expected a dozen batches of cookies over the school break.

I straddled the line with my right foot in my future library and my left in the front yard, ripped the corner off the bag of flour, and walked

backward, bent at the waist and leaving a powdery white line to out-
line the house. I had been moving fast, conscious that the clock was
running on the backhoe, and didn't look up at Jimmy until I reached
my starting point. He gave a little salute while I pulled the string out of
the way, dragging it across the yard with two of the stakes flopping
along behind like fish on a stringer. I saluted back, feeling like one of
the guys.

Jimmy carved perfect trenches into the earth, and the idea of our
house merging deep past the surface sent a thrill through me. Digging
deep was never easy, but it was always worthwhile. I wound my pink
string into a ball. Everything would have to be used and reused for us
to come in under budget. I leaned the stakes against a tree and carried
the empty flour sack to the car. " 'Self-rising,' " I read from the label.
"Don't I wish."

If wishes were fishes, we'd all cast nets, my grandma used to say.
And wasn't that the truth? I wasn't much of a wisher anymore, though;
I wasn't watching the stars or pulling off flower petals while waiting for
good things to find me. I was building them.

Jimmy pulled an old stump and an enormous root system out of the
general area of our future refrigerator and loaded it on his trailer next
to his backhoe. We exchanged a fair amount of dirt and flour with a
vigorous handshake, and I wrote him a smudged check with only his
first name because I hadn't quite understood his last name despite the
three occasions I'd asked him to repeat it.

"Know how to set da rebar?" he asked, truck door open and one
foot on the bent, mud-encrusted running board.

I angled my head toward the oak where I'd propped the stakes and
pink string. A fat bag of black rebar chairs rested against the oak like
a lumpy pillow.

"Shit." Jimmy spit a nauseating brown stream. "Better off usin'
rocks in dat clay mess. Got a mini spring yonder." He pointed at the far

corner of my den. "Wear yo hip waders." He laughed and I joined him. Might as well. Once I sorted out what all that meant, it would probably be funny.

"Thanks, Jimmy. I'll be calling you for the Donna Fill before long."

He nodded and pulled away, no doubt with a fine story to tell at the next job site.

I had barely squeaked through the ground breaking even with a professional on site to fix my mistakes. Now that I was all alone, the gaping foundation holes were as daunting as pathways to the underworld. Even repetitive viewings of geo39th's wise overview of footings hadn't managed to make me look like an expert. If I went back and watched the video, I was willing to bet I'd see a line of chalk or paint when the backhoe ate a hole in the earth. He had probably imagined that any imbecile would know enough to take that step. It went without saying. You couldn't leave the strings and stakes up for the dig. That would be just plain stupid. And even though geo39th had sworn by the rebar chairs, he wasn't working in red clay. And what was this about a mini spring? I walked around the trench, my courage as unstable as the wet earth.

The far corner where Jimmy had directed his laughter was closest to the neighbor's pond. It was still a good 250 feet from the water, but there was no question he was right. The neatly squared corner held at least six inches of water, and the water was pooling higher and building to a stream moving toward the front of the footing.

"Hip waders? All my boots have heels." I kicked a layer of mud off my old running shoes. They weren't going to be the ideal footwear for the construction project after all.

Look at your feet, I heard Matt say with a contemptuous snarl. And as badly as I wanted to feel superior and strong and a million years away from the effect of his shaming, I didn't. I felt inadequate, like I was a failure with big feet and a small, small mind. What made me think I could build a house? I had just made a fool of myself, breaking ground with our self-rising Christmas flour. The loan officer would flash me a classic smirk for that one—and I deserved it.

I pulled my muddy shoes off into a shopping bag and drove back to the house in cold stocking feet. The image of Caroline's tornado house that had been perfectly clear in my mind that morning had faded into a blur that barely felt real. Balancing the kids, work, and building a house felt impossible. What had I been thinking? I had a big software project to roll out. My mystery novel, which I thought of as my future, had a weak protagonist and a weaker plot. I had freelance articles to get to the newspaper, and we needed the cash to keep paying the bills. It wasn't going to be easy. What had Mr. Rothschild been thinking? The bank had been insane to loan me money; I was a terrible gamble.

Hershey greeted me with a stripe of fur on her back raised into a Mohawk. The house was quiet and empty.

I had less than an hour to work on an article before the kids came home. Hope would pick Roman up on her way, and he would be clingy and cranky after a long day in day care. I felt a little clingy and cranky myself, so that suited me just fine. Everything worthwhile had run out of my mind, leaving me raw and empty. My editing progress sucked even more than usual, and tomorrow's deadline loomed closer and more impossible by the minute.

The courage I hoped to find building a house wasn't going to drop in my lap; I was going to have to hunt it down and trap it. Fifteen minutes before the afternoon chaos arrived, I stretched out on my bed with my eyes closed, my mind buzzing with to-do lists. Years ago, I had tried guided meditation but had never mastered it. There had never been a time when I needed to clear the space between my ears more than that moment.

I talked myself through what I remembered of the old meditation CD. Squeeze and then relax your toes. Your calves. Your fingertips. Feel a warm breeze passing over your body. A bright light rose up and wrapped around me. Had that been part of the CD? It was peaceful, so I floated awhile, weightless and empty. The CD man had told me in a low, gravelly voice that people often met their true selves on deep meditation journeys. My true self was superb at hiding, and I wasn't sure I wanted to meet her anyhow. I shivered, losing my concentration. What if I found Caroline there, standing in the upstairs window, framed by the red curtains? Even though I admired that imaginary woman, I was afraid to meet her, afraid she would narrow her eyes at my weakness, my fear.

Breathing deep, I fell weightless in the center of the warm light. I opened my eyes—not for real, but in the little dream world—and someone was sitting cross-legged near my right hip, chin pressed on his chest to look down at me. It wasn't my true self unless my deepest soul was an elderly black man with a sun-weathered face and narrow, dark eyes.

He sat perfectly still with his hands in his lap. His lips stretched flat, expressionless, and I had the sense there were few teeth behind them. His eyes felt wise and a little world-weary. He was trying to tell me something with those eyes, and I hoped it wasn't another damn secret I was supposed to intuitively absorb. I was tired of life's coded messages. I willed him to speak, to tell me the grand secret of life. He didn't say a word, just continued looking down at me, rarely blinking but stretching it out long and slow when he did, like he was falling asleep and waking again. His name was Benjamin; I knew that without him saying.

Tell me I'm going to be okay. Tell me we'll make it. Tell me something I can believe in. But his dark eyes took in every minuscule detail of my soul without giving me anything back. The strange man simply existed, nothing more. Then Hershey barked and the front door swung in to bounce hard against the doorstop. The bright little world vanished.

I felt calmer, more in charge, like I was able to take a full breath for the first time in years. But I was also a little afraid of the old man. Who was he? And what if I didn't like what he was there to tell me? I bit my bottom lip. Life had tossed me some hard deals; whatever the old man had to say, I could take it. I promised myself I'd try it again, maybe every day, until I really did find my true self and understood the island man's presence.

The kids announced homework and school drama. A teacher had been put on leave for an investigation, a janitor had helped a special-needs kid after a bad fall, and one of Jada's friends was going out with the boy Jada had liked for two years. Hope and I made pork chops, potatoes, and corn on the cob, with Roman serving up plastic cakes and cookies on mini dishes while we worked. He wasn't clingy after all, but slow and quiet without his afternoon nap.

After cleanup, Drew and I drove the seven miles to the job site while the girls did homework and took care of Roman. I had a concrete truck scheduled for the next morning to pour the footer, but the rebar had to be in place first. Instead of boots and hip waders, we had put our feet into tall bread bags and secured rubber bands around the ankles before putting on our running shoes. It kept the water a thin layer away from our skin, but not far enough to keep us warm.

Even in the South, December was cold. When we leaned over the edge of the trench to lop off roots, it was twenty-eight degrees and falling by the second. My feet were dead numb by the time we climbed down into the trench. Drew handed down ten-foot pieces of rebar, which is a half-inch steel rod used to reinforce concrete. I spaced the bars out in the trenches, hands so cold that the only thing saving my grip was the ribbed surface designed for a better concrete bond. We made four parallel lines of rebar all the way around the rectangle of the house and the smaller rectangle of the porch. The mini spring Jimmy pointed out had become a gusher. Drew affectionately named it the Ink Spill.

Our gloves did little more than hold a cold layer of ice water against our hands. Someone had probably invented a waterproof glove for this sort of work, but none of the videos we watched had mentioned it. I had never in my life imagined being so cold and miserable. Playing in four-foot snowbanks in a Wisconsin winter was warmer than being sopping wet in an Arkansas December. We used rocks to prop up the rebar, like Jimmy had suggested, but even they sunk in the mud slop faster than Gilligan in quicksand. Drew insisted the rebar chairs were exactly the thing we needed, so we ripped open the bag and propped a few in place. They looked like four-inch-tall traffic cones with a crescent support at the top to prop the rebar. In theory they were perfect, but their little heads vanished before we'd reached the end of the first trench.

After sunset, I turned on the headlights and we kept working with no noticeable progress. Somewhere along the way, we caught a case of the giggles. One of us mentioned that the Ink Spill could turn into the Ink Tsunami, and we imagined waves of water barreling through the trenches—which unfortunately wasn't much of a stretch. Drew literally rolled around on a grassy spot, breath gone with laughter, while I sat next to him and smeared laughter tears with clay.

By then we had managed a system of placing flat rocks and then propping the rebar chairs on top of them. The rocks acted like miniature footers for the holders and the rebar was at least visible above the mud. "I'd say that's a professional rebar job," I said when I could speak again. My cheeks ached from smiling, and I loved the feel of happy tension. Our laughter needed to be pulled out and exercised more often.

"Think it will hold up Inkwell Manor?" he asked, then laughed even harder, gasping until I started to worry about him.

"What? What is it? More Ink Tsunami?" I was laughing, too, but without a target.

He shook his head. "It's Sinkwell," he managed between belly laughs. "Sinkwell Manor!"

"And it's a wrap," I said, peeling off my gloves and dragging mud-encrusted tools to the car. I twisted the key so the interior could heat while we packed up and put our shoes in shopping bags. We had flip-flops for the ride home.

We sat inside for a couple of minutes, the headlights shining on the trenches that had undergone another magical transformation, looking barely big enough for two rooms let alone a whole house. The heat sobered us while we worked through the painful sting of defrosting nerves and vessels. My nose tingled. I put the car in gear, and Drew turned on the dome light to search for his phone. I caught sight of my hands on the steering wheel and said, "Oh!"

Drew jumped and held his own hands up to the light. Like mine, they were a dead purple-gray from fingertip to wrist. We laughed most of the way home, now and then managing a word or two. "The gloves! The ink. Inkwell!"

We made it home before eleven, me hoping the ink would wash off and him hoping it wouldn't. Hope gave us a thumbs-up when we lied and told her the work had gone perfectly. Jada and Roman were long asleep, both in my bed.

It was almost two weeks before the footing was poured. First an ice storm set us back, then the holidays, then an overbooked concrete company giving priority to contractors they knew. The delay gave us time to draw plans for a 450-square-foot workshop to store tools and supplies. It was obvious that hauling tools and supplies back and forth between houses was going to get more and more difficult. So we made a basic two-by-four frame with stakes pounded in to hold it straight—or what passed for straight in our amateur construction world. This way, when the concrete truck finally backed up our long drive it could pour both at once. At least that's what I imagined.

In reality they made two separate pours a week apart. The foundation pour didn't have to be smoothed much, just enough to prop concrete blocks on top. But the shop pour would actually end up being the permanent floor, so we rented long-handled floaters and did our best to make it perfect. Despite being a lifelong perfectionist, my definition of the word had relaxed dramatically over the past few months. "Good enough," I declared when my biceps were burning and my feet were heavy enough with dried concrete to sink me in the neighbor's pond for good.

Our nine-month construction loan was well under way, but our house was not. I pretended we could make up the time during easier phases of the build. But a little voice told me there was no such thing, and it grew more and more difficult to hear my own determination over the voice of reality.

−8−

Fall

Black, White, and Gray

An alarm woke me and I tapped buttons across the clock, searching for that sweet snooze spot. No matter what combination I hit, the noise continued. I sat up, heart thumping when I realized it was my phone. There hadn't been a middle-of-the-night call in years.

I said something that resembled "Hello," dimly noting that it came out a lot more like "Um-mah-oh."

"Cara? You okay, honey?"

And then I was as fully awake as if the voice were inches from my face, one hand holding a knife and the other sketching an idea for a laser scanner to revolutionize the postal system. My next phrase sounded exactly like "Shit." I sat up and turned on my reading lamp, expecting to see him on his side of the bed with a wild gleam in his brown eyes. He wasn't there, of course, because he was on the other end of the phone. His papers and books were on the floor, but his side of the bed was empty and cold. He had been in his office when I went to sleep. We'd joked about the weather and he had laughed like a perfectly normal man. It worked that way too often, the normal days stretching into months until I doubted that anything was wrong at all, until I believed him when he said that it was me, that I just overreacted when he worked too hard. I clutched the phone tight enough for the plastic to groan. The light left me feeling exposed—spotlighted—so I switched it back off. "Adam? Where are you?"

"It's so good to hear your voice. God, I've missed you," he said, sounding like the old Adam, the good one, the one before all the insanity. "How are the kids?"

"They're fine. Really good." And I realized it wasn't really true. I had never been a skilled actress, and hiding Adam's vacationing mind was growing more difficult. But he had seen them earlier that night over supper and even managed part of a conversation. Why was he acting like he hadn't seen them in years? My heart beat so fast I imagined it sounded more like a purring kitten than a human organ. The back of my head started to throb, and I could feel an artery pulsing in the side of my neck as though it were trained to gallop along quickly in preparation for Adam's next rant.

"I'm so glad. They're good kids. Smart."

I rolled/fell out of the bed and made it to the door and then out into the den, doubled over like I'd been gut-punched. "Where are you, Adam? Are you in the house?" I pushed open his office door, forbidden territory. He wasn't there, and his desk had been swept clean. The monitor and desktop computer were gone, keyboard and mouse cords trailing like long fingers pointing out the door. My head pounded. I could hear Adam breathing fast and nervous on the phone, but he wasn't saying anything.

Tiptoeing even though my heart felt louder than my footsteps could possibly be, I checked the rest of the house. Hope and Drew were sleeping the comatose sleep of preteens. Jada's floor was scattered with dolls, so I couldn't get close enough to check her bed without risking a broken limb or puncture wound. She rocked sideways and mumbled something when I flipped her light on and off. Even at three and a half she was prone to nightmares so terrifying that I didn't like her to tell me about them. I convinced myself that the reason her waking hours were so carefree and happy was because these nighttime demons chased her worries and fears away. The alternative looked too much like hiding, or avoiding—too much like me.

"Tell me what's going on, Adam. Talk to me."

"They got too close. They're putting things on my computer now. Messages. Words. Numbers. I can't let them get everything. Not all of it. If they just take my thoughts, steal them right out of my head, then I can't make the deal. I need the money for you and the kids. I'm going to take care of you. I can do that. I can take care of you."

Facing as many doors and windows as possible in the den, I curled into the corner of the sofa, phone pressed bruise-hard to my ear. I could hang up. I could just hang up. He was so far past understanding that nothing I said would matter anyhow. But I had spent too many years doing what I imagined to be the right things. The safe things. The things that would be right enough to level his mood. *Don't set him off, please don't do anything to set him off* had been my internal chant long enough to become a personal motto. I didn't know another way to think. Placating and pleasing Adam was a mind-set I didn't know how to escape even though we had been talking about separating, giving his mind a break from the chaos of the kids.

". . . is what she said. So, we'll do that tomorrow?" he asked.

"Sorry, I'm not really awake. What time is it?" I pulled the phone away, relaxed my fingers when I saw how contorted they were from my grip, and then checked the clock. A flash of anger made me flush. I could have checked other clocks in the house if they were reliable, if Adam didn't change them. Even with the phone away from my ear I could hear his sigh. He had important things to say and I damn well better turn off the useless prattle in my own head to hear them. Wandering minds were disrespectful. Unacceptable. "Sorry, I didn't catch all of that. It's two in the morning."

"It's two thirty-six, Cara. Two thirty-six A.M." He enunciated the words carefully, anger creeping between the syllables.

"Yes, Adam, so it is. What about tomorrow?"

"We have to go somewhere. Probably far away. Somewhere noisy so we can talk. This isn't how it's supposed to be. Things are getting out of hand and it can't be like this. I can't be separated from the things that matter—from my family. You will always be my family. We'll grow old together, just like we always said."

The words were the right ones to say, but I could hear his fist thumping against a table or desk on every fifth word or so. Something metallic rattled after each thump, maybe a spoon. I yanked a fleece blanket off the ottoman and pulled it over me in a tent. Instantly, I felt better. Safe. Bulletproof.

"We haven't made any decisions yet. We can talk at home. I can't just leave the kids. Why aren't you here now? Where did you go?" I held my breath, waiting for the storm.

"Remember when we decided the diving in Cancún didn't measure up to Cozumel and took a day trip for a drift dive? Twenty-seven hours of taxi, bus, taxi, pedicab, ferry, taxi, dive boat." He laughed, slow and real. "Rinse and repeat for the trip home. The dive was incredible, but you got so sick."

It had been a really spectacular trip. Just the two of us to stay connected, to keep our love alive. And things hadn't been so bad at home then. He had just started to look in the rearview mirror a little too often and fill one too many yellow legal pads with pages of dots and dashes. It was the leading edge of insanity, when things could still be explained away. He had been eccentric and charming rather than slap-ass nuts. The good old days.

"Is there any coast you haven't puked off in a dive boat, a spot we've missed? Maybe you'd like to turn green down under?" He laughed again, his fist thumping faster and the spoon dancing in a jingle.

He laughed so hard that the laughter faded to little throat clicks before billowing back out in a full belly chuckle. "Do you remember the old man with the ponytail who fed you grapes? They'll make you feel better, he says. But you puked them starboard before he had time to reach for the next handful. He was a persistent old hippie."

No laughter this time, and I knew why. He was making connections and closing circles. That little man, sun-damaged enough to be a skin-cancer poster child, was now part of *them,* part of the conspiracy to trick him out of an invention worth millions. He was no longer merely the grape man, but an idea thief, one in a long line of spies who stretched back to Adam's childhood.

"I've got to get some sleep," I said. "The kids are doing fine. We're fine. Let's leave things like they are for now. Come home and get some sleep. I don't want to talk about it anymore. Not now." I heard him drawing in a long breath, filling his lungs until they were near bursting, but I remembered to add, "And we're not going anywhere tomorrow."

"You're not going to shut me out. You are my family. If we don't stick together, we won't be safe. None of you are safe, Cara. Not you, and not the kids. You could die! Is that what you want? Do you want to die, Cara?"

"We need some rest. It's too late for either of us to think right now." It was a lie. I was thinking, all right: crystal clear. I was thinking of what he could do to me, to the kids. How easy it would be for his mind to slip even further. I was thinking he had to get away from me for good. For better or worse—I'd promised, I knew I had, but not with my kids' lives. I knew then that he had to go. Tomorrow, he had to go for good.

He fake-snored and then laughed. Even morphed and turned tinny by the cell phone, the sound terrified me. I hung up. My shaky finger jabbed hard against the phone, turning the ringer off. Radio silence.

His stories had always been tight and believable, with a long backstory and an enormous cast of characters too fantastically detailed to be made up. The first time I took him to see a psychiatrist it was to deal with the stress of his big deals, not because I didn't believe they were real. Years later I would question whether dozens of situations, dozens of people, even entire families ever existed outside of Adam's head.

Maybe if I could have pulled him through the door more than twice the shrink would have spotted inconsistencies, but Adam violently refused to go back or take any medication. The shrink and the meds were both part of a devious scheme, he said. The psychiatrist was another idea thief, just like the guys at work, like the bank teller, like our neighbors. I was playing along to keep my name off the enemies list, but that tactic had run its course. It was only a matter of time for me. There was nothing I could do to help him, and little I could do to help myself. I felt very small coming to terms with how big the thing was that had gone wrong with him. The half-moon was perfectly framed in the den window, and that made me angry. How dare the moon hang there so beautiful, as though someone hadn't just shouted, *Do you want to die, Cara?* Not just any old someone, but the man who had promised so many things and meant it, and might have kept all his promises if only his mind had stuck around. I wrapped the fleece blanket snug and went back to my room, snuggling up to a pile of pillows and holding tight.

I thought about calling someone for help, but who could I call without making things worse? Calling the police, a psychiatrist, or even my mom would infuriate him. Besides, I'd learned that lesson. Being a tattletale makes the bullies hit harder, and no one, not even your family, can save you. Sleep felt close, but just out of reach, so I practiced breathing deep and relaxing every muscle from my toes up. By the time I reached my neck, I was in the quiet, peaceful place where meditation had been leading me.

When Adam unlocked the front door, I woke and picked up the phone. It was four, and the caller ID said I had ninety-seven missed calls from an unknown number. He didn't come into the bedroom, and I went back to sleep instead of checking on him when I heard the door to his office close. I didn't have the strength for another round of paranoid ramblings.

The next alarm was the real thing, and I didn't have time for snooze. I woke Hope and Drew for school and got breakfast on the table. Jada could sleep a little longer before I took her to day care and went to my college classes. My stomach clenched when I tried to work out a time to tell Adam he had to leave.

He didn't answer when I knocked on his office door or when I pushed it open and called his name. An odd, sour smell hit me, promising that things were very wrong before I had the chance to see. I took a step back, pulling the door with me. Whatever it was, I didn't want to know. I'd rather just close the door tight and never open it again. But of course that wasn't the right thing to do, so I pushed in again, walking fast.

He was on the small green sofa in only his underwear, sitting upright with his chin on his chest. He might have been only sleeping. But he wasn't. A dozen pill bottles were on the sofa next to him. Handfuls of pills had spilled on the floor and the cushions, technicolor droplets of life or death. He had thrown up on his chest and a throw pillow that I'd once embroidered with a poem. A yellow legal pad balanced on his left thigh. No business plans, no equations, no patent ideas this time. It was a suicide note with ramblings so insane they read like a bad movie script.

Part of me thought what a relief he must feel to be at peace.

The pills hadn't been his first choice of suicide, I knew that. A long sword was next to him and a shorter dive knife. On the floor was a book about Japanese honor deaths, suicides by a knife to the stomach. He had told me before that he thought it was a good way to die.

I noticed his chest move up in a shallow breath. Back down again and up. I scanned the room, looking at everything but his chest, thinking about everything but the decision I had to make. Not long ago I would have said there was no question, I had to try to save him. But that was before I'd seen the torture every day had become for him and everyone around him. That was before I knew that I had to make him leave and that even then he might never stop torturing us.

If I walked away and closed the door, waited just a little longer, he would have what he wanted. Was that the merciful thing to do? I didn't ponder the idea for as long as it felt. I went to my bedroom and called 911, finding it impossible to speak in more than a squeak of a whisper.

Then I went out to the kitchen, where the kids were still eating their cereal. "Adam's sick and an ambulance is coming to get him," I told them. "He'll be fine though."

Hope and Drew nodded, reading the lies on my face and not bothering to ask questions that would never get straight answers. I called my mom then, and she pulled in beside the ambulance, dressed for work. She got the older kids off to school and played with Jada while they wheeled Adam out the door. He didn't wake up or even move a muscle. I still didn't know if I had been too much of a coward to do the right thing.

A tall, lanky police officer asked me all the wrong questions, and I didn't have the energy to spoon-feed him the right ones. I was going into shock, and no one seemed to notice until my mom wrapped a blanket around my back and hugged me. Then the falling-apart began in earnest.

By the time the police left, Adam's mom had arrived. I didn't want her in the house, maybe because I felt more guilt there. I ran outside barefoot in my pajamas. It was cold enough that I regretted not grabbing a coat, but I didn't turn back. Ivana, Adam's mom, had parked with the front wheels on the slab outside the garage, one back wheel on the driveway and one in the grass. She was standing with her phone pressed to her right ear and her hand at her neck, clutching at a gold shawl that belonged with a cocktail dress. Her eyes were frantic, smeared with yesterday's makeup, and her hair was frizzy. A pair of delicate blue house slippers with fuzz around the ankles completed a list of fashion faux pas Ivana Petrovic would never commit under normal circumstances.

"No, Sophie. We are not going to sit back and wait," she said, then snarled at the phone and disconnected the call with three more finger jabs than necessary.

"What is—"

"Do you know what's going on? Why he did this? Tell me about his note." Her eyes were huge and unblinking.

My heart ached for her. This was how I would feel if something went wrong with my son. "I don't know. He went somewhere last night and called but he wasn't making sense. He was . . . 'manic' is the word, I guess. It was after midnight though, and I didn't answer when he called back. He said—he said things that weren't nice. It was crazy talk."

Her phone rang and she sucked in a breath through her teeth. "It's Crevits. Officer Crevits." She stared at the screen, pale enough to pass out and incapable of answering.

"Sit down," I ordered. "Give me the phone and sit down."

She held the phone out, straight-armed, and the second I took it she scurried around the car to sit in the driver's seat. I didn't linger over the idea that it was the first time she had ever listened to one of my suggestions.

"Hello? This is Cara."

"He's awake and speaking. Just thought you'd want to know."

"Thank you." I relaxed, more relieved than I would have thought I'd be. "What did he say?" I asked, hoping it was something to clear things up, to make them okay even though that wasn't really possible.

The officer sighed, probably regretting his good-deed phone call. "He said he didn't mean to wake up." He gave me a few seconds, then continued. "He couldn't tell us how much he took or which kinds. He had a real variety. Mostly prescribed, most not to him."

"I'll tell Ivana he's awake," I said, tipping sideways until I had to grab the hood of her car for support.

"What? Speak up."

"Thank you."

"There's more, but it's, well, I'm not sure what the hell it is."

He hesitated for the space of at least three slow breaths, and I took the time to breathe deep until the dark edges cleared from my vision. "What did you find?" I whispered, imagining terrible things.

"Guy down the street from you said he practically beat down his door last night. They had talked once about lawn mowers but didn't really know each other. Adam said he needed some paper, a pen, and a phone. He filled two whole notepads with scribbles and made some phone calls. The guy just left him to it and went back to bed, but when he saw the ambulance and blue lights at your place this morning figured he should report it and give us these pads of notes and things."

I heard him suck in another breath and wondered how bad it had to be to upset a police officer. Then Hershey leaned against my leg and I remembered just how bad it could be.

"The guy said his cat was in the room, friendly kind of cat who likes everyone. But now this morning it's terrified and hiding and they can't get near it. Bunch of fur is missing from its back half. Guy is freaked out and doesn't know what to think." His voice was flat, as if he was trying to wipe the possibilities from his mind.

"I don't know what any of this means," I said. "He leaves messages for people, and he thinks they leave them back for him."

"Jesus. Like alien people or what?"

"Regular people. Businesspeople. But I need to give Ivana an update. Did he—is there anything else?"

"Nah. That's enough, isn't it? Jesus. Poor damn cat . . . Tell Ivana I'll see her at the hospital. We'll need a statement about—I'll call you for it later."

I hung up and pulled the passenger-side door open. Ivana's forehead was on the steering wheel. Her lips were moving.

"He's okay. He woke up and they talked to him a little."

"Come with me." She wasn't exactly pleading, but nearly so.

I wanted to comfort this lost mommy. I wanted to be there for her even though she had never been for me. But I had my own kids to comfort. "The kids, Ivana. I can't leave Jada. I don't have anyone—"

She waved her hand, dismissing me, and pressed her head back against the headrest. With a breath so deep it should have popped her lungs, she became fully herself. Shoulders back, chin up, steely. Yugoslavian royalty. She took her phone from my limp hand and waved it at me. I stood up as she started the car and barely had the door closed when she started rolling it back down the driveway.

I felt like a failure for not going with her. A betrayer.

Cold and emotionless though she might be, I felt sorry for Ivana. She could never escape his manic, creative genius or his depressive, crazed anger. And while I hoped she'd have better luck forcing him to get treatment, I knew she'd fold under his anger and taunting just like I did. He was no joy to live with. His sulky moods and short fuse made the average day tense and chaotic. Worse, his weeklong silent treatments were a hellacious torture. His narrow-eyed glare reminded you by the minute that you had displeased him in some way you would never be privy to.

Something had to give, though, and it would have to be my connection to Adam. He was too dangerous. It might have been my life the voices told him to end, or the kids', or even the whole house gone up in flames. He had tipped clean over the edge into a dark pit of madness, and I had no confidence that he could climb out.

After Jada was settled with cartoons and the older kids were off to school, I discovered that my laptop had been split open and gutted. No more hard drive. My assignments, the book I'd started writing, and hundreds of photos were gone. He'd probably tossed them in a ditch or lit them on fire, whatever the voices demanded to keep the people in the trucks from getting them.

Jada helped me bake cookies, chocolate chip because they were my favorite and I needed the calories to face down the stress.

By late afternoon my mom called. As a mental-health therapist, she had been allowed to see Adam on her lunch hour.

"You've got a decision to make," she said. "He told me some things and there's a lot more going on than you or I imagined. He needs to go to the state hospital. I called and got a bed for him, but he won't go voluntarily. Either you sign to have him committed, or the hospital will have to release him."

"He'd be furious if I did that. There's no telling—"

"He's already furious, Cara."

"Because I called for help."

She was silent. Waiting for my decision. She didn't have to confirm it. I knew when I called 911 that I'd be in trouble. Damned if you do, and damned if you don't.

"What will happen?" I asked, even though I already had a good idea of how these things worked.

"Once he's in, he can't leave until they say he can. You can't get him out. No one can. There is no easy way to take it back."

Relief flooded through me. He might get help, a magic pill to clear his mind . . . and it would take the responsibility away from me. But handing him off for the doctors to deal with felt like taking the easy way out. A cheat to keep the kids and me safe. "I think he's bipolar. Really bad. He'll be there a long time," I said, scared and hopeful.

"That's the theory," Mom continued. "But in reality he's quit his job and has no insurance. They'll keep him long enough to get him stable and then, because they have a dozen critical people waiting for the next open bed, they'll send him home."

"Home?" Not my home. Not anymore. I couldn't.

I could guess how things would go down at the state hospital. They'd give him pills to level things out and quiet the paranoia. He would quit them no more than a day or two after his release. I could watch him at first, make sure he swallowed them morning and night. But then I'd start to settle into the belief that everything was fixed. All better. And one night at 3:25 A.M. a tiny wiggle of paranoia would slip past the drugs and whisper that he shouldn't take them. The medicine was poison, or mind control, or a plot to dull his creative genius. He'd skip just a few, just to test the idea, and when his mania returned and set him on top of the world, he would know beyond any doubt that the pills were bad, and that would be that. More looney times. More days like this one.

Time. I'd have to buy some so I could form a plan. "I'll be there in twenty minutes to sign."

—9—

Rise
Shop Not Shopping

On the first night of Christmas break, I couldn't sleep even after finishing an old Stephen King novel and starting DeMille's latest. My reading had turned a hundred percent to action settings far removed from my own, and a touch of the supernatural was a bonus. Roman had fallen asleep later than usual after a late nap, and he was on the other side of my bed, kicking off the covers faster than I could spread them back over his cold feet.

Using my phone, I updated a building to-do list and added notes to a file for my mystery novel. Still, the sandman refused to visit. I wanted to blame it on my double serving of pie, even though I knew digestion-related insomnia was for people with more simple lives.

Pouring the house's footing had been a wake-up call. Not only was the project a million times more difficult than I had imagined, but it was a mere metaphor for what I really needed to do. I had fooled myself into believing that building a physical house was the same as rebuilding our family. While we might still use the physical build to accomplish the personal one, they were two distinctly different creatures and required individual diets. I felt enormously out of my league in both cases, like I'd adopted a Saint Bernard and an elephant.

I needed to meditate, to find peace with myself and let go of the past, before I could build my future. But I was afraid of what I would find if that bright world reappeared when I relaxed my toes and let the essence of myself float away. More specifically, I was afraid of who I would find. I didn't have any real-life friends anymore, and I'd grown afraid of the two imaginary people I had adopted as allies, as frightened of meeting them again as I was of my unlocking-door nightmare playing a rerun.

Caroline had been my inspiration for the house, a strong woman who wasn't afraid to express her opinion, to stand up for herself, to build a new life when the old one was blown to pieces. I'd imagined her encouraging me, lending a sisterly shoulder when I felt all alone. But somewhere along the way her voice had turned from empowering chants to vengeful whispers, and I was beginning to think she was little more than a dark side of my own mind. In order to banish Caroline, or at least rediscover the positive elements of her spirit, I would have to come face-to-face with another unnerving spirit, Benjamin.

The old man, thin-shouldered and withered from sunlight, had seen me naked. Not skin naked, but soul naked, and that was scarier than revealing the stretch marks on my tummy or the mole under my right breast. I had started moving past feeling like a victim of Adam and Matt, which sounds like a good thing, but my angry thoughts of revenge were dark enough to scare me. Blaming them on Caroline, a spirit I'd made up, wasn't going to hold for long. And if they were really and truly my thoughts from the start, then I knew that Benjamin would see them. And the things from before—like that I'd stayed with Adam and let my kids be damaged by his insanity, or that I hadn't left Matt even when he slammed my pregnant body into walls or left bruises on my neck—Benjamin would know those things, too. I imagined him snarling in disapproval, looking away in disgust, and saying, "You should have been more like Caroline. She would never jack things up like you have. Caroline, come here, sweetheart. Show Cara how to fix this mess. Take pity on her."

Without even considering that my focus would call him up, I pulled the covers to my chin and slipped directly into my meditation world instead of sleep. The light was there, warm and inviting enough that I forgot I was afraid to enter. Caroline didn't show herself, invisible as always, but Benjamin was there, cross-legged and looking deep into my eyes. I didn't want to be afraid of him, I wanted to get him talking. So I did the only thing I could think of, a move my grandpa had taught me many years ago: I took away my enemy's bargaining chip. No one could make me feel paralyzed or manipulated by secrets if I didn't have any. I opened my mind and welcomed him without restriction.

Go ahead, I told him. *Weigh the good and bad of me.*

Once he knew every little corner, I could move on from that dreadful place. If he didn't like what he saw, then he could move on, too. He was part of my own mind, a creation of my subconscious, which had to mean I could boot him right out if I wanted to. As soon as I thought it, I knew it wasn't true. I did not create Benjamin, he simply was, and I had no more power to boot him out than to make him speak.

Chin a notch too high and avoiding eye contact, I must have looked like a defiant teenager. *This is me, damn it. This is who I am and what I've done. Take it or leave it.*

Benjamin didn't move, just watched me with his slow-motion blink the only proof he wasn't a statue. His lip didn't snarl in disgust, and his eyebrows remained smooth, relaxed. The furrows on his brow were from age and smiles, not disapproval. I had the sense that he was not only watching me, but watching out for me, and then I slept. There were no nightmares and no lectures from Caroline, and I now understood that those were two different things.

Roman and Jada were playing upstairs when I woke. The sun was up, but it was a cloudy, gray winter day, the sort made for sleeping in and watching movies with repeated rounds of hot tea, hot coffee, and hot cocoa. Not for us, of course, but for other people. For people who left house building to the experts.

I made coffee, smiling over how necessary the dark brew had become. I'd never been a coffee drinker, only taking small sips on occasion, and then only when it was more cream than brew. While I wasn't exactly drinking it black these days, I was certainly turning more mainstream, with a touch of cream and barely any sugar. Jada and Roman slid down the stairs on their butts, fuzzy pajama bottoms turning the ride slick. Still, it looked more painful than any spanking they'd ever had from me.

"Pie! I want apple pies and roast beast!" Roman shouted, right hand raised as though he had triumphantly slain the beast himself.

"That's exactly what Christmas pie is for," I said, cutting a slice of apple for myself. "For breakfast." I had always started baking the desserts early so they were spread out over the entire holiday break. "You'll have to wait until Santa comes to eat the roast beast though."

Hope joined us, making a plate of beef-and-bean burritos for breakfast. Jada had cereal, dropping a couple of fresh cranberries in the milk in place of strawberries. We all laughed at her puckered face when she bit into the first one, and then harder when she stubbornly bit the second. All berries are not created equal, dear child.

I glanced at Drew's door at the top of the stairs, wishing he would join us but knowing he would more likely wait until the kitchen was empty before he poured himself a mug of coffee, blacker and more manly than my own, and carried it back upstairs to drink in front of his computer.

Hershey and I did a quick search of the front and back porch, looking for signs of anything out of place. Then I spread out the plans for the workshop on the table and erased the window. Every window I'd ever seen in a shop was covered over with stacks of lumber or shelves of nails. We would have electricity out there for overhead lights, and in order to get the riding lawn mower in I'd put a garage door at one end to let in plenty of sunlight. Besides, I was nervous about framing windows and doors. One less would make everything easier. The lumber was already on site, wrapped in plastic ribbons like an enormous gift. Building the shop would be perfect practice, like framing a mini house.

Drew finally came down for a cup of coffee and stood over my shoulder with it, looking at the plans we'd drawn on the back of Jada's math homework.

"Want to try out that nail gun today?" I asked, expecting him to resist.

"Sure. What time?" he asked, standing taller.

"Let's get dressed and go. Nothing else to do around here today."

The kids dressed in construction clothes and old coats faster than I'd ever seen them get ready for school. I wondered if they would be so anxious to pick up a hammer a month from now, or six months. The novelty would wear off for all of us, but hopefully our determination would not. If they gave up, I couldn't finish on my own. No plan B. No way out.

The city wouldn't let me put in my own temporary electrical pole, which was probably a good call on their part. So I called an electrician who promised to do it cheap if I picked up the parts and had everything waiting for him. I'd done my part, even securing the box to the pole and using a post-hole digger to put it in place—a job I'd rather not repeat anytime soon, in the red clay with more quartz rock per square inch than there were chips in Hope's overloaded chocolate chip cookies. Weeks later, the electrician had delayed a dozen times, and we were left with no power to run our tools or lights.

A generous neighbor, Timothy, had offered to let us run an extension cord down the hill, past his pond, and to his pump house to run any tools we needed until the pole was hooked up. Timothy was tall and lanky, a Yankee transplant who embraced Southern living so fully that he planted okra and black-eyed peas in his garden and even had a pseudo-Southern twang that made me smile for its precision and proper grammar. I had had no intention of taking him up on his kind offer, but on that cold December morning it's exactly what we did. I plugged in the tiny air compressor I'd bought at a discount hardware store and fired it up. Drew hooked up the nail gun, eyes alight. I pretended to defer to him because he was the one who had read the instruction manual, but I was secretly as terrified of the wicked-looking gun as he was delighted. To him and every other fifteen-year-old boy on the planet, it looked more like a zombie-killing machine from a video game than it looked like hard work.

Jada collected large rocks to make a fire ring at the back of the property, and Hope gathered sticks to make a fire. Roman filled a bucket with sweetgum balls to use as kindling. I hadn't actually made a fire outdoors more than a couple of times in my life, but I had a pack of matches, a thick old phone book, and piles of determination. We needed a warm, central spot for breaks, a place that felt like a vacation, even if it only lasted minutes.

I laid out the first shop wall, starting with a straight run that had no surprises. This phase of the build was called framing. I knew that much even if I didn't know exactly how to do it. The frame of a house would actually be better described as the skeleton. But skeletoning a house sounds too much like a horror novelist's verb, so nailing together all the rib-like boards that hide inside the walls is called framing instead. I started with a sixteen-foot-long two-by-four that would become the top of a wall. Every sixteen inches I marked the edge of it with a penciled "X." Then I made a matching one for the bottom of the wall, laid the two of them on the concrete slab eight feet apart, and ran eight-foot two-by-fours between them. The workshop was large, thirteen by thirty-three, so we'd have plenty of long, straight stretches to practice.

"These two-by-fours suck," Drew said, helping me line them up with each "X" on the bottom plate. "Look at that one, it's twisted like a ribbon, and full of knots."

"Yeah. They don't even seem to be the same length. Do you think that matters?"

He shrugged. "I think they just gave you the crappiest stuff they could find."

We nailed the first wall together and found that length did matter—a lot. "We'll have to take it apart," I said, "and trim them all to the same length."

He started measuring and decided on the length we would use, marking each board with his new neon-orange construction pencil. "Are you sure you ordered the right wood?" he asked.

And of course I wasn't. There wasn't a single part of this project that I was sure of. "I said two-by-fours. The salesperson asked 'Eight-foot?' and I said yes."

Drew started in with the nail gun, both of us jumping a little with each shot, and me terrified that he would put one through my legs as I knelt on the wall to hold the crooked boards in place with my weight. Even through our fears, we were grinning like fools.

"Looks perfect!" he said.

I held back on the victory dance. "Jada, come help us with the wall!"

She stood at one end, Drew stood in the middle, and I stood at the end that needed to line up with the front of the slab. We heaved the wall up, little Jada pushing with all her might, leaning forward until she was a diagonal line, braces glinting in the sunlight. It was exhilarating. We were powerful heroes who had created a recognizable wall from a pile of mismatched sticks. The wall wobbled and undulated in a strong gust of wind, reminding us that we were human after all. Drew nailed the first brace in place. I put washers over the bolts sticking out of the slab and tightened nuts over them. Then we stood in a line off the slab, Roman on my hip and the older kids next to me, admiring a job well done.

"We can do this," I said, relieved and energized. "There's the proof." As though framing one basic wall was proof of anything more than our determination. But it was a lot more rewarding than the concrete work had been. It rose above the ground like a living thing.

"Can we have a fire now?" Hope asked. "Roman's pants need to be dried out."

"Marshmallows!" Roman shouted, a campfire image he'd gotten from television rather than a real-life marshmallow roast.

I knew it took a lot of courage for Hope to ask. When she was five, an obsidian candle holder had exploded on our dining-room table, and the wax pool had ignited across the surface. It had taken only seconds for me to put it out, but it remained part of Hope's psyche forever. She wouldn't go to fireworks displays and paced in worry circles if I lit too many candles at once. Before that day, an open fire in an outdoor pit would have been just crazy talk to her.

She had constructed a pyramid of small sticks over crumpled phone-book pages. Any Boy Scout would have been impressed. I lit a match and held it to the "P" page. Prim, Primble, and Prime were licked away by the orange tongue. I had expected to need most of the matchbook for our first fire, but that tiny flame was all it took. Jada handed me branches as big around as my wrist and a thick log with damp fungus along one side.

Hope stuck long branches in the ground outside the fire's ring and hung Roman's pants and socks from them. "Poor lonely pants, with nobody inside them," I said, quoting from a favorite Dr. Seuss story that had always scared my kids into a tight snuggle at bedtime. Roman giggled at the pants and poked the muddy thighs with a stick. They wiggled and danced, making him giggle more. He was already wearing his backup clothes. With all the puddles on site he would be rotating hourly from one outfit to the other. He had plastic bags between his socks and shoes but clearly needed a pair of rubber boots. It was yet another way we were unprepared for the reality of a job site.

We framed the entire workshop by that afternoon, including a thirty-six-inch entry door but excluding the garage door. I wanted to read more about that before we tried to build the heavy header to go over the top of it. In addition to the braces nailed to stakes out in the yard, we cross-braced the walls with long two-by-fours nailed from the top of one wall down to the bottom of the other. I had no idea how sturdy it was without the rafters, so I wasn't taking any chances.

The hollow structure was long and narrow. "It looks like a ship," I said when we all stood back to admire the work.

"Like a whale, with the ribs and everything," Jada said. "A whale with his head chopped off."

"Chop. Chop. Chop." Roman whacked a spindly branch against the two-by-fours at the front corner.

I held my breath, worried that we couldn't possibly have done it, built something solid enough to stand up to a two-year-old. But the shop held up to his chopping, and to a strong wind that blew a pile of leaves into a whirling dervish. I closed my eyes and smiled. It was the first time I had built something so much larger than myself.

Roman threw his stick down and rubbed his eyes. A low whine led into a wide yawn. He had been pulled past his endurance point after another day he would have described as one of the best of his life if he had the words. Mud, rocks, sticks, and two-year-olds are the best of pals.

I found a pattern for rafters that night and an example of how to draw a chalk template on the slab so each rafter could be laid out, matched up, and built identical to the last. It was a great method, and it was too bad I hadn't read about it in time to use it. Our slab was criss-crossed with a network of braces that we didn't dare take down.

The next morning, Drew and I modified the idea by pounding stakes into the ground for a rough template. I made what felt like hundreds of diagonal cuts for the crosspieces, and he nailed them together. Later I would learn that we'd used twice as much lumber as we needed to, building a roof that would take a ten-foot snow load. It may have been sturdy, but it wasn't anywhere near perfectly straight.

I eyeballed the surface we'd need to cover with four-by-eight sheets of plywood. "It ain't no church," I said. It had been my dad's saying whenever a project strayed just left of perfection.

"More importantly," Drew added, "it isn't *my* room."

The next day, I met a guy named Pete at the lumberyard near a mountain of two-by-fours. He was stocky with red hair and cheeks, a fireplug of a guy tucking away a pinch of mint tobacco. He was born right in Little Rock and had never left the state. "Don't see a reason anyone should leave a perfectly good state," he said. I learned this and a lot more because he had absolutely no rules about personal space. He was also overflowing with building tips and personal information that crossed all lines of oversharing. We traded project stories and he gave me his card in case we needed a hand along the way. (I've no idea what clues he'd picked up on that suggested we might have one building emergency or another.)

I tucked his number away with no intention of calling a stranger in to our family project. But when he explained the ordering error that had made framing our shop a hundred times more difficult because of the shoddy boards, he won me over. Best of all, he was the first person I'd encountered who believed I could build a house without a hint of a loan-officer smirk. In short, I liked him.

"Those eight-foot two-by-fours is for scrap stuff. Like building a frame for concrete, nothing that matters much if you run up on a twist or bubble. Cheap, but you can't use 'em for framing. No one does that." He laced his fingers together over the top of his little potbelly, much in the way a pregnant woman might. "Biggest problem if you frame with 'em is they're near eight-foot long."

If, he had said. *If you frame with 'em.* At least he hadn't said *if you're stupid enough to frame with 'em.* Because by my reddening cheeks and averted eyes he must have guessed by now that we had done exactly that. "That's right though, isn't it? A ceiling is eight foot; so is Sheetrock and plywood. So the two-by-fours should be eight foot, too. Shouldn't they?"

"You got a top and bottom plate. Don't forget. Use an eight-foot board an' nothing will fit right. Too tall. A dead-on stud is what you use for framing. It's ninety-two'n five-eighths, not ninety-six. Top and bottom plate make it add up right."

Well, that was perfectly obvious. At least, it was now. Why I hadn't thought of it before was beyond stupid. Because I had nothing to lose at this point, and because I was growing accustomed to looking like an idiot, I asked, "So if a person *did* use them to frame something, like maybe a shop, what would they do to fix it?" I looked at the toes of my shoes, expecting to see my courage seeping out in a puddle right there on aisle twenty-three. "I mean aside from ripping it out and starting over?"

"For a shop I wouldn't rip nothing apart. You got some extra work though. Need to cut strips of plywood to make up the difference—put it at the top, under the eaves. Siding'll cover it. But that won't fall right either, so you'll have an odd siding piece at the bottom, most likely. Inside'll be the hardest to make right. Hang your paneling or chipboard, whatever you got planned, then I'd double up some one-by-fours for trim along the base. That's what I'd do."

Thank everything that's holy I hadn't ordered the lumber for the entire house yet. I also thanked Pete for his help and we shook, though he seemed tempted to hug me like a long-lost relative he'd finally found between the treated lumber and the eight-foot two-by-four not-studs.

"Call me anytime you're in a bind. I've built a house or two, and I'll help you out for twenty-five an hour. Can bring a buddy who'll work for the same. Get you past worrisome parts and leave 'til you need us again."

I left believing that little Pete was as big, brave, and noble as any knight in shining armor. And I had no doubt there were dragons in my path.

Drew and I followed Pete's advice to finish the shop walls. The plywood strengthened the structure, so we felt a lot safer climbing around on the roof to nail up the plywood and tar paper. I realized we never should have put the rafters in place until the plywood was up. It had been dangerous and unstable to climb around on the hollow walls with flimsy braces. Again, I was happy we were learning these things on a smallish shop rather than a full two-story house, where every disaster would be multiplied to a dangerous scale that could turn deadly. I had never once thought the project was dangerous when it was on paper, not more than a sliver or smashed thumb, but on site, the potential for sawn-off digits and falls from a deadly height loomed large.

I hired a garage-door company to install the door after we had the header in place, which proved to be a good decision, based on the difficulty they had getting it to open and close smoothly. We had the shop watertight and locked up by the end of Christmas break, though it wasn't finished by any stretch. It was missing siding and shingles outside as well as insulation and paneling inside. Drew wanted to keep going and finish it out with tool benches and pegboards, but I was determined not to let it turn into a distraction from the house, no matter how afraid we were to tackle the fifteen hundred cinder blocks stacked around the foundation. The purpose of building the shop first had been to have a place to store tools on site. We would work out the details later. Our construction clock was ticking and we had a lot of house to build by September 13, the bank's final inspection day.

They had already completed the first inspection, to make certain I was spending their cash on a house instead of crack cocaine, and the city had also sent an inspector over, prior to the pour, to make sure I had the rebar reinforcement in place.

Everything was signed off on and ready except our courage. Oh, and the electricity and water. The electrician hadn't shown up yet, and the plumber was failing at every turn. Yes, I was the plumber, but that didn't stop me from being mad at what a failure the hookup to the city main had been so far. I was still trying to work out how to get the 250-foot trench to the house dug, and since the water main was on the other side of the street, I had to get someone to bore under the street to get to it. In this case, I was in over my head in a literal as well as a figurative sense.

All in all, I was still confident that we would nail this project—pun intended. I had even bought tiny dollhouse furnishings for our stick house so Jada and Hope could put bookcases, a Victorian sofa, and framed pictures in place. Hope crocheted miniature rugs and let Roman march his Lego people around as long as she or Jada was helping him avoid booby traps.

He wasn't the only one skipping over land mines. I still watched my rearview mirror for Adam and woke in the middle of the night convinced that Matt stood over me, hands reaching for my neck. Fi-fah. When I was anywhere but the job site, I felt small, incapable, and as weak as I had for too many years. Hershey patrolled the yard with a silent promise to keep us safe, her tail dipping low between her legs when she ran across a suspicious scent. I wondered if dogs remembered the details of their own trauma like humans. Doggy PTSD. I hoped not.

I was up late on Christmas Eve, catching up on projects for work and even writing a few pages. I had trouble falling asleep, even though I was beyond exhausted. I eventually meditated my way into a dream-less rest. Benjamin seemed to have vanished after I had finally let him in and felt at peace with him. I missed his little land of timeless light.

Dim winter sunlight woke me, but I tucked my head under the comforter and willed myself to go back to sleep. Roman yawned in the bed beside me and lifted his arms over his head in a full-out stretch that two-year-olds do best. He had no clear memory of what Christmas meant, and it hadn't crossed his mind yet that it was a special day. Next year would be different. When he was three, we would probably have trouble getting him to sleep past four on Christmas morning.

I slipped out of the bed and tiptoed into the den to plug in the Christmas-tree lights. Hershey growled and I heard a noise outside. Even though we hadn't seen him in a couple of years, I'd never stop wondering if it was Adam, especially on holidays and birthdays. The lights blinked in a repeating pattern, all red this year, like little warn-ing lights. Danger. Danger. Danger.

Jada, my only morning child, giggled and made me jump. She sat cross-legged on the sofa, red snowflake wrapping paper peeled back like flower petals from a small box she'd pulled from her stocking. According to our complex family Christmas rules, stocking gifts were fair game to early risers, but tree gifts had to wait for the family.

Roman ran toward me, sleepy-eyed and red-cheeked. He stumbled, caught himself, and ran to the Christmas tree.

"Santa!" Roman yelled. "We can open!"

"Go wake Drew and Hope!" I said. "We'll open when Grandma gets here!"

His palms slapped the wooden stairs. "Up. Up. Up," he said, moving faster than I'd like.

I put a pot of milk on for old-fashioned cocoa, which would

accompany our traditional Russian tea cakes for Christmas breakfast. My grandma Doris had started the tradition, and I couldn't see any reason to end it. Cookies and cocoa were a dream team.

Hope and Drew thundered down the stairs with Roman, their enthusiasm almost as fake as mine. They had been taught to push down the bad stuff and carry on. Hiding secrets had been a family talent for too long for us to let loose of the habit easily. We would work on it, I promised myself that, but not today. I was exhausted from working too many jobs and then hitting the construction site until after dark. The festivities would sap the last of my energy.

"Ho! Ho! Ho! Who wants cookies?" I carried a tray with each of their favorite Christmas-themed mugs and a pyramid of cookies into the den. I'd spiked my mug and Drew's half full of strong coffee before adding cocoa, and he closed his eyes to savor the first steamy swallow. The smile that followed looked genuine, and I returned it, thinking of him rolling in the mud and laughing at the job site. It was a good memory, a favorite one, and I now believed we would collect enough of those to outweigh the bad ones we'd been stockpiling for too long.

My mom's van pulled in before I had time to eat my cookie.

"Grandma's here!" Jada squealed.

"Grandma brings cookies!" Roman said, running for the door.

As always, she brought the real spirit of Christmas with her. We hadn't seen her in a couple of months, and her dark hair had grown long, making her look very close to her Native American ancestors.

Her van was loaded to the roof with food and gifts, all wrapped to perfection with huge bows and ribbons. She was my best friend in the whole world, and the only one who knew even half of what had happened with Adam, with Matt, and during the other messy times in my life. Domestic-violence victims don't often have friends, and they rarely manage to hold on to family ties. Somehow Mom and I managed to stay close, but I had hid enough that it wasn't perfect. I would make things better after the house was finished. We'd make time to rebuild things that had started crumbling years ago when she and Dad divorced. I hadn't noticed when I stopped looking forward to the future, but now that the skill had returned I built tomorrows in my mind like neatly stacked bricks.

The idea that things would be perfect after the build was like an incessant monk-like chant that followed every thought on every topic. After so many years of bad times, I needed to believe the good times were right there within reach. Even more, I needed to believe that my own hard work was bringing them closer. I wanted to see evidence that for the first time in my whole life my future was in my own control.

It wasn't. But if we knew how out of control our lives are, how would we ever muster the courage to turn the next corner?

We opened gifts slower than usual, taking turns rather than tearing into our individual piles all at once. Our heaps were smaller, too, and they had an obvious construction theme. We opened tool belts, work boots, and rubber-coated gloves like they were the hottest pieces from this season's Milan fashion show. Jada tried out a chalk line on a large sheet of wrapping paper while Hope took selfies in her pink hard hat. When I opened a handmade coupon book from Jada, the kind promising the usual hugs, concrete mixing, chores, and wall framing, I realized that somewhere along the way we had all stopped pretending and were actually enjoying Christmas.

Right on the heels of that holiday joy, something ugly bubbled in me, a bold anger toward Adam and Matt for the years of unhappiness. It came from someone else—from Caroline. I imagined setting their minds on fire with fear. For a second, I imagined towering over them at two A.M. and showing them what it meant to be afraid—to really be afraid.

I had laced a length of sparkly gold ribbon through my fingers and pulled tight enough to make fat, purple sausage fingers. With a deep breath, I released the ribbon and balled a sheet of blue snowman paper into a tight wad. Conquering my fear and building confidence was good, turning myself into a mirror of Adam or Matt was not.

"Did you put the chicken in?" Hope asked.

I cringed. "Sorry. I got so wrapped up in making the perfect cocoa I didn't even think about dinner."

"Roast beast!" Roman said. "I want roast beast!"

"How did you know we were having roast beast?" My mom tickled him and pushed a button on his new ride-on fire engine. Sirens wailed and a deep voice said, "Put the fire out! Put the fire out!"

He laughed and turned on the revolving red light that should have come with a seizure warning. Jada pushed him around the house, skidding dangerously sideways around corners. I opened my mouth to tell her to stay out of the kitchen, but Hope beat me to it.

"No firefighters in the kitchen! Grandma and I are making spinach dip. Christmas dinner is postponed until two. And if you drive through this kitchen again, we'll be eating *you!*" She chased the two of them, banging a wooden spoon on a mixing bowl.

They sped out, laughing like she wouldn't really whack them with the spoon if they rode through again.

Drew scrolled through options on his new phone, the one gift that had nothing to do with construction. His headphones were back in place. I scooted in close and looked over his shoulder, pointing out a Scrabble app without speaking. The techno beat from his headphones meant that he needed space, but I didn't want him to slip as far away as he had before. We started a game of Scrabble, which I was destined to lose without spell check. It was a lazy game, both of us trying harder to make ridiculous words than score points.

Jada and Roman rounded the corner, both wearing capes, lipstick, and monster-claw slippers. Hershey jumped out of the way, carrying her enormous holiday bone to a quieter spot near the laundry room.

"I a superhero!" Roman put his arms out and raced around the room, cape floating behind him through the maze of new toys and tape measures. "Presents! Ho! Ho! Ho!" Roman said, zipping past and tripping over his monster slippers. He skidded on his tummy for a couple of feet and pushed himself up, crying hard enough to smear his lipstick. I scooped him up and grabbed a handful of tissues to mop up the tears and smears.

"I smell roast beast," I told him.

Roman laughed, twisting to get down. I pulled the slippers off before I set him free.

Hope and my mom put the finishing touches on a spectacular meal while I set Great-Grandmother's china around the table. My pumpkin and apple pies went in the oven just before we sat down. They would be piping hot by the time we finished, though no one except Drew would have room for pie. The rest of us would save it for our midnight snack.

Dinner conversation centered on Hope's college list, Drew's latest inventions, and Jada's plans for the WNBA.

Roman fell asleep with his spoon dipped into the last of his dressing. A smear of mashed potatoes formed a Nike swish above his left ear. Jada looked ready to doze, too, blinking frequently, eyes locked on her empty plate.

We spent a lazy day around the fire with Christmas movies. Mom jumped up frequently to clean or fix something around the house or fold a load of laundry. Near dark she went out and weeded my front flower bed, even though the house was up for sale and it wouldn't be mine much longer. She held strong to her forgiving heart and her attitude of helping everyone else tend their garden even when her own heart was heavy with loneliness and endless frustration caring for my disabled brother. She had a habit of staying excessively busy in order to keep from looking too closely at her own problems. Boy was I glad I didn't inherit that trait.

Jada and Mom were up the next morning singing over breakfast preparations. Mom had always sung her way through chores when I was a kid, and I picked up the habit from her. But while she had a beautiful soprano voice, mine was a croaky alto. The kids learned young to turn the radio up loud for my sing-alongs.

One day off was more than we could afford, so we slipped into our construction clothes and headed out to work while the rest of America hit the mall for sweater sales and marked-down tinsel.

Mom took on the task of organizing our jumbled mess of muddy tools in the shop. She designed shelves for the back wall and helped Drew hang his long-awaited pegboards over a sturdy table that became our workbench. Drew had adopted an annoying habit of saying "Cool beans," and Roman chose that day to mimic him, shouting "Cold bean!" when he found a lump of sparkly white quartz or a fat squirrel to chase around a hickory tree.

I was restless and a little irritated, feeling like we were wasting time when the house was so far behind schedule. But other than shuffling blocks around, there was little work to be done until I figured out how to lay the foundation. And since the edge of the pond was iced over, it was clearly too cold for mortar to set properly. The real source of my irritation was exhaustion. We were only a month into the project and the weather was as awful as the work. I wanted to quit so badly that I spent hours making mental lists of excuses to pack it all in, and followed that with hours overwhelmed with disappointment for my own weakness.

My stomach rumbled while I filled the wheelbarrow with rocks and dumped them into the tire ruts from parking in the muddy backyard. While I generally organized meals of crackers, granola, and jerky on the job site, Mom had planned ahead with a gallon of chili, cooking it on her dad's old tripod over the fire that Jada and Roman fed with sticks, two-by-four scraps, and popping sweetgum balls.

When Mom called us all over for a late lunch, we washed up with a thermos of icy water and tipped over five-gallon pails for our chairs. Mom had lifted a length of plywood across two sawhorses and lined it with Styrofoam bowls, Fritos, and shredded cheese—a construction-site buffet. We ate slowly, cupping the bowls and warming our noses over the chili steam.

"It's hot," I told Roman. "Even after you blow on it, be careful of the beans."

"Cold beans, Drew! Hot chili, cold beans," he sang.

Hershey roamed our fire circle, watching closely. She had always been a fire dog, shoving me out of the way if I got too close and barking if a flame escaped along a leaf trail. Drew gave her a small bowl of his leftovers and she settled by his feet, eyes shifting hopefully between the rest of us.

Mom told stories about her own childhood in rural Wisconsin after her dad returned silent and dreamless from World War II. We listened until the half of our bodies facing the fire was toasty.

"Cold beans, cold butt," Roman adapted his song.

Warm heart, I added silently.

I still wanted to quit, don't get me wrong. But I knew I wouldn't, and neither would the kids. We had navigated the worst of our isolation and crossed over the bridge that had held us apart. The construction project was still half impossible, but building our family no longer was.

We closed up the shop and moved concrete blocks around until our numb toes and red ears led us home to defrost. None of us would list that year as the best Christmas ever, but in a dozen quiet ways it may have been the most important.

–10–

Fall
Karma Points

My phone rang just as I was climbing into bed, and I froze, balanced in an awkward yoga pose that would be titled *startled half-recline*. I tried to talk myself out of answering it. My heartbeat stampeded through my chest and ears as I remembered other late-night calls. I wondered if I would ever hear a phone ring after dark without remembering. I sat, drew my knees to my chest, and answered, my voice weak and insignificant.

"Hi," said Sophie, Adam's sister, making the short word somehow apologetic. "I just left the hospital. Adam got a really good doctor, Dr. Christe."

I waited. Even though I knew it was mean, it was hard for me to want any connection to him after he had scared me so many times. After he had forced me to be the one to decide if he woke up from the latest suicide attempt or not. I was angry. It was impossible to direct anything but sympathy at the ill Adam, but I was plenty angry at the good Adam for abandoning me when I needed him. Sophie knew I didn't want him to come back to my house. She knew I didn't want him around my kids. She knew how scared I was. She knew I had a right to be. But she also knew how I had loved him.

"I thought it might help if you come by and talk to Dr. Christe. He changed the diagnosis." She exhaled loudly through her nose, twice. "Mother says Christe is wrong, that he's a kook and doesn't know her boy, but he isn't wrong, Cara." That exhale again. Three times.

Time enough for me to wonder if her anger might turn into a twin of her brother's anger, or his madness.

"It's schizophrenia," she said in a rush. "Dr. Christe said schizo-affective, actually, but that just means schizophrenia and bipolar both. I would have supported Mother that the doctor was a kook if I hadn't seen him myself. I mean, he was always a bit different, you know? But in a charming way, like an eccentric genius, not someone scary. Or that's what we all thought. Everyone but you, I imagine. You knew more of the truth than any of us. Didn't you?"

I should say something. I knew I should. But I was caught between an unexpected desire to weep and a need to cheer over the news that other people finally knew there was something really, really, seriously wrong with Adam. In some bizarre way the news validated a hope that this also meant less was wrong with me. But underneath my cele-bration was a growing realization that this grave news was only the beginning of terrible days ahead. Schizophrenia was a big deal. Adam wasn't one step away from slap-ass nuts; he was all the way there. Still, I had no words for Sophie. I felt irrationally angry at her, as though she should have known enough to whisper these truths to me before I had promised my life to him.

"I know you aren't planning to stay with him, that you don't want to have contact, but Dr. Christe thinks you should know what to expect. He thought it might help you explain it to the kids, and—" She squeaked out a tiny sob. Sniffed. And then cried full-out.

I felt like a real bitch for being mad at her. She didn't deserve to have this in her life any more than I did. And unlike me she didn't have the option to wash her hands of the responsibility. "I'm sorry, Sophie. I really, really am. I knew it was bad, and that it had been getting a lot worse over the past couple of years." My turn to take the deep breaths. "But I had no idea it was that. I didn't. Maybe I could have done something different to help him if I had known. Maybe I could have convinced him to see the doctor again, to take some medication." I didn't need her to tell me I couldn't have, and she didn't. Maybe she was mad at me, too. Maybe she thought I should have whispered it to her at some point along the way. We had both been too hopeful, too optimistic, too afraid to see the truth, let alone tell it. Adam and I had been married for two years, and small signs began four months in.

"The main thing is to keep the kids safe. Dr. Christe thinks he can give you enough information to help. Maybe not to predict, but to have a better idea what you're dealing with. You know, for the long term."

I didn't want him to be any part of my long term. I wanted him out of my life for good. Away from my kids. I was all the way done. If this doctor could help me understand how to keep him away, then it would be worth it. But there I was, lying again. The real reason I was agreeing was because Sophie was crying softly on the other end of the line and I felt guilty abandoning her with what still felt like it should be partly my responsibility. "Okay," I said. "When should I go?"

"I'll be there first thing tomorrow morning. Come before noon." Her tears cleared up so quickly I had the uncharitable thought they had been fake. "Don't bring them with you. The kids. Don't bring them to the hospital."

I hadn't considered even telling them I was going, let alone taking them with me. Jada was only a toddler and the older kids would be at school. But it said a lot that she didn't want them to hear. It might be useful news, but it wasn't going to be good news coming from the esteemed mouth of Dr. Christe. "Where," I asked. "Where do I go?"

"I'll e-mail you the address." Silence. We had nothing personal to say to each other, maybe we never had. It was all business these days—very bad business. "Thank you, Cara. It makes me feel better that we're trying everything we can."

We hung up without saying good-bye, and I was standing in the doorway of my bedroom, with no idea when I had walked there. I looked at my phone, surprised to see that it was past midnight—officially April Fool's Day and I officially felt like a fool for agreeing to meet Sophie. I climbed into bed and stared at the black flower of the ceiling fan, wondering what Sophie had meant by "trying everything we can." To keep me and the kids alive? That must be what she meant. Because what else might we try for? Schizophrenia had no cure. I had read enough about it for a minor character in one of my many unfinished novels to know that much. Only pills to quiet the moods and voices.

Did he hear voices? He'd never said he did, but I didn't have to think back far to know that he had been listening to shadows for a long time. He was outrageously paranoid, which I had attributed to the drinking, and the pills he sometimes swallowed with vodka. But no, he had been paranoid even when he was sober, and I had been hiding too deep to see it. Many of the times I'd guessed him to be drinking, he had probably been stone-cold sober.

It was hard to believe how long the crazy stuff went on before I suspected anything was wrong. It's easier to be fooled than I had imagined. Adam would come home and tell me mundane things that happened at work. There was no reason to doubt a story about what someone else brought for lunch, or a mild squabble between employees. Then he mentioned his favorite coworker's name and described the guy's family. He brought recipes home from the guy's wife. Hundreds of story details built on each other until one day the stories became bizarre, but still possible. Still, why would I doubt them when they had built on one another for years? Until one day I figured out that the best friend didn't exist, at least not in the real world where I existed. This guy, his wife, his kids, his recently deceased grandfather, his restored antique pickup, and his basset hound, they all existed only in Adam's head.

Sorting what actually happened from the tall tales was impossible. The crackers and fresh honey the imaginary family sent me from their imaginary bees was real. Like all good legends, I suspected, some stories had a grain of truth even though the real plot line was miles away.

If Adam had opened his eyes one Tuesday morning with full-blown schizophrenia, I would have recognized it immediately. But while I was going to school full-time and taking care of three kids and the house, the baby steps he took toward madness were excused, overlooked, and misunderstood until he had arrived at his final destination.

Morning came too quickly and the long drive to the hospital was too short. I had expected Sophie to be happy and grateful to see me. She wasn't. She was as uncomfortable and quiet as I was while a nurse guided us to a room with Dr. Christe. He half stood to shake my hand and we exchanged names as though we didn't already know them. He was grinning in a slightly unnerving way that probably felt more natural to his loose-minded patients than to their families. His dirty-blond hair was slightly mussed, but in a way that even I had to admit was a little sexy. Sophie looked absolutely taken with him.

He sat on the business side of a small pressed-board desk with cherry-colored veneer pulling off at the corners and seams. The room smelled like lemon furniture polish, which felt suspicious given the layers of dust and the absence of any real wood to polish. When he gestured to the only remaining chair in the room, a beaten-up red pleather office chair with wheels, I made an awkward wave to Sophie and sat. The space was so cramped my knee was pressed against hers. And when the nurse in pink elephant scrubs, which I thought were in poor taste, moved to pull the door closed, I almost bolted for it. Instead, I coughed and sputtered, "Can we leave that open, just partway? The air is just a little . . . well, I need some air, is all."

She raised one eyebrow, looked at the good doctor, and then left without pulling the door.

"I can imagine this is difficult for you," he said with a practiced sympathetic lowering of brows and a slight nod. "But it's important everyone who may have contact with Adam be aware of the way his mind works these days. Recognizing certain signs will help us keep him on track."

And keep us alive.

"Do you know anything about schizoaffective? Have you read some things?"

I nodded, struck mute.

"Well. You can probably identify which symptoms match Adam's better than any of us. So the important thing moving forward is to recognize when these manifest and alert us if they get worse."

Worse than tossing my computer hard drive in a Dumpster? Worse than trying to take his own life? The good doctor seemed to want me to speak. But most of the things circling my brain and fighting for my tongue were completely inappropriate. I wondered if everyone who sat in this chair was afraid of saying the wrong things. Words that might warn a nurse to bar the gates and lock them in, turn them from a guest into a patient.

"Worse than what?" I managed. "Because if they get worse, who will be alive to note changes?" It wasn't what I planned to say when I opened my mouth, and from the way his jaw opened and closed, it wasn't what he expected to hear. Not exactly politically correct? Was the danger of insanity a secret? Even here?

"Based on his response to medication so far, now keep in mind there are more we can try, and we will, but based on the effects to date he isn't going to get complete relief from medication. Some people really can control their symptoms with medication, mind you, but other cases are more complex. We can't expect he will ever behave perfectly normal, but we can expect improvements. It will be difficult to answer your question about what might be worse until we establish a new baseline for his behavior, a new norm." He stared at me, hard little eyes drilling holes in my skull.

Well, that was a useless mouthful. I clenched my jaw, wondering if airborne truth serum was a thing, and if it was, if it smelled like lemon wood polish.

"I'll tell you what might be the most useful." He turned a soft, sweet smile to Sophie. "And you tell me if you disagree, okay?"

She nodded, and smiled, and her cheeks turned pink.

I rolled my eyes, a completely involuntary reaction.

He turned back to me, and all sweetness melted away. "Let's go have a look, shall we?" He stood, towering over us, at least six foot two, which I never would have suspected behind the little desk. His chair must have been lowered nearly to the floor.

I didn't move even though Sophie stood and was hemmed in by my knees.

"He won't be able to see you. It'll be fine." He fluttered his fingers, waving me toward the door. "A picture's worth a thousand words."

I had enough pictures burned into my mind to last a lifetime. I didn't want to see him. Not even if he couldn't see me back. I had the feeling he would know I was there, sense me, and I didn't want to be on his mind in any way. Another part of me worried more about the opposite, about my reaction to seeing him. Would I feel enough compassion to take him back? I couldn't imagine that being a positive thing for me and the kids.

But Sophie put her hand behind my shoulder, lifting and pushing.

The Brookins Family.

Cara with the borrowed, broken concrete mixer.

Hope and Roman guard the sand for the mortar.

Jada butters mortar on the rough footer.

Cara and Drew plan a roll-up door for the shop.

Cara stacks foundation blocks. Again.

Roman tests danger level of foundation walls.

Cara works two shovels, chopstick style.

Roman naps. Everyone else is jealous.

Drew practices for zombie warfare.

Jada and Roman nap between chores.

PHOTO COURTESY OF VIRGINIA BARRETTE

Hershey protects the garage from ducks.

PHOTO COURTESY OF THE AUTHOR

Cara and Drew. "If it starts to fall, just let go."
PHOTO COURTESY OF JADA BROOKINS

Grandpa Bruce, showing us how we should have done it.
PHOTO COURTESY OF THE AUTHOR

Roman with his frog boots, pink duck, and favorite puddle.

Hope wrestles Roman back down the stairs.

PHOTO COURTESY OF THE AUTHOR

Drew imagines big things.

PHOTO COURTESY OF THE AUTHOR

Jada and Roman guard Grandma's soda and snacks.

Hope dives into the stain work headfirst.

Grandma builds frames for concrete countertops.
PHOTO COURTESY OF THE AUTHOR

Roman builds concrete castles in the countertop.
PHOTO COURTESY OF VIRGINIA BARRETTE

Roman prevents Hope from leaving to cook dinner.

PHOTO COURTESY OF THE AUTHOR

Quills the duck grabs a snack from Cara.

PHOTO COURTESY OF DREW BROOKINS

Cara muds and tiles a bathroom floor.

Cara vacuums Sheetrock dust in the kitchen.

Grandma, Roman, and Jada show how strong we've become.

"It will help. It will be good for you to understand. Dr. Christe wants to help. He knows what's best."

Sharp words wanted out but I held them behind my teeth and got to my feet. I refused to lead the way, waving for the good doctor to ignore Southern hospitality and precede me. He rocked forward and back, shaking his head until he was sure I wasn't budging. If there were dangerous people in straitjackets lurking around the corners, I wasn't going to step blindly out among them. Part of me knew that I was being unkind, I was stereotyping, but another part of me had already seen enough to know that this time the reality was even more frightening than stereotypes had ever suggested.

Sophie walked beside Dr. Christe through a maze of blue-green hospital hallways with me trailing behind, mentally jumping into a fighting stance every time we turned a corner. When he swiped his card beside a set of double doors and pushed the one on the right open, I held back, frozen with fear.

"You aren't going to see anything worse than what you've already been through," he said, soft and gentle. This time his lowered brow looked genuine.

I walked past him, to where Sophie was standing in front of a long window, silent and stone-faced. On the other side was what I thought of instantly as a dayroom, even though I wasn't sure where the word came from or if it was actually correct.

Each corner was arranged with a round table, neatly lined with four chairs. To my right, a game of chess had put one of the players to sleep, a reaction I could sympathize with. A woman working a zillion-piece puzzle rocked sideways, performing a complex pat-a-cake with herself each time a piece fit in place. All in all, they looked more normal than I expected. A half dozen patients were sitting or standing in pairs and talking, as normal as if they were planning a barbecue or bragging over how the kids were doing in school. They all wore street clothes, though the quality ranged from teen-boy holey to designer chic. If it weren't for the doctor and three nurses keeping an eye on them, I would have guessed they were family members rather than patients.

The idea unnerved me, that the dividing line between patient and visitor was so thin. But it also reassured me that I wasn't the only one who might have missed the signs until it was almost too late, that insanity can be totally invisible unless you really want to see it. The door on the far side opened. It had a small security-glass window guarded by a bulky man who probably made more money moonlighting as a bouncer. A man wearing blue scrubs shuffled in, his slippered feet sliding forward in six-inch increments. His head angled down, chin to chest, and even though the hair was familiar, he was too small and round-shouldered to be Adam.

"Oh," Sophie said, stepping back until the backs of her knees bumped a chair. She tipped down into it without looking to make sure her aim was straight.

I stood behind her with no intention of staying long enough to make myself comfortable.

Dr. Christe sat a seat away, long legs stretched forward and arms propped on the backs of the chairs on either side of him. "One of the first things we do to give the patient a break, a little rest from the voices, is to medicate them until the voices stay silent."

He pointed at the shuffling man.

I forced my eyes to follow the line of his finger, and this time the man was Adam, looking old and lost. Vacant.

"Adam's voices are stubborn things. Some people don't need much at all to quiet things down. This is how far we had to go to silence Adam's voices, though. Damn near as far as you can and stay conscious."

Christe leaned forward, knees on his elbows, observing his specimen like Jada watching fireflies in a jar. "We won't leave him this far under. Next step is to teach him to deal with the voices we can't eradicate. Help him learn he doesn't have to do everything they say, and he doesn't have to answer them. We'll try to help him tell the difference between what is real and what isn't."

"It's all real to him," I said, my voice stronger than I expected it to be.

Dr. Christe turned to look at me, but I was watching drool pool on Adam's chest. The effort of keeping his mouth closed was too much and he'd given up trying.

"Yes. It's real to him. But we'll do our best to help him make good decisions," he said.

A powerful wave of pity washed over me. Adam had lined my bed with knives while I slept. He had lied to me and tortured the neighbor's cat. He had told me terrible things that I would never know for sure if he had done or only dreamed. But I could see that on some level it was out of his control. A disease had stolen his mind, taken his family, haunted him with horrors none of us could understand. I had vowed to stand by him in sickness and in health. My guilt surged as strong as my pity. I had abandoned this poor drooling man, kicked him out of his home and had him involuntarily committed after his mind fled through no fault of his own.

But how could I take care of three kids and still have time to nurse a gravely ill man? Sophie must have asked about supplies and care packages, because the doctor listed things Adam could and could not have. The priority was clothes. "Patients do better when they have their own clothes. They feel more like people than patients. But no belts. No shoestrings. No jewelry. And he'll need toiletries, too. Skip the dental floss—it's practically unbreakable, you know. And the toothpaste has to come in a pump, no tubes. Even plastic tube corners are sharp enough to slice a wrist."

I tuned them out. If he really wanted to kill himself, wouldn't a shirtsleeve or pant leg work every bit as well as dental floss? "I'm going to get going," I said, standing and walking to the door. "I can see how bad he is. I knew that." I hadn't, though. I hadn't known how bad he was. Even after I heard he had given a sales pitch to an empty room, I had never imagined he was this crazy. All the way gone. Schizophrenia. I expected Sophie and the doctor to protest, tell me how much more there was to see and learn, but they didn't. Sophie looked like she'd been punched in the gut. I felt guilty for leaving her to deal with everything.

"It's good that you came. Any time you have concerns you can contact me. I'm happy to help. Do you have questions before you go?"

I shook my head, but then realized I did have one. "How long will he be here?"

"We'll get him stable and then treat him as an outpatient. Things will get better after he qualifies for some medical assistance. He's uninsured at the moment."

He could see I wanted more than that. I wanted the whole truth.

"Three to five days."

Like most things over the past few months, it was worse than I thought. Three to five days of safety. I nodded and walked out the door alone.

I would have to tell the kids a little about what was going on before Adam was released. It might help them to know that his mind was messed up and he wasn't doing things out of spite. Life was never what you thought it was going to be.

My mom always said a person isn't given more than they can handle. But that was only the first step of a lovely thought. I had moved on to step two, and it was less lovely. A person has to let go of the things that are too big and dangerous to hold close.

−11−

Rise
Sounds Easy

The kids said they didn't have homework and I didn't push it even though I had a feeling they were bending the truth. We needed to get away, out of this house, out of this mind-set. We needed to feel the physical stretch of moving heavy objects and the mental stretch that reminded us we were eating the elephant bite by bite, doing the impossible, building someplace safe.

So we went to the job site, this time with a small battery-powered CD player from the garage. The speakers were tinny and weak, but Drew had made an upbeat CD with a mix we could mostly sing along to. Even Roman danced to the beat while he waded into puddles whispering to himself, "Don't get muddy. Stay out of the mud."

Hershey came with us, even though she would be a muddy mess on the way home. She'd been lonely at the house. And though I didn't want to admit it aloud, I worried about the old girl. Tail wagging lazily, she followed Roman, nudging him now and then like a wayward pup.

Hope and I ran neon-pink strings from wooden frames I had pounded into the ground at each corner. We hung a line level from the taut string to get a level mark for the top of the first block row. The house was on a slight incline—or at least it had looked slight—so the foundation would be highest in the front corner under my library and lowest in the back corner under the kitchen. What had looked like a difference of only a few blocks when we had eyeballed it was actually about six feet. That would put my library floor nearly eight feet off the ground. This wasn't what I had imagined, and I started to worry about the block-and-fill foundation plan. It wasn't too late to build a different type of foundation, with a wooden floor that would leave the space under the house empty instead of filling it in.

I decided not to settle for that. With everything in our lives feeling hollow, I needed our house to be connected to the earth. We all needed solid ground under our feet.

We moved blocks until the sun faded and Roman's teeth chattered behind mud-smeared lips. We slipped into our flip-flops for the ride home, singing the whole way because singing felt good and silence did not.

Roman zoned out in front of a cartoon after brushing his teeth. The other kids went to do the homework they had said they didn't have, and I leaned back on the sofa at Roman's feet with my laptop. For the first time in a long time, I made solid progress on my novel. A surprisingly gruesome murder took place that I hadn't planned on, and I refused to analyze what that might mean. It wouldn't take a professional head-shrinker to track the subconscious correlations.

I knew it had been a successful writing night when I woke to three pages of "d"s on the screen. Almost always "d"s when I fell asleep, even though I wished just once it could be "z"s for a laugh. I carried Roman to my bed, having given up on sneaking him into his own bed. In a few months or a year he would go on his own, but maybe neither of us were ready yet.

I rolled intentionally on my side, curling into a ball to search for sleep rather than meditation time. Even though I always felt more grounded and at peace after seeing Benjamin, something about the experience still frightened me, and I didn't have room for more fear that night. He and I would make peace, but courage doesn't come like a lottery check, it is earned hard and slow, like Sisyphus pushing the rock uphill.

Monday at the office I was glad to sit in a cushioned chair and rest my back. I was also happy to lose my mind in the analytical process of writing code. But after I picked the kids up from school, we rushed to the job site and discussed a plan to get water hooked up.

The city had let me pull the plumbing permit with no evidence that I could tell one end of a pipe from the other. And no, one end of a pipe is not always the same as the other. The permit office seemed to have as much confidence in my ability to learn from YouTube videos as the bank, so I gave it everything I had.

I finally discovered that I could hire a crew with a drilling contraption to bore a hole under the road to hook the water pipe into the city main. Nearly waist-deep in mud, I struggled to look professional, wiping the end of the muddy pipe in my armpit and then holding it up with my knees to smear it with purple PVC prep and glue. The pipe wasn't much larger in diameter than a garden hose, which looked pitifully small to supply an entire house. But I'd watched videos, read articles, and even asked the guys at the home-improvement store, and the verdict was unanimous. The basketball-size pipes I had always imagined carrying rivers of water down the street and to my house did not exist. Even the city's line down my street was only about the size of my ankle.

I managed to glue in another twenty feet before I capped it off. That left me a nonfunctional water line about 230 feet from the front of the house, which even under my very loose definition of success these days barely qualified. It wasn't a step backward, so there was that.

A trencher was the next step, and my old tractor friend Jimmy had promised to call me back with the name of a guy who had one.

I was still battling the electricians—on the phone, I mean, since I'd yet to see them in person. They had snuck in once when I wasn't around to wire fuses and a shutoff into the temp box, which hung crookedly from the four-by-four I had mostly secured in the mud. The city had told them which main pole to hook my line to, but the person who owned the land around the pole blocked the dirt road with a locked gate and refused to let the electricians enter. As much as I hated conflict, I would have to deal with them eventually. I imagined the conversation starting with "I don't care if you're cooking crack back here or planting fields of funky stuff, I just need to hang a wire on that tall pole. I won't see or hear anything else that goes on—I swear."

While Roman and I waited for the trencher one afternoon, the electricians nearly gave me a heart attack when they drove right up behind me. The two of them rolled out of the car and landed on their widespread feet, the truck door releasing a cloud of funky smoke that nearly blew me over. Naturally, they were in a fine, mellow mood and friendly as could be, each munching a family-size bag of Funyuns.

Between crunches, the tall one said, "That man ain't gonna let you over there. Not ever. Says you'll cut a gas line if you dig to the pole."

"But you ain't got no choice. City says that's your pole, then that's your pole," the shorter, wider man said, wiping Funyun powder on his flannel shirttail over a trail that proved it wasn't the first time.

I raised my eyebrows and waited for them to tell me something I didn't know, but nope, that was pretty much all they had. "So I guess we have to go over there and talk to him? Explain things? Tell him he has to?"

"We?" shorty said. "You got a mouse in your pocket?" They both laughed too hard to notice the way I leaned on the bumper of their truck and sniffed away looming tears.

"Mouse," Roman said. "We got a mouse. Meow." He eyed their snack and I realized he could be inhaling some residual smoke standing this close, so I carried him to the shop.

The electricians sauntered over to admire the pole, which was actually standing straighter than either of them. Hershey followed, vacuuming a trail of crumbs.

Since we were running out of things we could do on the job site without a better understanding of foundation work, I didn't have much to keep me busy while the electricians did their thing. I wiped the dirt off a curved piece of metal Jada had dug up. Then, probably because I was in the mood to hit something, I pushed a ladder under the shop door, pulled the nail from my pocket—Caroline's nail—and hung the curved metal over the door. It wasn't exactly a lucky horseshoe, but close enough. Caroline's nail was now a solid part of our build. Her life connected directly with ours.

"Be back next week," skinny electrician said, picking at a hangnail. "Already contacted One Call to mark lines for the dig."

"You ought to let him know." Shorty nodded through the forest at where the neighbor's house had started to look a lot like the house of the witch who cooked Hansel and Gretel.

I nodded, though I didn't really think I had the courage to do it.

Roman waved while Tweedledum and Tweedledee backed a crooked line down the hill, waving back like happy two-year-olds.

Things were starting to feel out of control. Only a month in and we were so paralyzed by the idea of setting the blocks that we did nothing more than shuffle them from one spot to the next each day. Even though I had given my perfectionist-self permission for small mistakes along the way, I knew the foundation was not a place for mistakes of any size. I still believed plan Bs were for sissies, but I was willing to accept the label.

On the way home I called Pete. "Any chance you can come by and get us started laying block?" I asked, voice quavering.

He agreed to meet me at the site that evening—and I believed him. I believed him the next two times, too, because I had no plan C.

Optimists tend to believe what they need to be true and damn all the scenarios that are more likely to be true. But every so often fate smiles and the good things turn out to be true after all. Saturday morning when the kids and I arrived decked out in full construction gear, ready for a full day of work but with no idea what that work might be, Pete was there waiting with a cell phone pressed to his ear and a toothy grin that almost made me forget all the times he had stood me up. He clapped the kids on the shoulder like he'd known them since they were knee-high.

"Biggest problem here is your services. Electricity makes things a damn sight easier, and water is as necessary as a rifle in a rabid coon pit. Can't do mortar without it."

I looked at my boots, feeling like the author who turned in a manuscript without any punctuation. The services had been my responsibility, and I had failed. Worse, when it came to water, the only thing holding me back was fear. Through my shame, I still had to smile over the rabid coon pit remark. This conversation was a million miles removed from my ordinary life. I smiled, imagining my editor's voice in Pete's body: *Commas make things a damn sight easier, and end marks are as necessary as a rifle in a rabid coon pit.*

". . . good thing you have that." Pete pointed across the slop of Sinkwell Manor toward my neighbor's house.

I raised my eyebrows, hoping it was a joke.

"Get those pails out the back-a my truck, kids!" he yelled, and the kids obeyed. "Fill 'em up with pond water. We got a foundation to build."

Hope and Drew didn't bat an eye, just hauled up as much water from the pond as they could carry—which was more than they could have carried a month ago. Moving the concrete blocks that would be our block foundation had muscled us up a little, and we were no longer horrified by head-to-toe mud immersion. In our minds we were practically professionals.

Pete pointed at Drew. "You're the mixer. Water, one part mortar powder to three parts sand, and then a bit more water go in the wheelbarrow. Attack it with a hoe until you have peanut butter. Got it?" He didn't wait for an answer. "Keep the water coming, Hope. Little Sis is going to do the trowel work. Mom—because she's already used to it—does a little bit of everything. Whoever falls behind, she'll get ya back on track."

It was a surprisingly smooth operation, even if it was a slow one. Drew set up next to the hill of sand Jimmy had delivered to the backyard. We kept it covered in a giant sheet of plastic to keep it pure for the mortar work, which was torture for Roman. I marked off a corner for him to play in while Drew and I experimented and eventually got the peanut-butter mortar mixing down to an art form. Hope and I took turns hauling water, with Drew stepping in when he was caught up on mixing.

I made a path out of planks for the wheelbarrow and kept moving it to wherever Jada and Pete were slowly settling one block at a time onto the concrete footer. Jada globbed trowels of mortar in place with a narrow trowel that looked like a pie server, and I was proud of her for diving in without complaint or fear. Her cheeks had neat lines of mortar in stripes that looked like war paint. Pete followed right behind her, setting each block down in her mortar bed, and then using his own, smaller trowel to slather the end of the block with mortar before leveling it with the neon-pink string stretched corner-to-corner. The string had a line level suspended in the middle to make sure every layer of the foundation was perfectly level.

Once we had a rhythm going it went faster, but it was still going to be a long process before the layers of eight-inch-tall blocks added up to a wall more than six feet tall. My shoulders tensed as I watched Pete slide in twelve-inch increments down the sixty-foot-long back of the house and then slog through the muddiest side by the Ink Spill, which was about thirty feet. When he rounded the corner to the front of the house, he put his hands on his hips and stared at me. His exasperated look probably had something to do with me hovering over him and willing speed vibes at him with a laser-like stare. Still, he didn't scare me; a guy on his knees with his hands on his hips is not intimidating, even if he is wearing his baseball cap backward.

"Got a job for ya," he said.

Was that a loan-officer smirk I saw on his oh-so-friendly face?

"You put these blocks here?" He waved at the blocks we'd spent weeks lugging around and stacking neatly near the footer.

I nodded. Slowly. I had a good idea what was coming next. So maybe a guy on his knees could intimidate me after all.

"Too close to the footer. We'll have to build scaffolding on the high parts. Hard to level block any higher than your waist so we'll have to climb up to it."

"So . . ." I waved at the long line of blocks. Well over a thousand of them. "We have to move all of this?" My voice squeaked a tiny bit.

"Hmm. 'Bout half." He pushed onto his feet and stretched, laughing a little.

Every other sentence came out with a little laugh. Still, I couldn't help noticing that this one carried more mirth than his average.

"See that root there? The one that looks like a dog? Start a line there."

When I turned my head sideways and squinted, the root Jada had dug out of our future kitchen did look like a puppy. I lifted a block off the top of a stack and started the new row. Drew raised his eyebrows and shook his head at me when he brought the next wheelbarrow load of mortar and shoveled it onto a warped piece of plywood that Jada and Pete used as their mortar palette. My boy was wise enough to know when mistakes were funny straightaway and when the humor had to wait patiently for pissed-off to take its leave.

We worked until it was too dark to see. We had just started the second layer of block, which was depressing, especially when I looked at the seven-and-a-half-foot-tall marker at the front corner. This phase of the project was going to take a minute or two longer than the weekend I had allotted.

Drew and I cleaned tools in the icy water at the edge of the pond. The neighbor, Timothy, came out and offered to let us run a hose to his pump house. "I only use the well for landscaping, so I won't even notice if you tap in, especially this time of year."

We thanked him profusely and made plans to get back to work early the next morning.

The ride home was silent. We were learning to balance a teeter-totter of emotions. On one side there was the huge feeling of accomplishment to see the house rising out of the ground; on the other side was the sense of enormous scale that left us feeling like we were fighting an impossible battle. Then, of course, there was the fact that we all felt like a bully had tossed us off the teeter-totter and stomped on us for three or four hours. Everything hurt. It was impossible to distinguish muscles from joints. We were one big ache, and somewhere at the back of our minds a dim voice reminded us it would feel even worse in the morning.

Building an entire house in nine months had never looked more impossible.

Later that week the bank inspector stopped by and said the same. Naturally I spouted all sorts of optimism about our skill and determination, even though we had never been skilled and our determination was failing as the days and weeks passed.

We connected four long hoses to stretch from Timothy's pump house to our backyard, but the water pressure was low enough to make it barely worth the trouble. We left the hose in a bucket for a trickle-fill while we continued hauling one pailful after another up by hand from the pond. After we got moving, the hose would cut our trips by almost half, and that was worth it. We had moved into February by the time the blocks were all set, some with Pete's help and some on our own. I paid him by the hour, and by the time the Donna Fill was delivered to fill the entire space we had created with the blocks, I realized I could have hired a crew to set the blocks in two days for about the same price I had paid for us to labor over it for more than a month. Telling myself it was a solid, character-building experience didn't make me feel much better.

According to my careful schedule, we were supposed to have the entire house framed already. Instead, we stared in awe at a pyramid-size mountain of Donna Fill—which is a by-product of crushing granite. The gray powder is finer than sand but not quite as fine as talcum powder. We had twenty-seven dump truck loads of the stuff. Jimmy said it was the small dump truck, not the big one, but there was no such thing in my book. A dump truck was a dump truck, and our mountain was sized extra-large. Our block foundation was like an empty pit, and we had to fill it all the way to the top with the Donna Fill powder and pack it down tight before we poured the concrete slab floor on top of it.

We named our powdery mountain the slush pile and tackled it one shovelful at a time. It seemed impossible that we could move that much dirt in a lifetime, but it turned out to be impressive how much a determined woman could move in sixteen hours of lift-and-toss action.

Roman was in heaven. He settled into a corner with a bucket of rocks that Hope and Jada had painted to look like cars. They were nothing elaborate, but when they were lost in the mud we could paint replicas rather than worry about a hundred dollars' worth of Matchbox cars fossilizing in our foundation. When we got too close with our shovels, he shooed us away. "This is *my* Donna Fill," he said, drawing a line around his elaborate roads, holes, and hills. He was one of the only two-year-olds on the planet who not only had Donna Fill in their vocabulary but also had a working knowledge of its potential in sand-castle construction and tunnel stability, and its tendency to swallow painted-rock cars.

To the rest of us, it was the gray curse of the sandman from hell. We had Donna Fill in places it should never have gone. Our cars and house were coated with it. It got in our hair and our eyes, and I even found a handful in the bottom of my purse when I searched for a mint in the grocery-store checkout line.

It took us just over a week to fill in the basement-like space inside our block walls, so we were walking near the top block, where our slab would be poured. In the back corner of the house we were about eighteen inches off the ground, but in the front we were more like eight feet up. We weren't ready for the slab yet, though; first we had to pack the Donna Fill tight and run the sewer lines.

I rented a walk-behind Wacker packer and let it drag me around the surface. The device looked a little like an oversize push lawn mower, but weighed two hundred pounds and had a smooth plate across the entire vibrating bottom to pack the Donna Fill down tight.

The kids hauled loads of Donna Fill in after me to fill any voids created by the compression. We pulled strings tight across the surface to find uneven places that needed a shovelful added or taken away. More packing, more shifting powdery granite from one spot to another, and then even more packing until it looked as smooth as the roller rinks of my childhood. Couples' skate, everyone!

We finally finished the trench from the street to bury the water line up to the house and glued a vertical line of pipe together with a spigot on the end. The idea of having fresh drinking water on site made us all ecstatic, so it was with much fanfare that I attached a hose and turned it on. Then with less fanfare I ran to the street and turned the valve I had forgotten to open that would allow water up the pipe. When I gave it a second try, pointing the nozzle at a tree and whispering a mixture of curses and prayers, Roman clapped with delight. "Momma's peeing on the tree!" he shouted. Then he froze, eyes wide, hands tugging at his waistband, and feet hopping in the familiar I-gotta-go-now dance.

Drew shut the hose down while Roman took my place by the tree.

Pete hadn't been around in a while, but I called him for help with the sewer lines. I was terrified to place them myself. If I measured wrong, our toilet would sit outside the bathroom, and the washing machine could end up in the hallway. Not only that, but the wrong angle on a pipe could funnel sewage in the wrong direction, namely, back into my house.

"Sewer lines're easy," Pete told me over the phone. "Only one rule to remember, shit flows downhill. You get that right, everything will work out."

We muddled through with a little help from him and a lot of help from YouTube. He said he would stop by the day before my plumbing inspection to check things out.

Since I had to take half the day off work anyhow for the inspection, I scheduled a photography session that morning to get some new shots for my book promotions. I was up early getting my curls under control and trying to remember how to apply makeup. My mind was so clearly somewhere else that the photographer mentioned a faraway look in my eye like it was a bad thing. He was a trouper, but the final selection was filled with forced smiles and worry creases on the way to a migraine. I selected several almost at random, ran out of the studio and then back in twice before I had my purse, my phone, and the photo CD.

To my surprise, I actually found Pete at the job site, checking plumbing lines and adjusting a couple of the caps. Every open end, like where the toilets, sinks, and washing machine would eventually hook in, had to be temporarily capped. Then we filled the lines with water through the open end of one pipe elevated about two feet above the rest, where the city inspector would observe.

The surface of the Donna Fill had large white PVC lines running flat along the surface with the capped-off pipes sticking up like too many straws in a milk shake. The inspector's water level had to hold steady to prove I didn't have any leaks. He hung around and gave me building tips in between dropping subtle hints that I was insane for trying to build the house with my kids. I was a nervous wreck. If he found a leak, I had no idea how to repair it aside from cutting out faulty joints and then splicing new pipe in with an even higher risk of leaks because every repair would add at least two extra glued joints.

We passed on the first test and I caught myself reaching out to hug him.

The inspector checked our electric box and found we had electricity. I had no idea how long it had been hooked up, since I hadn't seen the electricians after the Funyuns day. The box passed inspection and we would now be able to power tools from our own meter.

We were left slightly shell-shocked by the amount of effort involved in the foundation. In fact, it was a part of the build that hadn't even crossed our minds back when we were building a stick house and drawing the plan. We'd had to dig deep, literally and figuratively, just to get everything to a solid ground level that felt like the start of a real house. From this point on, we would be spending a lot less time on our hands and knees in the mud and a lot more time reaching over our heads.

That self-rising flour had worked after all. Inkwell Manor was rising from the earth like a live creature with important things on her mind. Before we went home that night, we each dipped our hands in red clay and made a print on the block at the front of the house. The primitive cave-art on our massive concrete structure made me smile.

"We made this," Hope said.

"With our own hands," Drew added with a half smile that was all the way real.

We went home aching less than we had in months, maybe years. The bones, muscles, and joints still ached, but we were all beginning to realize how unimportant those aches were in the construction of a person.

That week I hired two unknown finishers to manage the slab pour. I needed it to be professionally smoothed, since I planned to stain it as finished concrete flooring. It didn't cost much more to pay them than it would to rent the concrete tools, so it was worth the cash. Despite a few tense moments when the trucks arrived too close together and dumped yards of concrete faster than we could manage, everything turned out close enough to perfect for me. Our house and our shop had a solid foundation, and it was starting to look like my relationship with the kids did, too.

Projects at the office were overwhelming enough to send me home with brain bleed every day for the next week. Programming was a great job to pay the bills and satisfied my inner geek, but office drama and deadlines were harder to handle on three hours of sleep a night.

Whether it was healthy or not, I started using a hammer to deal with stress. Thankfully, I had plenty of things to pound on without looking completely out of my mind. The kids had fallen in right behind me with the work-till-you-drop method of healing. Since most of the time they appeared to be feeling better about themselves instead of worse, I deemed it a success.

On a warm day in late February, after we ate some of the best blueberry skillet cakes on the planet, we dressed in our construction clothes. Hope packed a cooler into the trunk while Drew piled in tools. Hershey crowded in the back at the kids' feet, her head on Jada's lap, eyes darting from her to Roman.

It felt different driving up and seeing a smooth, hard slab. None of us had walked on it yet, and for a few minutes we stood and marveled over the solidity, half wondering if it was a mirage that we'd sink right through.

Finally, we stepped forward together, all smiles. It had been no small feat to make it this far. Standing eight feet off the ground to overlook our kingdom, I felt like we'd summited Everest. An inordinate amount of fist pumping, squealing, and cartwheeling took place. And just like an Everest climber, I became newly aware of the hazards of a descent. We were up out of the mud, but we had farther to fall. Roman could tumble right off the edge. We needed walls fast. We set out to put them up, certain of one thing only: Nothing is as easy as it appears on YouTube.

"Stay back, Roman. Stay away from the edge, okay sweetie?" I dashed toward him.

Drew snatched him by the arm, and then to take the sting out of it, propped him up on his shoulders. "Whoa! Look how tall you are!" he said.

"I a great, big, little, giant!" He lifted his arms high and roared.

"We need to build a safety fence around this slab," Drew said, peering down over the eight-foot corner where Roman had teetered seconds ago. Broken blocks and shards of hardened mortar littered the ground.

"No time for temporary safety nets. Let's build some walls. Until then, we'll keep taking shifts watching Roman. Jada has the first shift today." I spread a copy of our pencil-drawn plans on the floor of our future laundry room. Drew and Hope knelt next to me while Jada and Roman ran off the slab to hunt for tadpoles in the puddles.

"Where do we start?" Hope asked.

I wiped a hand over my face. I had no idea where to start. "The library," I answered, as though it were the gospel truth. "The south wall is a wet wall, so we know exactly where to put it." That was true at least. The big white pipes to carry wastewater down from the upstairs had to be sandwiched inside a wall. We walked back to that side of the house. Drew and Hope were wearing their tool belts, and I strapped mine on while we all stared down at the sewer line poking up through the slab.

"I've got the tape measure." Drew shook the hundred-foot reel tape at me.

"Who has the chalk line?" I asked.

"Jada!" Hope yelled. "We need the chalk line!"

Jada looked down at her feet and ran through the mud field to the back corner of the property, Roman trailing after her with an empty pail and muddy net. Her tongue stuck out a little while she worked the knot tying the chalk line around a fat hickory tree. Even though I was sixty feet from it, I could see neon-orange rings around the tree from the ground up to her shoulder height where she had tied it. I hoped it hadn't been hanging there as her limbo line through any rainstorms.

"Fourteen feet is what we planned." I waved Drew to the corner. "Measure out and see how close we are with the pipe." I made pencil marks at three points and was pleased that we were almost exactly on the mark with our plans. But we hadn't really understood how large the pipes would be when we drew the plans, so we would be two inches off on the other side. The wet wall had to be constructed with two-by-sixes instead of two-by-fours, to allow room for the four-inch sewer line coming down from the toilet.

"No more playing with the tools, Jada. They aren't toys!" Hope snatched the chalk line and picked stray bits of dirt and bark away before winding it up.

"Ask me before you play with a tool. And even if I give you permission, they have to be back in the shop before we leave the site."

Jada nodded, still looking at her feet.

"You can use my tools." Roman offered his mud-crusted net with a grin.

"If you and Roman gather sticks and sweetgum balls, I'll make a fire later," I said, knowing it would be just the thing to cheer her up.

They ran off, swerving for maximum puddle exposure. Less than an hour on site and their jeans were already splattered with red mud from ankle to butt.

Hope wound the chalk line in and shook the case to recoat the string with fresh chalk powder. We stretched the line and popped marks for the library walls, carefully leaving spaces for the French doors. Then we went back to the laundry room and marked it out. That pipe was off by about three inches. Still not the end of the world as far as amateur builds went.

I felt powerful, moving whole walls this way and that like giant chess pieces. The kids were getting into it, too, really feeling the house as a three-dimensional space for the first time. By the time Jada and Roman asked for lunch, all the downstairs walls were marked. It had taken longer than I expected, but I was a firm believer in measuring ten times and building once—or twice.

Drew built a fire in the rock ring and we sat around it with our sandwiches, each staring into the blaze and chewing in the same slow rhythm of the licking flames. I looked down and found my plate empty except for a piece of crust. I clicked my tongue and tossed it to Hershey. She caught it and turned her eyes on Jada, the most likely source of dropped food.

Roman was sagging in his mini lawn chair, sandwich gone and eyes closed.

I carried him to his pallet in the shop. Hershey looked forlorn to leave the food, but she followed and settled next to Roman to keep guard. I sat on a can of concrete sealer and closed my eyes. I just needed one second. The bucket tipped a little and a realized I had dozed off and almost fallen over.

Drew stood in the doorway. "Can we build a wall?" he asked.

I knew how he felt; I was anxious, too. "We have to mark the windows and exterior doors. Then we can try a wall."

"Sounds easy," he said, as though we hadn't already learned that none of this was as easy as it looked on paper.

We marked windows first, measuring a half dozen times, and then starting again. The interior wall placement had some leeway, but windows would be seen from the outside by other people. They had to be perfect. And since I hadn't even ordered them yet, I wasn't exactly sure what size the rough frame should be. We worked our way around the house and then added the doors and window to the garage, except the overhead garage doors, which would take a few more phone calls to figure out.

The number of decisions I had to make on the spot that day frightened me. There were no other adults to ask, *Does that sound right? What do you think?* It was all on me, and I was starting to feel the weight of it. It didn't take a genius or a licensed contractor to know that the decision overload would snowball over the next few months.

Because Drew needed it, we framed out one long, windowless, doorless library wall before we called it a day. The top and bottom pieces for the wall were sixteen feet long, just like they had been in the shop, but they were six inches wide instead of four in order to better insulate the house. I marked every sixteen inches on the top and bottom plates while Hope lined up the eight-foot-tall boards between them and Drew locked them in place with the nail gun. We couldn't push it upright, because we weren't sure how to brace a solitary wall that was eight feet off the ground at the base, but even flat on the ground it felt like progress.

Daylight was fading and Roman had gone cranky. "Let's head

home. We'll look at the walls again tomorrow. Maybe get a couple set in place." I wanted to build the walls as much as Drew did, but my understanding of framing the corners, doors, and windows was shaky. There were precious few purely straight walls in the open floor plan.

"Doesn't look like we did a thing," Drew said as we pulled down the driveway.

"Some days the work is invisible, but taking time to set it all up will make the next few days a thousand times more productive."

Roman named things out the window all the way home. "Horse! Red truck-truck-truck. That pond. Kid. See that kid? Motorcycle. Horse. That a school. School."

No one else spoke. Building was hard work, both inside and out. Without realizing it, we had learned to be very comfortable flat on our faces in the mud, where a fall wouldn't hurt as bad. Now that we were stretching upward, redefining ourselves, a backward tumble would really hurt. And when you've had a lifetime of people sticking their legs out on the school bus to trip you, it's hard to really believe this time will be different. This time you won't fall flat. This time you'll build higher and higher until you've built yourself a safe place.

While the kids showered, I made a chicken stir-fry with extra water chestnuts because Jada and Roman giggled over the way they crunched. It was the sort of night extra giggles might be needed. We'd all become pros at looking forward instead of back, but exhaustion slowed our forward momentum enough for the past to nip at our heels.

I pushed the stir-fry to rest on the back burner and ran to take a shower while the rice finished. Over the past seventeen years I'd become master of the speed-shower.

The kids were wet-headed and soapy-fresh when I came out. Hope directed Jada and Drew to set the table and move the food there while she made cherry Kool-Aid.

"Juice?" I asked.

She shook her head.

"Milk?" But I waved a hand as soon as I asked. We'd used the last of that for breakfast. The to-do list was long enough that things were falling off the tattered ends.

"Don't pour any Kool-Aid for me. I'll have water." I knew we'd run out of sugar next.

Jada and Roman were kneeling and standing on chairs at the dining-room table, peering into the stir-fry, when I carried drinks in.

"Oooo I see dem crunchies!" Roman said, clapping. The doorbell rang and he jumped, face stretched back like he was saying *Eeeeeeee*. He leapt from the chair toward me and I barely managed to catch him under one arm. He swung out and back again before I secured the other arm and pulled him close. I kissed his forehead, and he dropped his head to my shoulder, holding tight.

We were brushing at the edges of feeling safe and secure, but we weren't there yet. A neighbor boy selling discount shopping cards for his baseball team still set us all on edge, wide-eyed and pale. At least for now, only our hearts were running at marathon speed. Our feet were firm and unbudging. We were planting roots.

−12−

The Art of War

Hope was in middle school, Drew in elementary, and Jada in preschool when I put our home, the home we had shared with Adam, up for sale. I'd had a final divorce decree for several years by then and a restraining order for just as many, but Adam had never recognized either piece of paper. It was starting to look like nothing would keep him away.

"Some lady was looking at the house about an hour ago," eleven-year-old Drew said when I pushed through the front door after a too-long day of writing computer code.

"You didn't let her inside though, right?" I asked, scalp tingling, heart galloping.

"She knocked, but I ignored it. She was out by the sign mostly. Looked like she was doing something to it."

"Maybe it was the realtor?"

He laughed. "No. It was definitely not the realtor. She was wearing this big yellow beach hat, and maybe a bathing-suit top. Really weird. It's not even hot out. And it's cloudy."

I had a long commute in those days. Even though Hope was only twelve, she was in charge of Drew and seven-year-old Jada for almost two hours before I came home. Roman wasn't around yet. Most days my mom arranged her work schedule to be there when I wasn't, but she wasn't there that day. "It's good you didn't answer the door. You guys have to stay inside until I get home. Don't forget."

The strange lady in the yellow hat didn't set off alarm bells, but I walked down and checked out the for-sale sign by the mailbox. It was bright and cheerful, with red and blue bubble letters, but the idea of selling the house still made me sad. My kids had learned to crawl and walk there; we had celebrated a dozen Christmas, Easter, and Halloween parties there. And I wasn't leaving willingly for greener pastures. I was running away.

I opened the mailbox and flipped through the top few pieces of mail. A loose credit card slipped out and landed in the flower circle around the mailbox. Part of me wanted to leave it there in the petunias. I knew it was bad news.

A sale ad from the local grocery had a black line through "Current Resident," and a frightening name written above with a fine-tipped Sharpie. Adam Petrovic. The ink bled in little veins on the cheap newsprint as if a spider had written it with tiny webs. It didn't matter anymore that Adam didn't mean to be scary or dangerous. It didn't matter that madness had robbed him of his mind by no fault of his own. The only thing that mattered was the threat he represented to the kids and me. He was a very dangerous man.

My heart squeezed so tight it hurt. I understood how a person could really die of fright, their heart contracting tight enough to lock right up into a stone.

The next envelope, a Capital One application, had been cut open with something as sharp as a razor blade. The dark Sharpie letters of Adam's neat, all-caps handwriting were visible through the envelope.

"Car coming," Hope called from the front door.

A rush of blood flooded my face, and I blinked rapidly as I stepped away from the mailbox. I leaned down and grabbed the credit card that had perched in the branches as naturally as if money did grow on trees. All at once I was furious instead of terrified. If he had done anything to the house, anything the kids would see, I would call the police, let them enforce the damn restraining order—aka the most useless five-thousand-dollar piece of paper on the planet.

I wanted to ask Drew more about the yellow-hat lady, but I didn't want him to know it probably hadn't been a woman at all. It had been a disguise, something the voices had instructed him to wear. The credit card was shiny and new, and the name stamped on it was a combination of mine and his, Mrs. Adam Brookins. He had signed it in cursive with the same stitched-together Frankenstein of a name.

Adam was living with his sister about fifteen miles from my house. The only contact I had with the family was when he fooled them and quit taking his medication long enough for the voices to shout louder than his logic. The cycle repeated every couple of months, with him coming around the house and doing crazy things until I called his sister or the police and he was carted off to the state hospital until he was released over a promise to take his meds. Rinse. Repeat.

He wanted to believe he still owned me, and for all intents and purposes, he did. He owned us all, and his insanity was as alive in our minds as it was the first day we learned he was descending into paranoid schizophrenia.

I carried the mail to my room. "I'll change and then start supper," I sang over my shoulder, imagining they wouldn't notice the way fear had turned my voice high and trilling. I never realized how often I still watched for him until I found evidence that he had been nearby. Later I would inspect every inch of the mail. There would be clues there, hidden messages and underlined words, things he needed to tell me without letting *Them* know. Of course I'd never decipher the secrets. I was a terrible code breaker—he'd told me so for years. But it wouldn't stop me from trying, from hoping there would be a clue to what he might try next. Maybe, against all odds, a hint of how to stop it all for good.

He had been in the house again, and that was why we were moving. My clothes had been rearranged in the closet, color-coordinated from cools to warms. Taking a few seconds to mix things up made me feel better before I changed into shorts and a sweatshirt, my fall go-to casual wear. I checked my panty drawer, then laughed, not even sure what I expected to find there. Everything looked in order.

But in my bathroom, a long line of products had been arranged across the double vanity. If I combined the second or third letters of the shampoo, lotion, shaving cream, panty liners, and shower gel in just the right way, they would spell something, reveal something true only to Adam. I quickly rearranged them so I wouldn't be tempted to try.

All at once a knife blade of pain stabbed above my right eye. A pain like that would turn into a migraine if I didn't get control of it. Ten minutes. If I could just lie down for ten minutes.

When I lifted the sheets on my bed, two long columns of books slept peacefully. It was less terrifying than the knives he'd lined up there in the past while I slept, but only because I hadn't yet figured out what the books meant. The titles or the subjects would all add up to something in Adam's mind, and it could be sharper than knives. Could be a promise, a memory, an apology, or a threat. I would never be sure which.

I took a photo of the books—an even dozen. They weren't arranged alphabetically, and the first letters of the titles didn't spell anything. Eleven authors in a mixture of fiction and non-, with no obvious connection between the topics or genre. I had the idea that *The Art of War* was significant, and not only because copies of it occupied both the top-left and top-right corners. Blank yellow Post-it notes had been pushed between the pages at points in the text.

More hidden messages. More codes to break.

I cried a little because no matter what I did it wasn't enough to save us from the constant fear.

"Mommy!"

I threw the blankets back over the books and ran to Drew's room without taking a breath. He yelled again and I realized he was in Jada's room. I sucked in air, seeing spots and trying to ignore how bad the back of my head hurt, pain radiating down my neck and to my right shoulder. Adam's messages were almost always to me alone, and I could usually hide them from the kids. But this time, he'd gone further.

"Any idea what this is?" Drew pushed the toe of his shoe against one of Jada's shirts that had been laid out flat on the floor above a pair of her leggings, socks, and shoes. A primitive smiley face drawn on a sheet of plain white paper rested between the neck of the floral shirt and a sun hat. It would have been damned eerie just to see the clothes stretched out like a mini person, a two-dimensional Jada, but the smiley face took it up a notch to something terrifying. The blood drained out of my face and settled in my toes. For a minute, I thought I might actually pass out.

"Same in the each of our rooms."

I wavered again. I hadn't gotten used to the idea yet of just one of my kids laid out like a paper doll.

"I took pictures," Drew said, "and put the stuff away in Hope's room before she saw."

I could only nod. He was a step ahead and behaving like an adult even though he wasn't a teenager yet. He shouldn't have to think this way, gathering evidence and protecting his sisters from a glimpse of madness.

"Should we call someone?" he asked. "The police, or his mom?"

I shook my head. "I would if it would change anything, but it won't. There's nothing we can do."

If I told, he would punish me. Things could get a whole lot worse; I had seen them worse. My restraining order was useless. Even if they put him in jail, or back in the state hospital, they wouldn't hold him long. It was best to hold my tongue and my cool.

"We're going out for Chinese tonight," I said. "And I'll call his sister. I'll try to get her to do something. I don't want to keep calling the police. Boy-who-cried-wolf syndrome. We need them to take us seriously if we really need them." *When. When we need them.*

Drew nodded, looking around the room instead of at me. Running away was the last thing he wanted to do. But we were both as afraid to be in the house as we were to leave it empty. There were no solutions. No answers. We had no way out. Even selling the house and moving was no guarantee that he wouldn't just follow us.

For a long time, I had felt so sorry for Adam. Watching someone go insane was the most horrible thing I'd ever experienced. Despite all the things that were stolen from him, the knowledge that he had once had a family and loved them remained. But so did the realization that he couldn't be with them, and it was all shadowed over with voices whispering conspiracies and frightening solutions. My pity had long since been overwhelmed by my mama-bear protective instincts.

I had always known I would go to great lengths to keep my kids safe. But I'd never realized how hypothetical protection scenarios would feel in real life. Forget about going to great lengths. This was more than just what I would do to keep them safe, it was who I was willing to become.

The next afternoon I stopped at a sporting-goods shop on the way home, went directly to the gun counter, and rang the old-fashioned bell. I hadn't researched weapons for personal use, but I already knew what I wanted from the research I had done for the books Adam threw away with my hard drive. I had even taken a gun-safety class at this shop a few years ago to learn exactly what it felt like to load and shoot a handgun.

"Well, if it isn't little Miss Murder Book! Haven't seen you around in a while." A tall, heavy man with a mountain-man beard walked around behind the glass display case. His beard wiggled like maybe he was smiling somewhere beneath it.

"Hi, Bill. Good to see you, too." I smiled, surprised by how calm I felt given the reason I was there. "This time, I'm buying."

His eyebrows, or maybe "eyebrow" was more appropriate, rose. "Whoa, I didn't think you believed in having guns around. You sure about that?"

"What kind of price can you give me on a .38 Special?"

"Well ya see, I got more than one of them." His eyes lit up, eyebrow lifting further toward his hairline, which had been running from that brow for a few years now. "I know just the one. Don't go nowhere. I'll get it from the front. Have it on display."

He kept talking while he walked, and I took a deep breath. I wasn't in the mood to shop around. The one I wanted was the least expensive weapon that would reliably shoot bullets.

Bill was so thrilled with the little box he carried back that he practically danced his considerable bulk back behind the counter. "Looky here!" He was breathing heavily, a little bead of sweat sliding down his left temple. He opened the black plastic case to reveal the tackiest pink gun I'd ever seen. "Costs a little more because of the color. Women love it. It's a .38, too. Special gun for a special lady. Isn't that something? That's what the papers say. See here?" He held up a little brochure to prove that some advertising guy, probably someone with a college education, had actually come up with that catchy slogan.

I smiled, aware that it was a flat, meaningless smile but unable to even pretend that this was what I wanted. "Maybe something like this another time. Right now I want something plain. What can you give me the best deal on? Money's tight."

He narrowed his eyes and popped a blue Bic pen in the corner of his mouth like it was a piece of straw. "You all right, Miss Murder Book?"

"Just home protection. I'm fine, Bill. Thanks for asking." I pointed to a solid black .38 through the glass. "What will that one cost?"

"That's a little polymer frame. I could give it to you for three hundred fifty." He registered my sigh like a good salesperson. It's practically a lost art, the weighing of the sigh. "Had a guy trade a used .38 last week. Shoots fine. Tried it out myself and cleaned it up. It's in the back."

"Thanks, a used one would be perfect."

"Now it ain't nothing to look at," he said over his shoulder. "Been dinged up some." He disappeared through a swinging door.

I shifted my weight and slowed my breathing. Did I really want to do this? It was a point of no return. I shouldn't buy a gun unless I could really shoot someone with it. Could I do that?

"Like I said, not much to look at." Bill hurried back, or hurried by his definition, and pushed a half-crushed cardboard shoebox toward me.

I lifted the lid. It looked more dangerous than the pink one had. And Bill was right: This one had been tossed around enough to earn scratches and dings. I played it cool even though I really wanted it. "Looks like it's been rattling around in a toolbox for ten years, doesn't it? How much?" I looked away at the wall, trying to feign disinterest.

"It's a Smith and Wesson, and that's a good name even if it is old. But for you, Murder Book, let's say one-eighty."

I dropped the lid and tried a sigh, but wasn't loud enough to be heard over his own breathing. That was a lot less than I had expected. "I can give you a hundred fifty cash today."

He tugged his beard, but we both knew he would hold on to this one for a long time before just the right cheapskate came along. "Just for you, little lady. Just for you. And when you're rolling in cash over your next book, you come back and I'll give you some trade-in on that pretty pink lady? Special gun for a special lady. Okay?"

I smiled, although I was no longer sure I had another book in me. "When I'm ready to trade up, I'll come back by." On the way to the front, I added a twenty-dollar lockbox and a box of ammunition to the tab.

The drive home was too fast for the slow thoughts I had hoped to sort out. I paused after I opened the car door, holding my breath until I heard Hershey barking a happy welcome. Old habits, I thought, carrying my gun cradled like a baby. I liked the way she felt in my hands, heavy, powerful, and dangerous. The very same reasons I hadn't liked guns during my safety class. Things had changed a lot in the past few months. Not only things, though; I had changed a lot, too.

I pushed six rounds in and clicked the barrel into place, careful to point it at the floor. There was no safety on this model, and even if I liked the way the gun felt, I had a healthy respect for firearms.

"You need a name," I told her, tucking her in tight on a high shelf. I smiled grimly, knowing I had just the right one.

"Karma."

−13−

Rise
A Little to the Left

The kids and I had been to the house only once all week. A series of spring rains blew across the Midwest, threatening tornadoes and hail but not delivering anything more than minor floods. We fretted and fussed over how long we had spent drawing chalk lines and what might happen to our lone wall, flat in a pool of water on the slab. But whining about it got us nowhere, and we resigned ourselves to planning and watching how-to videos in the evenings.

Saturday morning I tiptoed into the kitchen and started the coffee. Either our pot was shrinking or my son had become a coffee hog. Whatever the problem, I refused to believe it had anything to do with my own consumption. A part of me—I mean a huge part—wanted to curl up and waste the morning away reading a novel. Something far removed from real life. But I wanted things to improve on a permanent basis, and hiding wouldn't make that happen. I plugged in the waffle maker and put Hershey out before going upstairs.

Drew's door was locked. I knew this without trying the handle, and thumped my knuckles on the door. "Sunshine in the forecast. Let's go build a house!" My voice was barely above a whisper, but I knew he had heard. In houses like ours, being a light sleeper was a well-honed survival skill.

Hope woke with a yawn and groan. She didn't like coffee, and hadn't yet learned that sometimes taste was irrelevant. In the adjoining room, Jada was awake, chewing her bottom lip and poking her finger at the old phone Drew had passed down to her. "Come help me make waffles," I said. "We've got a busy day."

"Is it raining?" she asked, jumping out of bed with a grin. Bright-eyed and bushy-tailed, my mom would have said.

"No rain. We're going to Inkwell!"

When we had filled up on waffles with cherry-pie filling on top and coffee with real cream, we loaded the cooler with an odd assortment of snacks and sandwich fixings and piled in the car.

The time away from the job site had everyone eager for physical work. Hershey was as happy as we were to see our mud-surrounded slab.

"I'm fishin' for frogs and fire," Roman said, arms up and eyes alight.

"Can I help with the walls?" Jada asked. "I want to build something."

"We'll take turns with Roman. Everyone gets to build." I felt a little like I was talking them into painting a fence, but there was no sense complaining about happy helpers. I would enjoy the mood while it lasted.

Sheets of plastic had kept most of our wood piles dry, but the slab had a few dips that held puddles. Roman pulled an inverted bucket over and sat on it, setting up a prime fishing spot between the den and the bathroom. He threw a tantrum when Hope swept his puddle over the side of the slab, but snuffled the tears away when Jada caught two tiny frogs in a muddy sippy cup we had left on site a week ago.

The one wall we'd built was swollen and twisted from soaking all week. "We could probably still use it," Drew said, scratching his head and chewing the inside of his cheek.

"Seems like a bad way to begin," I said, and that made the decision. "We're not settling for this. Let's drag it to the side. Once it dries out we'll see what we can salvage. Fresh start."

We rebuilt the wall, with Drew mastering the settings on the nail gun by the fifth or sixth nail. The next wall, the front wall of my library, had a window. We built the header and remembered fairly well how the half dozen YouTube videos had said to frame it. Drew couldn't stop grinning. By the time we had a handful of the exterior walls built, we had a system. Hope carried two-by-sixes over, and I marked the top and bottom plates every sixteen inches and made any cuts with the miter saw, forming headers, sills, and cripples for windows and doors. Drew and I worked together to assemble each wall, and then I knelt on the studs to hold them in place while he hit each joint with the nail gun. The entire slab was covered in sections of walls.

Jada leapt through the obstacle course of walls with Roman climbing cautiously behind her. "Can I help? Is it my turn?"

We had avoided the scary part as long as we could. "We're going to have to raise some walls and brace them. We're running out of room to build, and our measurements aren't going to be right for the next walls if we don't get these in place."

"One more," Drew said. "Let's build the inside wall between the den and library so we have something to brace these to."

He was right. But even after we built it, the idea of the bracing process made me nervous. A long, skeleton of a wall won't stand up on its own. We had to nail long boards on each end to use for support. If we had a wooden floor, we would have nailed the braces to the floor. With the concrete slab, we had to brace the walls against one another and nothing would feel stable until we had more walls up to increase support options. Houses were a lot flimsier than I ever imagined. I took a deep breath. "Library wall first. The one we rebuilt. We're going to need all hands on deck, and yes that means you, Jada."

I settled Roman in his mini lawn chair with a blueberry Pop-Tart, and we stood at the top of the wall, with Drew and me on each end and Hope and Jada spaced in the middle. Hope had rolled a thin layer of blue foam along the edge of the concrete floor slab, pushing holes in it with the threaded ties sticking out from the edge of the slab. The foam insulation wasn't used in every build, but I'd read about it and liked the idea of the extra insulation and moisture barrier. The ties were essentially extra-large bolts and would push through the bottom plate of the wall and help hold it in place during tornadoes or other potential disasters—like the crash of a poorly braced wall built by amateurs. They didn't actually hold the wall together, but they did snug it up tight to the floor. Slowly, and with grins wider than our fears, we walked our hands from the top down to the middle as we stepped forward. The holes we'd drilled in the bottom plate matched perfectly to the threaded bolts, and the foam insulation stayed in place. It was a minor miracle.

"Now what?" Jada asked.

I pretended I wasn't wondering the same thing. "Hope and Jada, hold the brace things. They'll work like handles while Drew and I get the other wall." We had nailed ten-foot two-by-fours at each end to brace against other walls, and they made decent handgrips to support the wall. I glanced over my shoulder at Roman. His feet were propped on a wall with our front door framed at one end, his attention split equally between the wall raising and his treat. Drew and I pushed the next wall up and met the corners together. The top-heavy window frame made it almost as wobbly as my nerves. "If it starts to fall, just let it go!" I told him, hysteria creeping into my voice. I had a nightmare image of the kids trying to stop the walls and plummeting over the edge of the slab with them. It was an eight-foot fall off this corner, which made me regret insisting that we start with the library.

Drew shot at least a dozen nails into the corner and was only half-way up from the slab.

"Let's not make Swiss cheese. Get it tacked and move to the braces." Our eyes met. He was just as uncertain about the stability as I was. "The corner's good, Jada. Let go of your brace and come here." I pulled a handful of large washers from the back pocket of my jeans and thumped my toe on the bolt end sticking up through the bottom plate of the wall. "Put one of these on each one. Then come back and get the nuts."

She ran back for the nuts, and finger-tightened them with so much enthusiasm that I worried she would strip the skin off her fingers.

Drew had done all he could with the braces until we had another wall. "Another interior wall next," he said. "I want to run a cross brace."

I nodded, but found I couldn't let go of my end of the wall. It might fall. We might have done it wrong. The whole thing could crash right over the edge. What if . . . I wanted to hold my hands over my ears to stop the million what-ifs. But instead, I answered the question. *If it falls over the edge, we'll pick it up, salvage what we can, and try again. That's what. Is that so bad? Can I live with that? Yeah. That's actually no big deal. Not in the grand scheme of things, anyhow. I can live with that.* I let go.

"We built a house!" Roman said, spinning in a circle next to his chair.

"Sit down, Roman," Hope said. "You can come see the house after we do one more wall, okay? Sit for just a little longer."

He sat with his fingers laced on his knees, watching like he might shout out a few pointers concerning our technique.

The next wall went up quickly but came with its own unique challenges. It didn't have insulation under it or the threaded ties to hold it to the slab. To keep it from shifting around, we had to bring out the big guns—and real bullets. A nail had to be driven through the bottom plate—the bottom horizontal board that vertical wall boards are nailed to—and into the concrete. This terrifying job was all mine. The nail gun hooked to the compressor wasn't powerful enough. I would have to drive the nails in with a device that looked a lot like a telescope but actually fired .22 blanks, blasting the nail through both wood and concrete.

I crouched at the far end of the wall, dropping the shell twice before fitting it into the middle of the tool. The three-inch masonry nail went into the business end of the power hammer. This was the closest I had come to crying since we started. I lifted the tool upright and took a breath so deep that my right ear popped. "Earplugs. I forgot." The delay made me so happy that I tried in vain to think up a reason for another one.

The kids watched with sympathetic grimaces. They could see that I was scared but weren't about to take my place. I lifted the gun, carefully choosing the right spot to rest the nail end, and tried the same trick I had relied on throughout this enormous, impossible project: imagining the worst possible outcome and reminding myself that we could get through it. What was the worst-case scenario? Oh, Jesus. I didn't even want to think about it. I lifted the hammer and after a practice aim realized I was just as terrified of smashing my hand with the hammer as I was of the crazy tool malfunctioning.

"Pretend it's Thor's hammer. Forget about the gun thing." Drew's voice was muted through the earplugs, but it still made me smile.

I lifted the hammer and brought it down hard. The .22 shell fired, and I swore I could feel the air around me expand and contract with the blast. The echo sounded for miles. Sulfur and burnt-paper scent drifted up. The tool wobbled in my grip and I let it go, more interested now in the results than in the weapon. I'd driven the nail clean in, crushing the little orange plastic cap around the nail head. The kids' eyes were wide, fingers still up by their ears, when I turned around and grinned.

"Nailed it!" I said, feeling damn proud of myself. But when I pulled the earplugs out, I could hear Roman whimpering. I hugged him and admired his latest frog-in-a-pail, Bufford. "Hope is going to play with you for a few minutes while we get this wall finished. Then we'll take a break, okay?"

"And a fire?" he asked.

"Maybe a fire. It's warm today though. We might not need one."

"I need one."

"Gather some wood and gum balls then. We'll have a fire."

He wove his way around and over walls to the low end of the slab in the garage and headed for the closest sweetgum tree to gather gum balls. Hope joined him, and I put three more nails in the wall with the nail shooter, shouting "Ears!" before each hit. The power behind the echoing blast made me feel strong and capable. Caroline would find excuses to use a tool like this. She would build things just for the joy of hammering them into concrete with a bullet. I had the urge to shout and roar a marine hoo-rah.

We had a late lunch, and then framed walls until more than half of the downstairs was complete. The structure gained stability once we had enough walls to brace and cross-brace each one into one or more of the others. It resembled a spiderweb in ways it probably shouldn't have, but at least it felt safe. Better overbraced than underbraced, I always say.

It was dark when we started packing up tools. Roman was worn-out. He and I had played for a while in the afternoon and let the older kids lay out a wall and raise it on their own. I couldn't stop smiling while I watched them push our kitchen up into a three-dimensional space. Their faces were almost unrecognizable. They were not the same kids who had slept with me on bedroom floors with a dresser in front of the door. These kids were self-assured. They were capable of anything. These kids were brave. Invincible.

Roman and I carried snacks, muddy clothes, and the cooler to the trunk. I thought the kids would get the hint that it was time to wrap it up, but they looked determined to see the entire first floor framed, even if it meant working by moonlight. "Get the tools locked up," I said. "We'll come back in the morning."

They let out a united groan, and I could hear their minds whirling for excuses. "We should spend the night out here. Camp out on the slab," Drew said.

That was exactly the right comment to swing Hope over to my side. "Mommy's right. Roman looks exhausted." She pulled the plug on the compressor and flipped the air-release valve.

Jada and Drew sighed wistfully but wound up cords and hoses without complaint. I took two steps toward them, and my vision faded around the edges. A lake of coffee couldn't compete against the effects of the sleep deprivation I'd been facing for weeks. Add some dehydration and inadequate calorie intake and it was no wonder I was at the edge of collapse.

Roman climbed into his car seat willingly, a sure sign of exhaustion. "It was a best day," he said. "A best froggy day. A twenty-eighty-five-three-hundred-froggies day."

"It was definitely a best day." I drank half a bottle of warm Gatorade, and the spots had stopped dancing through my vision by the time the kids closed the shop door and walked toward us, dragging their feet like zombies. The adrenaline rush of progress had pushed us way further than we should have gone. Every cell was depleted.

The drive home was so silent I thought everyone was asleep, but when I pulled into the garage they were all staring straight ahead, in a sort of shock.

I herded everyone in the door and made them sit at the table. Hershey collapsed two steps inside the door. None of us had the energy to cook. If I had any discretionary cash I would have ordered a half dozen pizzas. Instead, I carried two loaves of seven-grain bread to the table with the family-size jar of peanut butter, strawberry jam, grape jelly, and—my favorite—raspberry preserves. I added a pitcher of Kool-Aid and two pitchers of ice water. Before the peanut butter had made the rounds I had to refill both water pitchers.

We ate in total silence, all adjusting slowly to a new picture of ourselves and our family. The air was heavy with more than just the smell of sweat, mud, and peanut butter. It was charged with an energy from someplace deep, something primitive that had empowered the ancients with the stubborn determination to construct mud hovels with fingernail-scraped earth patted into bricks with calloused hands.

The peanut butter went around the table once, twice, and I stopped counting. Roman fell asleep after eating a full sandwich. When the bread was gone, we carried the jelly to the refrigerator and went wordlessly to showers and baths. Roman woke up enough to sit upright in the tub while I scrubbed him down but fell asleep again while I toweled him off. I carried him upstairs to his own bed, knowing there was no way he would wake up in the night.

We had worked as hard and as long setting the foundation blocks in place, but that work hadn't been as emotionally draining. The day of framing made the house real. It made our future real. For the first time in years, it made us real. We were relevant. We were alive. And we were going to keep on living.

I stood in the hot shower only long enough to rinse away the grime; I couldn't stay upright longer than that.

Other people, those whose spirits hadn't been pulverized, would have celebrated and laughed when the house was enclosed by real walls. There would have been high-fives and pats on the back. Our joy was just as real, but it was the kind you feel when you crawl the last mile on your belly and cross the finish line all the way empty. We would get to that place where we were full of happiness, but first we had to be emptied of sadness.

I fell into bed. Emptied from the top of my head to the tips of my toes.

As soon as I closed my eyes, Benjamin was there. I was asleep in seconds, but I saw the right side of his mouth lift in something that resembled a serene smile before he faded behind my dreams.

Sunday began in a series of slow-motion scenes followed by hours in hyperspeed. Breakfast was slow, the bacon salt lingering on my tongue even after I had finished my orange juice and the brilliant-yellow yolk glowing like sunshine on my toast. Drew and Hope were silent, a carryover of physical and emotional exhaustion. Jada crunched the crust of her toast. Crumbs coated her braces, and raspberry jelly dripped into the crease between her thumb and finger. She laughed easily from one topic to the next, even though I was the only one who appeared to be listening and I was mostly pretending. She was sweet perfection.

While the kids packed the car with a cooler and a clingy dog, I slipped out to the front porch for a minute alone to inhale and exhale.

It was ten thirty when we pulled up to Inkwell Manor. The kids hooked up cords and hoses without waiting for my instructions. "Do you want to put up another wall or play with Roman?" I asked Jada, knowing that she felt left out of the fun stuff a lot.

"We're hunting crawdads," she said, digging through a collection of shovels, rakes, and hoes in search of small nets on three-foot handles. Over the years, the kids had trapped countless swimming, crawling, and flying creatures in those stained old nets.

"I want green," Roman said, pointing at the blue one.

"Just stay by the ditch, not the pond. Don't let Roman anywhere near the pond." It was a mom thing to say. An ordinary warning exactly like countless others I'd issued over the past seventeen years. But this time my throat squeezed closed and a knife of pain rocketed through my stomach. Things were good, which made me terrified that they would swing back to bad in order to set the universe at ease. Long ago,

Adam had given me a scare about drowning kids that still hit my gut hard when I least expected it.

I leaned against the tool bench, head low like I was looking at something important and very, very small next to the vise grip.

"We need to start planning the staircase," Drew said. "The downstairs is almost finished!"

I forced myself upright. This was no way to live. It was time to focus, push forward, grow up. We were alive, and we might as well live. *Growing old isn't for sissies,* my grandpa used to say.

"I'm still researching the stairs," I said. "My math keeps going all wrong when I try to plan them. Every try ends with new numbers." I had left two messages asking Pete for help but hadn't heard back. "This skeleton frame may look complete, but it's just the first step. We have to add the top plate and ceiling joists next. And add the Sheetrock nailers and support nailers for curtain rods, towel holders, and shelves. There are holes to drill for plumbing and electric. The plywood has to go up on the exterior before we do the joists. Remember how unstable the shop was when we put the rafters up before the plywood? We don't want to try that here. Oh, and we have to mark every light switch and outlet since we don't have a formal electric plan. Trust me—we aren't going to run out of work before the stairs are built."

He had zoned out on me after the first few items on the to-do list, but I had needed dozens of work images to fill my head so there was no room for anything else. Seconds later, he flipped over a milk crate for the old radio and put on Bob Marley's "Redemption Song." Jack Johnson followed with some banana pancakes, and that yielded to techno, which demanded robotic dubstep moves from Drew. Bit by bit, we were filling our souls with good things. Replacing the bad memories with good ones.

I danced a few graceless steps and spun the heavy header for the pantry door in a circle, grasping it like a partner. The kids rolled their eyes. I liked it when they treated me like an ordinary, embarrassing mom instead of a fellow prisoner of war.

Hope held the cripples in place while Drew nailed them. She didn't even flinch with the pop and hiss of the gun. He was becoming a real expert, and we were all gaining confidence.

"Let's lift the kitchen wall. Clear more room to move." I loaded a .22 shell into the Ramset nailer, feeling reckless and excited about blowing a nail through concrete. We hadn't put nails in the exterior walls, because the bolts were there, but one of the bolts had stripped and wouldn't take a nut, so the nails would have to do. "Ears!" My voice was a stranger's through my earplugs. I smacked the top of the ram gun with a framing hammer and felt the numbing jolt in my fingers. A chunk of concrete flew off the side of the slab.

"Umm. Mommy? That wasn't supposed to happen." Drew dispensed his fifteen-year-old wisdom freely, especially when I'd done something stupid.

"Too close to the edge. Angled it wrong," I said, slipping in another nail.

"Go too far the other way and it'll go through your knee." He shrugged.

A dry hickory leaf drifted down and skimmed my cheek. I reloaded, wondering how effective a Ramset would be as a weapon while I sunk the next nail. Grins all the way around. The nail was tucked firmly through the treated bottom plate of the wall and into the concrete floor slab. The chip from my first attempt wasn't too bad. Since we were using all two-by-sixes instead of two-by-fours in order to get a higher insulation value, the wall would be plenty stable. A wave of shrugs passed from youngest to oldest. Nothing to worry about—it was unanimous.

"Meet the construction gurus of Inkwell Manor," Drew said. "Fear our superior skills!"

Within the hour we had a pantry and a laundry room. The entire downstairs—minus the three-car garage—was framed, at least in the most basic sense of the word. We could finally get a full sense of what it felt like to be in the space we would call home. Even though we could walk right through the stud walls, it felt more solid than the house we lived in. It also felt one hundred percent ours. But it wasn't only ours. It was flooded with an energy from deep in the earth, and the combined energy of a million women that I had grown accustomed to calling Caroline. We were not alone.

Jada and Roman tracked mud in and out of the house, and that's what it was now, not a slab but a house. They set up an elaborate potion-making factory in the kitchen. An inventory of buckets, cups, and paper plates loaded with a variety of soils, seeds, grass, leaves, and algae lined a bowed eight-foot two-by-ten. Baby-food jars of spiders, frogs, and a lone crawdad solidified their product line and made me worry a little about Jada's latest reading list. Maybe she should back away from Harry Potter for a while.

Over supper sandwiches, we wandered through the rooms, silently imagining our future. The sofa here. The secretary desk there. My mom's plant stand just here, with a stack of antique books angled on top and a mirror just behind it. We were all starting to feel very comfortable in the primitive structure. Trying it on like a second skin.

"Ready to try some plywood?" I asked, knowing it wasn't going to be as easy or as much fun as the framing had been.

Drew and Hope nodded, believing just the opposite.

The walls looked like the hollow ribs of a ship, three-dimensional but not solid. The next step was nailing four-by-eight sheets of half-inch-thick plywood on the entire exterior to create a more solid, stable structure. The library wasn't the most logical place to begin, and it was definitely not the easiest, since the slab was nearly eight feet off the ground. But I was a sucker for symbolism, so it was where we began, setting up two ten-foot ladders at the corner. Hope and I would have to carry the four-by-eight sheet of plywood up and hold it in place while Drew secured it with the nail gun.

"I'm set," Drew said from nearly twenty feet over our heads. He was standing on a ladder inside the house, ready to lean over the top and pop nails in.

Hope and I made it halfway up the ladders, single-stepping like little kids, before my ladder started going down. "Drop it!" I yelled, and because we had already planned for this scenario, we launched the wood away from us and I jumped from my ladder as it fell over into the mud. "Crap. I'd give anything for solid ground out here." The chunk of wood I'd propped the back corner of my ladder on to keep it out of the mud had sunk out of sight.

Three tries later, after sacrificing larger pieces of lumber for ladder stabilizers, we made it all the way up with the plywood. Drew stabilized it from the top, and after five minutes of "To the left. Now up. Wait. Maybe down a little? How does that look? Right. Just a little. Too much. Back left—but only a smidge," Drew finally yelled, "That's it! Hold it!" And he sank nails across the top and as far down as he could safely lean. "It's harder than I thought it would be to hit the studs. I thought I could eyeball it, but I keep missing." Judging from the frustration in his voice, if he'd been working alongside some friends instead of his mom, he would have peppered the statement with a half dozen curses.

"Just do the top and edges. That'll hold it. We'll figure out the middle," I said, still holding tight to the plywood to keep from tipping sideways on my ladder.

"Got it. You can let go." He disappeared behind our first solid wall.

Hope and I looked at each other, not moving. Letting go is always harder than you think it will be. When we finally climbed down and took a dozen steps back to admire our accomplishment, my stomach flipped over. The major ordeal had resulted in little more than a postage-stamp-size board on an enormous envelope. Hope and I sighed in harmony. No need to say it; we all knew this was going to be about as much fun as laying foundation block.

We walked around to the side of the house, by the unfinished garage, to get the next four-by-eight sheet, stopping beside Roman for a sample of the strength potion he'd mixed up for us. He zipped around after nom-nom-nomming an enormous bite from a green plastic shovel, throwing rocks into a puddle like they were boulders.

"Hershey likes it," Jada said, offering some to the happy Lab. She lapped at the green-gray mud, tail wagging. "She's going to be the strongest dog in history!"

"Any more and she's going to puke in the car. That's enough," I said. Then, when Jada's face fell toward a frown, I added, "If her powers become obvious, we'll be overrun with people trying to steal your secret formula. Best to keep this potion a family secret."

I held the shovel near my lips, nearly gagging at the moldy, rotten seafood smell, but I managed a string of eating noises. Hope was less convincing with her sample, but then we both made a huge show of lifting two sheets of wood like they were nothing. We made it around the corner before we had to dump one sheet off, prop it against the house, and then continue to the library corner for the next attempt.

The second sheet was a little easier, but only because it covered half of a window and Drew could hang out the larger opening to help us. Sheet number three was as slow and painful as the first had been. By the time it was up, we were all ready to go home. I had been up in the night long enough to be fully exhausted. I didn't bother telling the kids that it would get easier or go faster next time, because they wouldn't believe it any more than I did. It was slow, hard work. Period.

Tools and supplies loaded in the shed, and cooler, kids, and slightly ill-looking dog loaded in the car, we pulled down the long potholed driveway.

No one looked back.

We moved bedtime back an hour to pile up in front of the television with a movie and popcorn. Roman and Jada fell asleep almost immediately. I managed to eat my share of popcorn before I started dozing, but Hope and Drew were wide awake when the credits rolled. Well, their eyes were open, even if their bodies were noodle-limp with exhaustion.

I got up and turned off the television. "Get some sleep. Another big day of school tomorrow!" My attempt at cheer sounded more like mockery. They yawned, mumbled, and dragged their feet up the stairs, Drew's feet hitting as silently as a ninja's and Hope's like an elephant.

Jada was too heavy for me to lug up, so I pulled Roman's Winnie the Pooh blanket to her chin, turned out the lamp, and lifted Roman, intending to carry him to my bed. Only because I was too tired to go all the way up the stairs, I thought. But I reminded myself about the honesty pledge and admitted that it was because I was afraid. That was enough to make me stubbornly carry him up to his own bed after all. Fear wasn't in charge of my actions anymore.

That was still sort of a lie, but it was the truth I was working toward, so I let it slide.

I climbed into bed feeling very alone. "Help me, Benjamin," I whispered, closing my eyes almost tight enough to hold back the tears. "Help me find sleep."

As soon as I relaxed my muscles enough to sink deep into the mattress, like I was being pressed into a pad of Play-Doh, he was there, sitting cross-legged with his eyes closed, mouth closed, and mind open. He wasn't smiling, and I wasn't sure my impression of him smiling the night before was right anymore. Maybe it had been a warning, a grimace. But he wasn't there to share facial expressions that predicted the future. He meant for me to forget the future and the past and be right there in that single moment to find peace.

I did my best to throw the well-fortified walls of my mind down, to relax and be so fully myself that I became no one and everyone. I don't know how much of that I accomplished, or even how accurate my guess of his intention was, but somewhere along the line I had stopped questioning his existence. It didn't feel odd or embarrassing to know he was waiting in this meditation world. It felt natural and real. I drifted out, growing large enough to hold the whole house, then the country, the earth, and nearly large enough for the whole universe to fit inside me before I drifted to sleep.

The kids didn't make a sound all night, and neither did my dreams. They were silent shadow movies with neither a benevolent nor a malevolent intent. Benjamin was never part of my dreams; they were a place he sent me alone. I faced them like I did the day, with my chin raised in a false bravado that was becoming more and more the real thing.

-14-

Fall
Loyalty Won't Save You

I left work early to get new brakes on my car and made it home before the kids. Being in the house all by myself was a fantasy that almost never came true. Having Hope and Drew in elementary school and Jada in kindergarten made for a noisy life. I was smiling right up until I opened the car door and heard the god-awful noise. It was a hellacious animal cry, somewhere between a whine and a scream. It was the sound I imagined a forest animal caught in a bear trap might make. But it wasn't in the forest; it was coming from behind my house.

Sometimes I felt ridiculous, even paranoid for being afraid of Adam years after our divorce. I wondered if he had left a paranoia seed in my mind, sending me on my own path toward insanity. But then on an ordinary day I would come home before the kids and find a note, or a knife, or hear the pained scream of an animal, and know the paranoia was justified. He was never far enough away.

"Hershey?" I yelled, tears coming even though I didn't know for sure if the noise was her or some wild creature. I ran to the side door of the garage, wondering if it was safe and worried that the sound of my heart would announce me even over the animal shriek. I held back a sob when the scream grew louder. It was on my back porch, and since Hershey hadn't come to greet me, I knew it had to be her.

I pulled the back door wide and was standing on the concrete slab before I realized I should have grabbed a weapon, at least a knife.

Hershey was on her back, thrashing wildly from side to side like she had a thousand times before on a hot day when she found a shady spot of tall, cool grass. Her feet were taped together with clear packing tape. Back paw to back, and front to front. Her jaw was taped shut, too, a cellophane muzzle of packing tape, but she'd worked it open enough to make that noise, that god-awful noise.

"Shhhhh," I said, kneeling beside her and looking for wounds. The sidewalk was bloody but I couldn't see where it was coming from. "It's okay, I'm here, girl. I'll get you out. I'm sorry. I'm so sorry. I shouldn't leave you. I'm sorry." I was bawling. Snot, tears, and sobs like I don't think I'd ever cried before. I ran back inside and grabbed a steak knife, then returned to Hershey, trying to calm her so I wouldn't take gouges of her hide when I sawed at the tape.

Scissors would have been better, but one of the kids had forgotten to return them to the drawer. "How many times? How many damn times have I told them to put things away? You never know when you'll need them. When an emergency like—"

I started laughing. "An emergency like what? Like when a crazy man tortures your family pet with packing tape? That sort of emergency? Is that what my kids are supposed to plan for? Is that why I should yell at them about the damn scissors in the junk drawer?" Hershey's mouth was free even though the tape was still stuck across the top of her muzzle and under her lower jaw. But she could open it freely now and had quieted to a pitiful, high-pitched whine, intermittent, like she only had the strength to make the sound on every other exhale.

Her front feet were separated, but I'd nicked her with the knife on the inside of her right foot. It wasn't bad, but I would put some antibiotic cream on it. When the back feet were finally cut apart, she rolled over on her side, head in my lap, licking my hands while I rubbed her ears and spoke a million platitudes and promises.

I kissed the top of her head a dozen times, leaving a puddle of tears and snot. Her back was rubbed raw, the hair stuck in the smears of blood on the rough concrete. It wasn't as bad as I had thought it might be when I first saw the blood. Her spine was raw and would take some time to heal. There was no way to hide it from the kids, but there was no way in hell I would tell them the truth. God no. This was too horrible to tell anyone. I felt horribly ashamed.

I took my phone out and took pictures. I hadn't thought to take any when I had first seen her and didn't regret that even now. It would have been inhumane to delay even a second to get her out of the tape.

"Jesus! Oh, Jesus!" I wiped a hand over my face, trying to process why anyone, how anyone—no, how *Adam*—had done this.

I went inside for supplies, meaning to leave Hershey on the porch and come back out to clean her up. But she stayed at my side, her left shoulder pressed against my right leg. We walked to my bathroom like that, with me bent over to keep a hand on her rib cage, rubbing and patting in comfort.

Baby oil released the worst of the tape, but not without leaving bare patches. Her muzzle was the worst, where she had torn clumps of hair out working to open it before I arrived. She sat patiently, big yellow-green eyes on me the whole time. When I washed her back and applied antibiotic cream, she panted and moved her feet in a tiny dance, barely lifting them high enough for the nails to click against the tile. But she didn't try to get away, and she didn't whimper. She was safe with me, and she knew it.

Even when she had calmed down and eaten a bowl of kibble and drunk two bowls of water, my hands were still shaking and I had only just stopped crying. The kids would be home any minute and my head was pounding. I crawled on the sofa with an ice-cold washcloth on my swollen eyes. Hershey lay on the floor next to me, my hand draped over her.

When the door opened, Jada yelled, "We're home! We're home everyone!" A silly habit she had almost outgrown now that she was in kindergarten.

I smiled from under my mask.

The kids made the expected fuss when they saw the dog, and I sat up on the sofa, keeping the washcloth over my eyes. "She's just fine," I told them. "Got into a little scrape. I cleaned her up and we'll keep an eye on it until she heals." The washcloth trick wasn't going to work for long, and I wanted to be honest with my kids. But this time, oh God, this time was different. This time lies were going to have to do. "Give me twenty minutes to close my eyes, try to get rid of this headache. Then I'll start supper. Do your homework!" I tried to sound enthusiastic, but just sounded forced. My voice was hoarse and my nose was stuffy.

Hershey followed me to my bedroom and stayed next to my bed while I tried to get myself together.

After a few minutes, I started feeling weak and helpless and that pissed me off. "I can't just climb in bed with a cold washcloth on my head like some victimized woman in a black-and-white film," I said, tossing the washcloth and sitting up. I took a hot shower with Hershey sitting outside the foggy doors, eyes never wavering from me while I washed away the last of my tears. I was done crying. No more of that nonsense for me. This was my last straw, so to speak, and I felt a surge of power with the hot water.

I stretched my shoulder muscles under the steamy spray, hands clasped and reaching for the ceiling. "It's time to move forward. Reach for my dreams."

Hope and I made breakfast for supper. Eggs fried over easy with a side of toast and bacon had been my comfort food since I was a little girl. We added waffles to the menu, with my secret ingredient of almond extract in the batter. I always made the kids leave the room or turn away when I added it, banging around in the cabinets and knocking jars together like it was a complicated process and a long list of secrets. Waffles had never appealed to me much, but making them always put a smile on my face. Our waffle maker made four heart-shaped waffles, and no one on the planet can make heart-shaped food for their kids without it bringing a smile. Even better, instead of it beeping, singing lovebirds chirped when the waffles were perfectly crisp on the outside but just a step past doughy on the inside. I had dropped the waffle maker in soapy water years ago, meaning only to spot-wash it, and ever since the lovebirds had squawked a terrible, shrill noise that the kids never tired of imitating and I never tired of hearing.

While we consumed too much syrup, butter, and bacon, no one asked for the details of Hershey's injuries. They could see that I was at the edge of breaking. Even though I had put makeup on my red nose and under my eyes, it was obvious I'd been crying. And I was not one for frivolous crying. They had a general idea that it was something terrible, and Hope and Drew, at least, had no doubt who had done it. Maybe it was a survival mechanism in their own minds that warned them not to ask more, a little voice that warned that they knew all it was safe to know without taking a trip down looney lane.

It didn't help to remind myself that I had known he would keep coming back, that I should be prepared, that nothing he did was surprising or unexpected. I wanted him locked up. I wanted someone to protect me. But there was no place for him to go, no cure for what drove him, and no one to protect us but Karma.

I went out to fill the bird feeder while the girls did the dishes. I smiled every time I looked at the kids. Yes, I was aware that I was smiling far too much considering the circumstances. I wasn't sure if it was a fake-it-till-you-make-it mind-set, or if lunacy was already tugging at my fingertips, calling me a step closer, just one more step.

My hands were shaking so badly that I spilled a waterfall of sunflower seeds over the side. The squirrels would be pleased. I brushed seeds from my pant leg and walked toward the door.

Something caught my eye on the little table between our lounge chairs, the one for holding a tall cold drink on a long hot day. What do you know, there was a cup there, too. A clear glass mug half filled with cloudy water and chilled with a dead, white mouse.

Something was written on the mug with a black marker, but it was smeared and melting away. Fingerprints! I thought. They could get fingerprints from those smears. The idea almost made me laugh. It wasn't as though there were any question about who had been there.

I took a step closer, making out a few letters but intentionally trying not to read any words. The mouse wasn't solid white after all; it had black spots. No. It had words written on it in black marker, just like the mug. His tiny front paws were stretched up, like he was reaching toward the sky, inches from escape. His eyes were open and those little paws were still.

The blue plastic seed scoop clattered to the concrete, settling in the middle of an ugly brown stain.

After I had cut Hershey free, my goal had been to clean her wounds and apply antibiotic cream. I had been focused and working hard to look forward, not back. There was no doubt that I wanted to block out the memory of finding her there on the porch, but that was no excuse to have forgotten the blood smeared in a foot-wide stripe across the porch. Even worse, I had forgotten to look around for other things. It had never once crossed my mind, even though it should have been top of the list. Adam hadn't been as clutter-minded as I had. A screaming dog hadn't knocked him off his purpose. He had remembered to leave a telltale message.

I went inside and Hershey met me at the door, nudging my hand for reassurance after refusing to go onto the back porch. I rubbed her ears and patted her ribs until she lifted her head and tail. Then I grabbed a couple of plastic shopping bags and my phone. I slipped out to take a picture and dispose of the mouse.

"Sorry, little guy," I said when I tied the second bag closed. "I hope you find a mountain of cheese in mousie heaven." I hosed off the stain as well as I could, but would have to come back later with peroxide and a scrub brush. Cleaning bloodstains was on every novelist's list of skills that they researched but never expected to use.

I tried to keep thinking that way, as though this were research for some future novel. But I kept failing and slipping back to reality. Everyone knows that in a novel you shouldn't hurt the dog. People can be tortured, but never, ever hurt the dog.

Real life is a shade different from the novels, though. Sure, I was horrified and incensed that he had done such a terrible thing. I loved Hershey and felt physical pain over the assault. But the one pervading thought I couldn't shake was how much worse he could do to my kids. In the grand scheme of things, this was not the worst thing that could happen.

I only hoped that the worst wasn't yet to come.

–15–

Rise
One Cookie at a Time

Another round of rainstorms kept us away from the house, and I started to panic about the schedule. It was one of the rainiest seasons on record. The foundation had taken so long for us to figure out that we were months behind my original schedule. An experienced crew could have finished the block in a weekend for only a little more than I had paid Pete to help, and the saved time would have been worth ten times that. We had made progress, but I was making more bad decisions than I could afford.

Just when it seemed impossible to grab a stroke of positive luck, an angel showed up to pull us out of our muddy mess. He wasn't the traditional white-plumed, singing kind; in fact, this man didn't even believe in angels. But in our weary state, we welcomed the tall, stubborn German man who had raised me. He drove sixteen hours from Wisconsin by himself, his vehicle packed full with supplies and his head with ideas. I had more faith in my father's ability and knowledge than anyone I knew.

"Grampa Puttkammer is here!" Roman shouted, nailing the pronunciation and enthusiasm even while he hid behind my legs.

But nothing in life is simple. My dad was facing a major health problem.

Not more than a year before, on one of those Sunday afternoons when my Bradford pear trees were turning from sweetly white to electric green, my strong, always-healthy father called me from Wisconsin. "It's going to fall below freezing again tonight," he said casually, as though May frost were as common to me as it was to the Yankees. "The windchill might hit five degrees and the cat won't leave my lap. Did I tell you I ordered heirloom tomato seeds this year? And I guess they finally diagnosed that thing with my leg. Multiple sclerosis. It'll be a dry summer again. We just haven't had enough snow for the past few years . . ."

My scalp went tingly and my vision tunneled. This news was completely unexpected. Not the new garden seeds, the weather, or the lazy cat, but the relabeling of what I'd believed was a pinched nerve in his right leg. Dad had been taking care of my ailing grandparents for ten years, his own health ignored. "Multiple sclerosis, and snow," I said, not sure what the fumbling words meant. But when you talk to a Wisconsinite, every conversation has something to do with snow or the Packers, and football just didn't seem to fit. We talked medications and management, but with no cure and few successful treatments, there wasn't much to say. Even the words "I love you, Dad" lost bulky weight, bubbling up fragile and wispy across my tongue.

He was still a few years from his planned retirement and one of the most brilliant and active people I'd ever known. I said these things over and over, as though his wit, energy, and proximity to free time should have wrapped him in a blanket of immunity. The sudden, undeniable truth of Dad's mortality crushed the air from my lungs, and even when

I stood in my backyard with my arms lifted to the sky, the world no longer seemed big enough for me to inhale fully.

I was toppled by the reversal of who would be taking care of whom. Even though I was eight hundred miles away, I wanted to drop everything and run to him, slipping and sliding up his frozen sidewalk. But I had my own messy life to deal with in Arkansas, so I hadn't seen him as much as I needed to. And my messes just seemed to grow bigger and bigger. I didn't expect more than phone advice from him when I started building, so seeing him at my kitchen table sketching ideas on the back of my junk mail was an enormous relief. He was six foot two, lanky, and still looked strong as ever.

"So exactly how much do you know about building a house?" Drew asked.

"Oh, quite a bit," Dad said. "I built the house your mom grew up in. Course my dad helped. And all of his brothers. We had some friends who helped out quite a bit. And it was a lot smaller than the house you planned here. A third of the size, maybe. And it had a basement, so all the plumbing and vents ran down there, which made them easier to get to. Oh, and the roof structure was a lot different. Has to handle a hell of a snow load. But a house is a house. Nothing to it really."

The kids and I exchanged nervous half smiles. It was too late to fool us with dismissive remarks about the simplicity of building a house. And we were all too aware that a work crew of a couple of teens, a 110 pound woman, and a grandpa with a chronic illness was nothing at all like having a huge family and pile of friends over for an old-fashioned barn raising. Maybe Dad knew that, too, or maybe he's to blame for my congenital optimism.

"We'd better get my car unloaded," Dad said. "Put it off long enough."

"What did you bring?" Jada asked, hanging on his arm and bouncing on her toes.

"I came from Wisconsin, didn't I? I brought enough cheese that we're gonna need a wheelbarrow to carry it in!"

And he wasn't kidding. If Dad had a motto it would include the words "bargain" and "bulk." He had stopped at one of the Amish communities and bought a fifty-pound block of cheddar.

We spent the next couple of hours cutting it into blocks to bag and freeze. Fortunately, he had also picked up a half pallet of plastic bags intended for hot-dog buns. They were food-safe and perfect except for a smear on the printed logo that put them in a discount store. We had a lifetime supply of plastic and cheese.

We were binge-drinking slushies while we worked. "Whole flats of strawberries for a couple of dollars," Dad bragged. "Just because they were going bad. Cleaned up and frozen they make perfect slushies. I added grapes to the mix, too, half a trash bag for a dollar. Just can't let that go to waste. Think of all the work that went into growing those grapes and shipping them across the country. Might as well stick 'em in our head."

"Brain freeze!" Jada yelled. "I have brain freeze."

Roman ran in circles, laughing and drooling strawberry slushy. "My brain froze! I a ice cube in my head! Brain slushies!"

Just when I thought we had processed the last of Dad's gifts, he came in dragging two full-size coolers. "Turn the oven on," he said. "I brought turkeys!"

Yes, that was plural. Turkeys.

We baked through the rest of the day and all night. Then we stripped the turkeys clean, filling plastic bags with meat for sandwiches on the job site. We'd eat turkey and cheese until we gobbled and sprouted feathers.

Hope and Drew piled a final load of bags next to the pantry. I didn't look inside, happy that whatever we had it didn't need to be cut, shredded, blended, or stored in the now-packed refrigerator and extra freezer. The rest of Dad's treasures would be revealed soon enough.

Our first few days on the job site with Dad were spent planning more than building. It was no surprise that some of my original plans weren't the best use of space or materials, and Dad was nothing if not frugal.

Both of my parents believed in improving standard designs or inventing new ones. They dug a full-size swimming pool—with shovels—when I was six. They made plans for a build-it-yourself motorized glider and talked about building a car with a kit from a magazine. They fashioned custom tools and devices, Dad with metal and concrete, Mom with wood and fabric. They stood in the store planning how to modify and improve an item before they even made it to the checkout line. "Cut this part off, add a wheel here, put a rubber handle on this, and it will be perfect!" Dad would say, and Mom would nod, and rework the plan on the way to the car. They gardened and hunted, home-canning vegetables, fruits, and meat. They made our meals and furniture from scratch. Most important, they taught me that I could build anything I could imagine. Granted, they didn't expect me to dream quite so big.

"There's a better way to get this plywood on the exterior. Safer," Dad said. Then he drilled two small holes in the center of a four-by-eight sheet of plywood and threaded a rope through them while I gritted my teeth, convinced that he was ruining the sheet. "Now you can pull it up from inside the house, just one person guiding it from a ladder. You'll have a lower risk of head injuries at least."

He was right, of course. "What about the holes from the rope? Won't they let cold air in?"

"Those little pinpricks? It'll be a damn miracle if you don't have gaps big enough to put your head through in other spots. If they bother you, glue on a piece of foam or caulk them. No biggie. Least of your problems."

Perspective. That's what Dad offered. Not always the perfect opinion, but always an intelligent one. Having someone else to bounce ideas off was a relief. I wasn't alone anymore.

Roman toddled up after we had most of the downstairs plywood in place on a Friday night. "I a doughnut!" He was completely naked and had rolled himself in sand. Sugar-coated. The section of our sand pile that I'd roped off for him was his new favorite play place, even though I wasn't sure if I preferred it over mud.

Dad had brought a large collection of toy cars and trucks he'd picked up from curb trash on his daily walks. "Can't see any reason to put all that in a landfill when there's a lot of good use in it."

Dad's multiple sclerosis was impossible to ignore. He was still strong and had eased so much of my stress, but he had also added a sackful of new worries. He had to use a cane a lot of the time because he was off balance. When he tired out he got dizzy all at once, like a wave that knocked him down wherever he was. "When it comes over me, I'm done just like that. Have to sit down awhile. There's no arguing with it like you can with the regular kind of tiredness."

I arranged lawn chairs in strategic locations and forbade him to climb on ladders. He used the chairs and the ladders. One out of two isn't bad, I suppose.

Every other night he injected himself in the stomach with interferon. It wasn't a cure, but there was a small chance it would slow the progression of the disease and reduce the frequency of his weakness spells. He paid a high price with side effects, but bravely continued, since it was the only possible relief for the wicked turn his own nerve cells had taken.

He was tough, though, and he gave me the confidence to tackle impossible things like framing the three-car garage. I had put it off because the garage floor slab was four inches lower than the house, and the step down made everything more complicated. The step and some differences in the ceiling joists would make the ceiling tall enough for the garage doors while leaving the upstairs all a single level. In short, it was a complicated section to frame, and expensive because of the taller studs—each had to be hand-cut to exactly the right length—and the heavy headers above the two garage doors.

I had ordered our ceiling joists premade and was happier now than ever with the decision. They supported a lot of weight and needed to have enough room for the HVAC ducts and plumbing to run between the two stories. They had been ready for weeks by the time we were ready for them.

Dad supervised the joist delivery and a crane to lift them into place while I was at the office. I couldn't stop smiling when I saw them. The structure felt a lot more homelike even though the joists looked more like a rose trellis than a ceiling or floor. And as much as I loved being up out of the mud with the majority of our work, I had started feeling more and more nervous about how far off the ground everything was happening. We weren't even working on the second story yet and already a minor mistake could cause a serious injury. Why that had never crossed my mind back when we were building the little model house out of sticks, I'll never know.

To keep us safely on the ground as long as possible, I directed everyone to finish the nailers for Sheetrock and supports for towel and tissue holders. We planned gas lines and water lines even though we were nowhere near ready to install them.

Dad must have suspected what I was up to, because he started telling the stories about when he was drafted during the Vietnam War. They were stories about basic training, protests, and race riots in the capital. He told about hearing a visiting marine in basic who announced they didn't have enough people listed as ground infantry in the marines and were going to move some of the army guys over. "You, you, you, and you," the marine said, pointing right down the line of draftees. The next guy in line wavered, weak with relief. Dad said he would never forget the look on the guy's face. To be one finger point away from almost certain death and escape. It changes everything.

The stories varied, but the theme was consistent and relevant. Dad had been told by friends to keep his gaze steady and blank and never volunteer for anything. But he was my dad, so he rarely listened to advice even if it felt sound. He was restless and bored, so he held his hand up whenever they asked for a few volunteers, even if he knew he had no idea how to complete the task. Most of the time, he ended up in a better place because he jumped in and took action. He carried better weapons, learned more skills, and was well respected.

So when another guy showed up, pointing and assigning each draftee to their next duty base, Dad and a couple of other guys received a different assignment from everyone else in training. He was sent to Langley, Virginia, to take a position in the presidential honor guard, while most of the others went straight to Vietnam.

Dad was telling me to get my hand in the air, take action, quit staring straight ahead to avoid the beady eyes of danger. I might avoid the potential of a few bad things that way, but I was also avoiding the good.

I came home from work on a Wednesday, resolved and determined to get the second story under way. Dad had been spending his mornings at the job site and then coming home for a nap before heading back out with us for the late afternoon and evening. As soon as I entered the house that day, I knew something was wrong. A bowl of soup was half spilled on the breakfast bar in the kitchen, and everything was dark and quiet. Hershey cowered down, tail between her legs, and led me up the stairs.

My legs went numb. I was thinking of Adam, wondering if he had come back and done something terrible. By the time I reached the top of the stairs I knew thoughts of Adam were half distraction to keep myself from thinking about Dad.

I found him curled in a bed we had set up for him in our playroom. I'd never seen my dad look so small. He had pulled a quilt over his head and he was crying. "MS attack. Have to rest," he said. "Sorry."

The world spun wildly around him, rising and falling on waves that left him nauseous and weak. His words came out slow and slurred, and half of his face slumped in a mild palsy. With the help of an eye patch, his dizziness subsided after a couple of days and he was on his feet again. The attack had taken a toll, though, and I knew that every attack meant additional, permanent nerve damage.

The attacks would keep happening, no matter what he did, but there was no denying that stress made them worse. I worried that I had caused it. My crazy project had taken him down a notch, stolen away some of his life.

We were all tired and we were nowhere near the end. Was it worth it? For a house? Nothing more than a damn house?

But somewhere deep I knew that we were building more than that and we had no option to quit. The supplies were piled up and we still couldn't afford to hire someone else to puzzle them all together.

Sometimes, when you raise your hand and jump in, there is no going back, no way out. And sometimes, that's exactly the sort of commitment a person needs in order to make a profound life change.

It was time to move forward and up, so that's exactly what we did. Dad was at least as stubborn as I was, so he was right there with me. "I'll go out to the house with you this weekend, make a plan for the next stage," he said while Roman and I were planning supper on a Friday night.

I nodded, avoiding his eyes and my own guilt.

"I want peanut butter and eggs!" Roman said.

"Don't you want turkey?" Dad asked, smiling crookedly.

Roman rolled his eyes. "I can't eat more turkey in my life." Then he raised his eyebrows and grinned. "Can we have cookies?"

"Maybe one cookie after supper. Spaghetti sounds good. Everyone likes spaghetti." It was one of my dad's favorites and he hadn't been holding much down lately.

"Some garlic bread would be good," Dad said. "Get me a piece of paper and I'll draw what I came up with for the water heater in the attic and some storage up there. I might have the knee wall figured out in your room, but the rafters are going to be hell. No way around it."

"I'll make cookies," Roman said.

"First let's make your spaghetti." I tweaked Roman's nose. "One crisis at a time."

"One cookie at a time," he agreed, hands on his hips and nodding like a bobblehead all the way to his booster seat.

I couldn't remember if March came in like a lion or a lamb, but April was all lion. We had been deluding ourselves with the rosy idea that the second floor was going to be exactly like framing the first floor. Crawling around on the ceiling-joist beams, we all learned valuable lessons. First, the kids learned how terrified of heights I was, a fact I had hidden well to that point. And second, a glaringly obvious thing we had all overlooked: In order to build the second floor, we had to somehow move all the lumber for the floor, the walls, the ceilings, and even the entire roof from the muddy spot outside the garage up to said second floor.

Dad gave us some great suggestions, but he wasn't going to be able to lift as much as he would like to. He was still unsteady and tired easily. I dubbed him the project supervisor. A lifetime of yelling instructions at Green Bay Packer coaches through his television screen had primed him for the job.

"Can't we hire a crane?" Hope asked. But she knew we hadn't budgeted that. Paying for the joist construction and delivery had put us at the red end of our budget.

"This is an old-fashioned build. Like the pyramids. All hands on deck. We can do anything."

"I wish we had more hands," Jada said under her breath.

So did I.

Drew called a couple of friends over for a few hours on Saturday. In exchange for some sandwiches and sodas, Taylor and Bret spent the day hauling lumber. I could tell by the look in their eyes that they wanted to flee, but I made the best use I could of their help for the day. The boys had spent precious few hours in the sunlight away from their computers, so introducing physical labor was a shocker. I kept Taylor on the ground with me, hoping his exceptional height would be useful. We slid a four-by-eight sheet of tongue-and-groove plywood off the stack and lifted it so we were left holding a four-foot side. Drew and pasty-white Bret each grabbed a corner and pulled it up, making a stack up top. We tacked a couple of boards in place so they would have a safe, elevated work space, and then carried on moving nearly two-thousand square feet of plywood up to the elevated platform.

The boys were eating a mountain of turkey sandwiches and dreaming they were done working for the day when I remembered the bathtubs. We had my oversize garden tub and a traditional bathtub-shower combo to move upstairs, and I had been wondering how the kids and I would get them there on our own. They had to be framed in the rooms where they would live because they were too large to fit through finished doorways. Getting them up before the walls were framed was essential. I kept an eye on the three sandwich-vacuuming boys and waved them over when they stood to leave. "We have just two quick things to move up and could really use your help before you go."

To their credit, both boys smiled politely. They weren't quite as good at hiding their true feelings when I led them to the shop and pointed to the final two things. But they dug right in and moved the tubs to what had become known as our launching point outside the garage. It took nearly an hour to get the garden tub properly tied, and we ended up using a couple of long boards that would later be part of the roof as a ramp to pull the tub up. The smaller tub-shower combo was much lighter, and since we had the ramp system in place it took only fifteen minutes to get it up to the second floor. The tubs looked like an odd art project balanced on the ceiling joists before the floor was even in place, but this build was nothing if not odd.

By the time I turned around, Taylor and Bret had made a remarkably fast and quiet escape backing down the long drive. I waved, but I'm not sure they ever looked back.

We had nothing left to lift for the day, and it was a good thing. I couldn't stand fully upright for the next two days and could barely sleep through my back spasms, which strengthened whenever I thought about all the lumber for the walls we still had to lift after the basic plywood decking was in place.

Screwing down the tongue-and-groove plywood for the subfloor was actually a lot of fun. It was fast progress once we got a system going, and it felt good to be up in the sunshine. But before we could move the rest of the lumber up, the spring rains picked up again. Work gave me a new project writing software for the city parks and recreation department. It kept my mind too busy to go mad with restlessness and guilt over lost time on the job. Dad made endless plans on scrap pieces of paper and cardboard, writing figures and prices in the margins. I offered him whole stacks of brand-new paper, but he is a recycling king all the way through. The rain gave him the time he needed to rest and rally for another round of work.

Pete called on a rainy afternoon. I hadn't heard from him in so long that I had worried we'd lost him for good. "I can come out and frame the stairs tomorrow. That work?" Pete asked. "Buddy of mine can help. Twenty-five an hour, each."

"Okay, but only if you can both work really, really fast."

He laughed like I was kidding.

The pair showed up the next day right on schedule, which was a surprise. The friend, who was introduced as Reggie, quickly became known as a Re-Pete. Pete and Re-Pete were the biggest love/hate paradox of my life, both my saviors and my downfall. Re-Pete had clearly spent a lot of time lifting weights and no time lifting a hammer. He eventually figured out what Pete needed him to do, but I was paying them both a lot of money for on-the-job training and explanations, not to mention dozens of Pete's famous anecdotes. I was a big fan of stories, but Pete couldn't walk and talk at the same time. Not a hammer was raised while he dished out tales about the cows and puppies of his youth. "Know what I mean?" he would ask for the tenth time in a short conversation, and I would nod vigorously, which he promptly mistook for enthusiasm when what I meant was *I've already paid thirty dollars for this story, get on with it!*

When we finally had the two-by-four rough staircase built, it was a double-edged sword. We could easily haul supplies—and my aching back—upstairs. But Roman could also go up to the enormous, empty floor where any two-year-old would love running laps. The front corner was nearly twenty feet off the ground, and that was heart-attack height for any mom.

"It's great motivation to get the walls up!" Drew declared. And he was right. Dad helped us mark everything with chalk, altering our plans significantly for the upstairs based on things we'd learned building the first story. Projects always looked a lot different in 3-D. We also found out how difficult it was to line up key upstairs walls over the downstairs counterparts so that plumbing and electrical could run straight down through. This had been easier to draw on paper than it was on plywood with a chalk line, but we eventually managed and started hauling two-by-sixes up, some by the stairs and some over the side of the garage. Each method had supporters, but in the end both were plain old hard work.

"Before we start framing, we have to figure out this final wall in my room." I pointed to a spot on the subfloor where I imagined that the wall should go. Inkwell Manor had a side-facing garage, and it was a full two stories everywhere except over the half of the garage at the front of the house. This would give the roofline some visual interest and make the house into something other than an enormous box. But even though I had looked through a dozen books and Web sites about building a short knee wall on that end of my bedroom and a steep pitched roof over that part of the garage, I still had no real concept of how to do it.

Dad ran his hand down his face and sat in a lawn chair on the opposite end of the enormous subfloor, so we had to shout a little to hear each other's pathetic ideas, all starting with "What if" and "Maybe."

We weren't making any progress. Finally, Dad lifted his palms in surrender and shrugged his shoulders. "The easiest thing is to just put another room there. You already know how to do that. Frame the walls all the way out and the roof straight across. Put a door in from your room."

"Another whole room? I don't really need that." But I was already making plans for it in my head. "And it will be a lot more expensive to do another whole room."

"Not really," Dad yelled. "The steep rafters, extra plywood, and shingles were going to be a lot more expensive, so you'll save some there. I'll bet it would be hell to shingle at that angle, too. You'd have to hire someone with a bucket truck. Really it's just the price of a little extra Sheetrock, flooring, a window or two, and your brick."

I paced the area that was supposed to be part of the outdoors but just might turn into another part of Inkwell. I wasn't convinced.

"Either that or hire someone to tell you how to do it the way you planned," Dad added, going for a wrap on the hard sell.

Pete didn't really know how to build what I had drawn for him, but said he could probably figure it out. I knew for sure that would cost me more than the windows and Sheetrock for the extra room.

I nodded at Dad, and we finished chalking the lines for walls.

Dad was up and moving around almost as good as new over the next few days. We framed the entire upstairs in a weekend. I renewed my incessant chant of "If it starts to fall, just let it go!" with every exterior wall we raised. My voice was more frantic than ever as I imagined my kids plummeting over the side. Finishing the upstairs was a grand accomplishment, but with sixteen-inch spaces between the studs it wasn't enough to keep Roman in, so he wasn't allowed upstairs without holding someone's hand, not until the plywood was in place. It took only three tries for us to figure out that we couldn't manage that on our own, so I called Pete back before we headed home late that Sunday.

"Re-Pete can help again, too," he said.

I hesitated, but decided I could be straightforward, since I was technically the boss. "Re-Pete doesn't seem to know a lot about building. Seemed more like a gofer than a builder."

"Fair enough," he said. "He has a lot to learn. Tell you what. Pay him ten an hour while he's learning." Re-Pete was still getting the better deal, but I agreed to the terms, ever optimistic that things would go better than the facts suggested.

Pete and Re-Pete only took a week to get the plywood on the upstairs, which was a record when it normally took me a week to get them to show up. Drew helped them with a lot of it, working after school until dark. If he hadn't been there pushing them forward and forcing Pete to work while his lips moved, it would have cost me triple in both money and time.

Dad worked from the ground most of the time, drilling holes in plywood and planning new and better ways to get the job done. He spent plenty of time on a ladder, too, and nothing I said would keep him down. "I'm only going up a little ways," he'd say. "This is nothing. I'm doing fine. MS means I feel like shit if I'm sitting at home or working, so I might as well be working. I rest when I get tired."

We spent a day cleaning up after the plywood was up and the ladders were happily pulled down for a while. We were eating lunch when a neighbor stopped by with his son. We'd met the son once before, but I couldn't remember his name and was too embarrassed to ask. The son was looking for work trimming trees, and he wondered if we needed anything tidied up. We didn't, but they enjoyed looking around the house, so I took them upstairs for a full tour.

"What we need is some help building the rafters. Any chance you know how to do that?" I asked, blinking often to keep the hope from dripping out of my eyeballs and pooling at their feet. They shook their heads in unison—the dad stepping square in a puddle that the son had just sidestepped.

"You really do need a roof, don't you!" he said, and thankfully didn't turn in time to see me roll my eyes like Hope.

"What about these windows and the doors downstairs? When do you cut those out?" He knocked on the plywood covering one of my bedroom windows.

"It's on the to-do list. But honestly I sort of suck with the reciprocating saw. It has a lot more muscle than I do," I admitted, stepping in a puddle on purpose.

"Probably take me less than ten minutes to do the whole house with my chain saw," the son said.

I raised my eyebrows, and probably dropped my jaw, too. "You could cut those out with a chain saw? No way. Not possible." I really thought he was kidding, maybe a little cruelly even, messing with the woman who knew nothing about building a house but was trying to do it anyhow.

"Really. An hour tops."

I bit my lip. When a thing sounds too good to be true . . . But then I thought, *What the heck? He wants to try it, let him try it. What could possibly go wrong?* "How much?"

"Fifty bucks. Doors and windows. Neat and trim."

We shook, and he disappeared down the stairs. I stayed in my room, too embarrassed to go down and admit to the kids and Dad that I was stupid enough to believe that this nameless guy could do construction work with his chain saw. Five minutes later, he fired up his chain saw in my bedroom. I shook my head: *There's a thing not every girl can say with a straight face.*

It took him about a minute to cut the first window, but the others went faster. He just dipped the tip of the chain saw through the wood and sliced down like he was drawing a line through butter. The perfect rectangle fell out somewhere around the kitchen downstairs. Definitely something to warn the kids about.

I ran for the stairs. Drew and Dad were already rounding the top of them, eyes wide. I grinned and left them to watch while I ran to warn the others. Jada and Roman came up to watch while Hope covered our lunch to keep it sawdust-free.

The entire process was so much fun to watch that I forgot to time him, but it couldn't have been more than fifteen minutes to do the entire house. He even ran from window to window to prove his point. The same job would have taken Drew and me a whole day of wrestling with the reciprocating saw. We would have left a jagged mess of wood along the edges and maybe a lost finger in the mix. The day was on my short list of favorite building days to date.

"Don't suppose you want to come back later and carve that hickory out front into a large inkpot and feather?" I laughed, happily handing him his fifty bucks.

"I'm not much of an artist. But if you need a hand with any other quick cuts like that, holler at me. That was fun!" He was grinning as wide as I was. "Wasn't really sure it would even work. Never done anything like that before."

Well, great. I'm glad he didn't lose a limb in the process. But really, even his confession didn't stop me from smiling.

"Worth every penny just for the entertainment value," Dad said, grinning wide.

–16–

Firefighters Have Hoses *Fall*

The spring talent show at Hope's middle school was a lot more entertaining than I had expected. Watching handfuls of awkward twelve-year-olds dance, sing, and act was a lot more fun from the parent side of the bench than when I had been a shy child working up the courage to take a stage. Jada had loved it the most. As a first grader, she had been starstruck watching the big kids.

She chattered and sang song bits all the way home.

"Mommy?" Hope's voice edged up, laced with fear.

Fortunately, the kids were paying more attention to where I was going than I was, because as I drove up our driveway, a red Honda headed down it straight for us. It was Adam's car, of course.

I backed out without looking for traffic, then took off down the road, dialing my cell while I took a corner through a neighborhood and toward town. If I had taken time to think it through, I would have headed straight for Ivana's. Her house was only a mile from mine, but in the opposite direction and there was no easy way to turn back now. Sophie's house was nearly ten miles away.

"Where are we going?" Jada asked. "I thought we were going home."

I was relieved that she had been too distracted to notice his car, as though ignorance were a thing powerful enough to keep her safe.

"Shhh, I have to make a quick phone call," I said, which was true, but I was also avoiding their questions for as long as possible. I glanced in the rearview mirror and ran my fingers through my hair as though primping was on my mind instead of a potential high-speed chase. Adam's car pulled closer.

"Still there," Drew said.

"How is getting away so easy in the movies?" Hope asked, her breath rapid and shallow, at the edge of panic.

I took three more turns and came out in another neighborhood. Ivana's home and cell number had rolled to voice mail. I didn't leave a message. If you can't say something nice, don't say anything at all.

Sophie picked up her cell on the third ring.

"He was waiting for us at the house," I said, as panicked as Hope had sounded. "I know you don't want me to call the police. I promised I'd always call you first. But we're in the car, and he's chasing us. You have exactly two minutes to get him away before I call the police."

"I'll call you right back," she said, but then cleared her throat and wasted several precious seconds to add, "Thank you, Cara."

I hung up.

I couldn't shake the image of him in that hospital, so doped up that he couldn't lift his feet or his lower jaw. Maybe that was the real reason Sophie had taken me there. To make me pity him—and her—enough to cut him some slack. But a car chase was a lot to ask of anyone. Even someone who had once made big promises.

My phone rang. It was Sophie.

"Still there," Hope said at the same time I said, "Hello?"

"He left his cell at the house. Mom answered it," Sophie said.

Ivana was home but hadn't answered when I called. So she was screening my calls. I didn't mind much since I didn't want to talk to her either, but this was an emergency. She should know I wouldn't call for idle chatter. I never had.

"I'll have to call the police. I won't let him put the kids in danger, Sophie. This isn't fair." As soon as the words were out, I regretted them. Since when did fair have anything to do with life? This wasn't fair to her either. She was in for a lifetime of unpleasant calls like this one.

Jada was crying. Hope was sitting backward in her seat to get a better view out the rear window. Drew was practically backward in the passenger seat.

"Everyone turn around and keep your seat belts fastened. I'm going to figure this out."

"Wait, Cara. Let's find another answer. He can't go through another hospital stay!"

I jerked around another corner, happy to see a main road. The neighborhood had started to feel claustrophobic, and I didn't know it well enough to be certain I was avoiding dead ends.

The closer we got to town, the safer I felt. There's safety in numbers, I kept thinking. But the first red light we came to nearly had me barreling through stopped cars like a bulldozer. Only one car separated him from us. If he jumped out and ran up to the car, we were trapped. The doors were locked, but windows are easy to break. I had a crowbar under my seat that would do the trick. Adam would have one, too. And crowbars were the least of our worries. A bullet would cut through glass like butter.

The light turned green and I spotted a fire station just up the block. A big American flag flying overhead. Freedom, that flag said. Safety. So I pulled in and started opening my car door, thinking I would run out. But I knew from the time we'd come down to donate to the pancake-breakfast fund drive that fire-station doors were locked up tight. If I ran for the door, and he pulled in and got out of the car, the kids would be alone.

I imagined ramming the big overhead doors. And then laughed. It was a single "Ha!" I couldn't believe how stupid I'd been. "Firefighters don't even have guns!" I shouted.

The kids laughed, too, even though it wasn't funny.

What the hell was I thinking a firefighter could do to save us? I had no idea why it had ever seemed like a good idea. He had pulled in behind us. I went around a handicapped parking sign and pulled around on the grass to get back on the road. I was headed for the police station, and wondering if arriving there would do me any more good than sitting in the small fire-station parking lot.

About the only thing that was clear to me was that I wasn't thinking clearly. I wasn't sure how to get to the police station. I wasn't sure I could get back home. And Hamot, Arkansas, wasn't exactly a bustling metropolis. The whole police force was around twenty-five cars and I was probably being generous.

I kept driving, and the fact that I was lost was most likely what saved us. Exactly what it saved us from was a mystery, but when I was making a three-point turn down a street I'd never seen before that was too far from town to be near a police or fire station, Hope said, "I'm pretty sure you lost him. I haven't seen him for a while."

"Me either," Drew said. "I was just about to say the same. You lost him."

"Who's lost?" Jada asked.

From the rearview mirror, I could see the wheels spinning, her eyes wide with memories.

"Remember how Adam was having trouble thinking clearly?" I said. "I think today was a bad day for him. He got confused. We'll all be okay though. Sophie is going to find him." I had the urge to drive to

Wisconsin, where my dad and grandparents lived. Home. We felt safe there. Nothing bad ever happened back home. Adam had never been there.

My phone rang. It was Ivana. I connected without saying anything. I didn't trust it to not be Adam.

"Cara? Is that you? Can you hear me?" she asked.

"Yes."

"You haven't called the police, have you?"

"Not yet. I was on my way there. To the police station," and as I said this I wondered why in the world I hadn't called them. I should have. Of course I should have. I had even said I was going to. I had meant to after hanging up with Sophie. I really had. The worst part was that I hadn't avoided the call to save him, I had simply been so wrapped up in my fear and the idea of getting to the station that I had lost the train of thought that would have made me call. I had panicked.

"He's home now. Adam's here with me. I'm having a talk with him. We've got it all under control."

I nodded, but I had started crying and couldn't stop. Couldn't speak. I had failed again. Failed to do exactly the right thing to save my kids.

"Are you still there? Don't go to the police. He's here and he knows he has to stay here. He isn't going anywhere. I'll sort this out with him. Okay?"

"Okay," I said, not even sure if the whole word got out before I had disconnected. I turned the ringer off and pulled into a parking lot, not even looking to see where we were.

"Pizza!" Jada yelled.

True enough. We were at a pizza joint. I handed my billfold to Hope. "Get two. Jada can go with you." I was still crying and wasn't sure I would ever stop.

I waved at the radio and Drew turned it on, starting with "Don't

Worry, Be Happy," which only made me cry harder. But that turned out to be the last outburst. I found a tissue package of questionable age in the back pocket of my seat and cleaned myself up.

Drew handed me a bottle of water, also of questionable age, that tasted like the hose water of my childhood. I smiled.

The pizza made it out in record time. No one had mentioned that they were hungry, but stomachs rumbled all the way back to the house.

I slowed at the end of the drive, planning to get the mail.

"I'll walk down and get it," Drew said. "Let's get this pizza in before Jada's stomach chews its way out to the box. I've never heard so much grumbling in my life!"

She kicked his seat. "We got the little packages of Parmesan cheese!"

I smiled back at her just in time to see her licking her lips. Who cared what chaos was brewing around us? A mini package of smelly old Parmesan cheese was enough to bring us around. We were too used to this. Too pliable from too many traumatic events.

We were also too deep to climb out. Too aware that sometimes the only safe place was behind a false smile.

–17–

Rise
What Is Down Must Go Up

Before we had boxed in the upstairs for good with plywood, we had enough sense to push the ceiling joists up through the studs. They were eighteen-foot two-by-tens and would have been difficult to get up the stairs and then turned to an open room where they could be fed up to the top of the walls. They sat in three stacks in my bedroom, and Roman had strict instructions to avoid them and the open windows, but otherwise he was finally free to run and play upstairs. I was relieved beyond words. The only thing we were missing to have the house in the dry was a roof.

Jada and I spent a Wednesday evening lifting the ceiling joists up to Drew, who straddled the middle of the wall between my bedroom and Roman's. Since it turned out to be the best place in the house to feed them up, we decided to put them all up there and then disperse them along the length of the house later when we nailed them in place. It was getting dark, so the goal was just to get them up there. My dad had gone back to the house to rest, and we were anxious to join him. We worked by the car headlights for the final stretch. By the time we had the last board up and our muscles were screaming, the thunder and lightning started. I hated the idea of leaving all those expensive boards up there in the rain after working for so many months to keep them dry, but the framed house had survived dozens of storms. We congratulated ourselves on a job well done over a handful of beef jerky and headed downstairs.

Roman and Hope had swept up the downstairs, an endless chore with mud, leaves, and sawdust covering everything anew each day. Roman was bouncing a dozen quarter-size Super Balls in crazy patterns through the house. It was clearly driving Hope nuts, but he was giggling so hard that no one with a heart would ask him to stop.

Hershey was flat on her side in the dining room. A small patch of hair was permanently missing next to her spine, but no one ever mentioned it. A Super Ball bounced off her hindquarters and her eyes barely flickered. Good old dog, she was. No doubt about it.

"Get all of them, Roman. There's still a red one in the den," Drew said, holding his hands out, already overflowing with balls. I had the ridiculous idea that they were cleaning up until Roman dropped a red ball in Drew's hands and he yelled, "Watch out! Here they go!" He flung the balls as hard as he could across the room.

Roman screamed in delight, running after them and then turning tail and running back when they leapt back at him, a delirious mix of terror and joy across his face. The balls ricocheted off studs, and each set out on its own wild path, thumping against us and Hershey, and then finally all rolling across the concrete, seeking out a low point. The shop lights hanging from studs with too-bright bulbs doubled and tripled the effect of the balls with wild shadows.

"Again!" Roman screamed, handing a green and white marbled ball to Drew. "Do it again!"

Hope rolled her eyes; the chaos was too much for her ordered mind. The rest of us were all in, gathering the balls and depositing them with

Drew. I caught Hope's eye and nodded up the stairs. She tiptoed up, and I knew she would go to her own room.

Drew put in four more rounds of ball-tossing glee, which had us all running and screaming after them like Roman had and then running back the other way. We could have gone on longer even though we were tired and hungry, but Hope came down to announce that the rain had really started. Even without the roof, it would be a while before it made its way down through the tongue-and-groove flooring upstairs to cover the slab. But it would, and we would have yet another mess to clean up. Sounding like broken records, we drove home, talking all the way about how much we needed a roof.

Jada was the first to throw up that night, but Roman wasn't far behind her. Hope started closer to sunrise, and I was glad she at least had some sleep. Drew said he felt fine and went on to school. I couldn't blame him; I would have run for the hills, too, if I had the chance. By noon, I was throwing up in between cleaning up the kids and handing out cans of ginger ale.

The stomach flu lasted for just over twenty-four hours, leaving us weak and pitiful. Dad avoided us all and by some miracle never caught it. My stomach hurt almost bad enough for me to forget how bad my back hurt. Drew was the only one unaffected, and he hid out in his room to avoid our germs. It was nice to hear rapid-fire automatic weapons echoing in his room again. It had been too long since he had time to get lost in a video game.

I thought about how I had been escaping with Benjamin and realized we each had our refuge. Jada had her dolls and toys, and Hope found peace in her craft or scrapbooking projects. I forgave Benjamin a little for leaving my kids out. Maybe they each had their own Benjamin after all.

It had rained through both nights of our sickness and most of the day on Friday. We were up bright and early on Saturday morning, even if we weren't bushy-tailed. We arrived at Inkwell ready to do some serious work on the ceiling so we could start the rafters, which I had a number of misgivings about building—but first things first.

Drew carried the compressor and nail gun up and I followed with nails, various tools, and supplies. "Oh, crap," he said, sounding a lot like Hope had downstairs when she saw how much water had pooled across the slab again.

"This sucks," he continued. "I mean, this really, really sucks."

I looked up and saw that it was worse than a few puddles. The ceiling joists we'd moved up on Wednesday had soaked up enough water to make them heavy and pliable. The weight had bent them down until they were shaped like mocking smiles rather than the rail-straight boards we needed. Maybe if we had balanced them up on end instead of laying them flat. Maybe . . . But there was no time for maybes. They had already dried in the morning sun. "Do you think if we flip them over?" I asked, knowing right away that it wouldn't work.

"We'll have to order new boards," Drew said. "Throw these away. They're ruined."

We didn't have the money to buy double supplies. And these were expensive pieces of lumber. One long board cost a lot more than two shorter boards that would add up to the same length, because they had to be cut from taller trees, which made them more difficult to make and to transport. "No way. We'll make these work. Just give me a minute."

He climbed up, shaking his head and flipping the boards up to balance on the short ends the way they were supposed to be.

"Let's get the first one nailed in, then we'll figure out the next. One at a time. We can make this work somehow. Maybe if I cut spacers to hold them the right distance apart?"

Dad made two spacers, which Drew nailed in place to hold the next joist exactly sixteen inches from the center of the first. We nailed it in place and it stayed straight, counteracting the bend in the warped board, so we did it again. It added a lot of time to the job, and it took a little more wood than we would have otherwise used, but we put spacers between every ceiling joist down the back half of the house over the rest of that day and all of the next. A job made at least four times longer than it should have been by our own stupidity. Live and learn.

The next week brought a line of thunderstorms that crippled the entire Midwest. Thankfully, our ceiling joists were safely in place and shouldn't suffer much from the exposure. The subfloor upstairs was another story. We had already purchased cherry hardwood flooring and were worried that the plywood would be too damaged to make a stable surface for it.

I finally reached out to Pete and admitted that I was too terrified to watch my kids crawl around on the upstairs ceiling joists—twenty feet off the ground in some places—to stick-build the rafters ourselves. He was sympathetic and suggested he could bring Re-Pete and another guy over on the weekend to get the roof on. I was so thrilled that I forgot I wasn't supposed to believe everything Pete said.

A tornado passed less than a mile from Inkwell Manor that week, peeling back roofs and tossing mobile homes around like Twinkies. "God hates trailer parks and Oklahoma," my dad said. The familiarity of his much-repeated line made me smile.

When we arrived on site Saturday morning, I was surprised that Pete hadn't beat us there. Drew wasn't, but he had been uncharacteristically sluggish and in a foul mood. I was even surprised at lunch when Pete still had not arrived. We stayed busy putting up Sheetrock nailers and sweeping away water puddles, but it was still irritating. I had a whole roof not being built.

By the time Pete called at four in the afternoon, I wasn't surprised anymore. Fool me once . . . okay so we were way past once.

"We got a call about some tornado roofs that needed fixing so we're working on that today," Pete said. "These houses are going to be damaged if we don't put the roofs back on."

So is mine! I wanted to scream. But it wasn't Pete's fault that I was a scaredy-cat. I should have ordered prebuilt rafters the way I had the ceiling joists between the two floors. Structurally either version would offer the same support, but it was much cheaper to stick-build them from scratch—at least, it would have been if I hadn't lost my nerve. Since we had already built the rafters for the shop, it hadn't seemed like it was a big deal. But stick-building on the ground level for a thirteen-foot-wide building is a lot different from stick-building in place for a thirty-three-foot-wide house from twenty feet in the air.

"We'll come by in the morning and get started on yours," Pete said, but I was pretty sure he was just saying what I wanted to hear, not what he intended to do. And as much as I hated to be, I was right.

The roof delay was more than just frustrating. It made me feel restless and powerless. We had worked for months to empower ourselves, and now the feeling was unraveling at my feet.

A week later and no closer to having a roof, we were cleaning the job site. Chunks of concrete blocks and wood littered the area around the house, and it had really gotten out of control. I was out front, tossing stuff in a wheelbarrow, when I stopped to take a good look at the house. I looked at it all the time, but this time I looked at it square-on, imagining it with brick covering the front. Something looked very wrong. It was off balance.

It was no secret that we had drawn the plans ourselves with little attention to aesthetics and no mock-ups of the exterior, but I had carefully measured the window placement to make sure that the six windows on the front of the house were evenly spaced—both on paper and when we laid out the walls. Still, there was a huge, unattractive blank spot between the garage window and the dining-room window. On the other side, the front door was dead center between the library and dining-room windows. That was exactly what threw everything off balance. The only way to fix it was to add another window.

"Hope," I yelled, "grab a tape measure and meet me in the dining room."

She didn't ask questions while I measured and marked a rectangle halfway between the two windows. I released her back to clean up around the backyard while I drilled a hole at the top of my three-by-five rectangle in the garage. In the absence of a chain saw, I threaded the large-toothed blade of the reciprocating saw through the hole and cut straight down. The corner turned out sloppy, but I made it and cut through two studs along the bottom, pausing in the next corner, trying to decide if I could make the turn without drilling a hole and deciding I couldn't.

In the silence between the saw motor and the drill, I heard screaming. "Mommy! Stop! What are you doing! Mommy!"

I turned to see all my kids gathered behind me. Even little Roman was red-faced from yelling, both palms out in the universal stop gesture.

"What?" I asked. "What's wrong?"

Drew stared at me, dumbfounded. "What are you doing? You can't just cut a hole in the wall! Have you lost your mind?"

I looked back at what I had done, sidestepping to make sure it looked even. It did. I could already tell it was going to look perfect. "The house was off balance. Needed another window. We'll just do the same thing upstairs, in Roman's room." I pointed over my head.

Hope raised her eyebrows, suggesting that the house wasn't the only thing off balance.

"It's too late to just change the plans," Drew argued. "We've already framed this. The plywood is up. You can't just start cutting holes in it!" He had moved from being scared that I was psychotic to angry that I had ruined a perfectly good wall.

I grinned. "Actually, I can! I can just come out here and cut a hole in the wall and put a window in it. If that's what I want, then that's exactly what I can do!" I started laughing then, hysterical laughter. I felt powerful again. In fact, I felt more powerful than I ever had in my life, and I was ready to start cutting again. I picked up the drill and made a one-inch hole in the corner so I could turn the blade.

"Go out front. Look at the house. This window has to be here. I'm serious. Go look." I waved them away, as anxious to get back to my cutting as I was to prove myself right. They went reluctantly, Roman on their tail with his little hands propped on his hips, mimicking their disapproval. Before they rounded the corner I had the saw moving again, making a mostly-straight line up the wall, and then I climbed on the ladder to make the final cut across the top.

The wood fell out with a lot less grace than the pieces had with the chain saw. This one was a lot heavier with the six-inch studs still attached. I grinned and waved to the kids, sticking my head out. "See what I mean! This is exactly what it needed."

Jada waved back, nodding and smiling. Roman did, too, because what could possibly be more fun than cutting a peek-a-boo hole in the side of a house?

Hope and Drew finally agreed that I was right: The house simply wouldn't have worked without the extra window. Drew returned, still red-faced. "We'll have to build a header for that. And cripples."

I stood back for a better look at what I'd done. "Yeah, I could have planned that cut a little better. We'll have to cut the two-by-sixes up higher for the header. It's actually going to be hard to do with the plywood on, isn't it."

He nodded. "But it will look a lot better. I'll start on the headers."

We were nearing the end of April without a roof, and the bank loan would close in less than five months. It was going to be impossibly tight to the finish. We couldn't do the insulation, cabinets, or flooring until the electric and HVAC were in. And of course we couldn't have the electric or HVAC put in without a roof. Everywhere we turned was a catch-22.

But we did have another window, and there is nothing quite like picking up a saw and cutting your own window straight through the wall to give you a new perspective on life.

The bricklayers showed up later that week. We had done the block ourselves and I knew it was solid, but I also knew it wasn't as aesthetically pleasing as I'd like the finished brick to be. So I hired a crew to put brick up several feet in the back and sides of the house and on the entire front. They would also build brick steps onto the front porch and columns around the porch posts.

We all marveled at how fast they worked, tossing armloads of bricks up to a worker on the scaffolding who caught them with a scoop of his tan arms, piled them up, and reached down for the next armload flying his way.

While they worked on the front, Dad started us on the siding behind the house and then he built a chimney around the triple-wall pipe for my woodstove. The siding made Jada and Drew happy. It was fast progress with a beautiful finished product. Everything we had done until that point was part of the interior skeleton of the house. The brick and siding were finish work. We pretended it meant we were almost done.

By the time we got most of the siding finished and all the brick was up, Dad had almost reached the end of his medicine supply. Because of the complex delivery schedule of the refrigerated interferon he needed for his MS, he had planned to leave when it ran out rather than change the shipping address.

I felt a little panicked at the thought of making decisions on my own again. Even if I would probably come to the same conclusions, I found a lot of comfort in tossing around the possibilities and hearing someone else say my thinking was sound, even another amateur. Dad no doubt felt my panic and doubled up his workload, staying at the job site all day while I was at work and the kids were at school and then continuing with us past sunset.

I shouldn't have been surprised when, only two days before he planned to leave, Jada ran into the house to get me. "Grampa fell. He's hurt." Her eyes had teared over and her fingertips pressed so hard on her bottom lip that it faded to a bloodless white.

He had been on the damn ladder again, putting the last of the siding on the chimney out back. I never got a clear answer about how far he fell or what he hit. He had made it to a lawn chair that was tilted crooked on a lump of concrete and he was holding his arm, already swollen and ugly enough that I wanted to take him directly to the emergency room.

"Now just wait awhile," he said. "I felt around. Nothing's broken."

He was trembling and his voice was quiet and high-pitched.

"We have to get your arm X-rayed. It could have a fracture, you can't feel that by poking around."

"Oh, my arm?" He laughed a little, but it was eerie instead of funny. "My arm is nothing. It's my back I hurt."

When he had caught his breath I checked out his back and found a knob the size of half a tennis ball next to his spine. I had never seen anything like it and couldn't even imagine what it was. But I knew what it cost. And the price was too high for a house.

The kids and I pleaded and insisted. I even threatened to call an ambulance, which only prompted him to prove he could walk to the car on his own two feet. Maybe I forgot to mention it, but my dad is stubborn. Glad I didn't inherit that annoying trait.

He took three extra-strength Tylenol and went to bed as soon as we got home. Then he rested another day and we packed him up for the drive home. He still insisted that he wanted to see his own doctor, because that would be easier for insurance. I still insisted that he needed an X-ray and probably an MRI of both his arm and his back. The sixteen-hour drive north was never pleasant, but this time it would be a special slice of hell.

I told him I loved him, thanked him for all the hard work, and then cried like a baby when he drove away with turkey sandwiches and sliced cheddar packed in a cooler next to him.

He called when he made it home and never told me what all the doctor said about the fall. I was glad that he went, at least, and trusted him to follow through while I picked up the pace on the build. Even with the boost of his help we were still impossibly behind schedule.

The kids and I spent a couple more long days cleaning up around the site. Brick and siding pieces had become a tripping hazard, and I wasn't going to stand for any more injuries.

We hauled everything to the dump after dark and ate a quiet supper that did not include either turkey or cheese. We'd had enough of both to take a very long break.

I felt tired all the way through. My back was protesting from another day of bending and lifting after it had finally mended from the last strain. I took a Tylenol and climbed into bed. I didn't go looking for Benjamin, and per usual, he respected my wishes. Sometimes I wanted his peace, no matter the cost, and other times it felt too fake to wrap around my shoulders, like a fairy-tale land that only I had access to. It didn't feel fair. I wanted peace in the real world, the world I shared with my kids. They deserved to travel forward without the weight we carried. And if they couldn't have it with me, then I didn't want it at all.

Benjamin was stubborn, but in a different way from me or Dad. He didn't argue with me. He had more effective ways to pull me in, and he was patient.

We stayed off the job site for a couple of days so I could catch up on work, or that's what I told myself. The truth was that I was physically and emotionally exhausted. And maybe I was once again afraid to move forward.

On Wednesday night, we all went to Inkwell to mark the electrical. I had no idea how our pot-smoking electricians could possibly wire the place without electrocuting themselves, but I had already paid them the required 50 percent deposit, and that was over five grand. Like too many things in my life, there was no turning back, no way out.

We walked through the house together to make sure we didn't miss anything. Each of the big kids was armed with a different color of spray paint. Drew had yellow to mark ceiling light fixtures. Hope had red to mark double light switches for fan-and-light combos and green for single-light fixtures. Combos of more switches received a red-green "X." Jada had white for outlets. It was her first time using spray paint, and she was wearing the giddy smile of a graffiti artist in front of a clean train. Each of them was also armed with a scrap of cardboard to prevent paint from dripping onto the floor. Or at least that was the plan. I followed with a clipboard, checking off which lights I'd already purchased and which were still needed.

Room by room, we arranged imaginary furniture and lamps, making sure every room was perfectly labeled. When we were standing in the den, which was the last room to mark, I stood in the exterior doorway, supervising the marking.

"There's the hardworking lady," a deep voice said from directly behind me.

I jumped and the clipboard went clattering across the floor, with me running after it and spinning to identify the voice at the same time. My legs tangled and I went down on my butt, heart racing and ears thudding.

Past the doorway stood a trio of young Hispanic men, visible only from the middle up because the floor was four feet off the ground and we hadn't built steps yet. They stood in a triangle, each carrying a fishing pole. The point man's tongue fluttered through apologies while the two taller boys flanking him stared with true concern and not the slightest hint of humor—which was a lot more than I could say for my own giggling offspring.

I held my palms up and attempted a smile. "I'm fine. Just fine. You surprised me, that's all. I didn't know anyone was out there."

"Yeah, we are going fishing," the point man said, ducking his head. "The neighbor there says we can." He nodded across the pond.

We had seen them fishing and had never thought it was a big deal. And since we had also seen them a quarter of a mile down the road having barbecues and listening to music, we assumed that they walked by our house to get to the pond. But I had never considered that they walked through our backyard. It was hard to remember that this had all been a field a few months ago, and using a well-worn fishing path would be a hard habit to break. It was fine with me if they kept using it while we worked, but I was jumpier than the average girl.

"We sit over there and watch you working every day and we say, 'That is one hardworking white woman,' and it's true. You are building a big house, right?" He ducked his head again.

I laughed, maybe harder than I should have, but I couldn't help it. Not only had they scared me half out of my mind, they had just made the most beautiful reverse-stereotype statement in history.

"Do you work in construction?" I tried to keep the eagerness out of my voice, but on the inside I was on my knees with my hands folded in prayer. I could certainly use skilled additions to my work crew.

The tall boy of maybe sixteen behind the spokesman, who looked about fourteen, answered this time. "Oh, no. We don't know nothing about making things like this. We are at the Chico's Restaurante on Highway 7. Juan is a cook. Maybe you'll come by sometime?" he asked.

"I love the cheese dip there!" Hope said.

I nodded, even though I had never had their cheese dip or anything else. "Good luck with the fish today." I pointed at their fishing poles.

"Maybe you'll join us?" They waved and walked away.

Drew pulled me to my feet as though the bizarre encounter hadn't happened. And since I was the one humiliated on my butt, and embarrassed to have three strange teenagers tell me that I was a hardworking white woman, I was equally willing to let the whole thing go. "What's next on the list?" he asked.

Hope marked the last outlet in the den, using a lot more paint than she needed. We were all feeling a little restless.

"We're getting more and more stuck without the roof." I held my hand up when I saw the look in his eye. "No. We are not going to try to build it ourselves." I chewed my bottom lip, afraid of what was about to come out of my mouth. "Why don't we start the plumbing?"

"How?" Drew asked.

I had no idea. I turned to a fresh page on my clipboard and walked to the garage, where the main water line came in under the foundation and up through the slab. "It'll be easy. We just trace a path from where the water comes in and pass it over each place we want water. We do this all the way up to the attic where the water heater will be, and then back down with the hot water. I'll mark down how many of each turn we need. Make sense?" I didn't look up to see if it did.

In a column down the left side of my paper I drew pictures of connectors (I would later learn they were called joints) that looked like "T"s and plus signs. Under those, I wrote "faucet," "sprayer," "toilet," and each of the appliances that needed water. I held it up to the kids. "See? We just make hash marks by each item for a count, and then I'll take this to the plumbing-supply store tomorrow. I found one in Little Rock that will give me a contractor's discount if I show that I pulled the permit." I had no idea if my method was close to a proper plan, but we had watched some plumbing videos and decided to use plastic PEX pipe, so I had at least a vague idea of the process and what the pieces looked like.

We made the hash-mark counts, and even though it was earlier than we would quit on an average work day, there was little else we could do. Everyone was quiet on the ride home, feeling restless under our time crunch. Waiting for other people to do work was the worst part of building the house. When it was our fault that things didn't get done, we were a lot more forgiving.

I didn't stop at the mailbox when we pulled in front of our other house, the one we lived in but didn't feel at home in, and I drove a little too fast up the driveway and into the garage.

"I need a vacation. Someplace with too much sun and sand," I said, half under my breath. And too much tequila, I wanted to add. I had never been much of a drinker, but it sounded like a great idea just then. It had been more than a year since I'd had time to go out and have a margarita and a plate of fajitas. I couldn't remember the last movie I'd watched in a theater. One of the early Harry Potter films, four, maybe five years ago?

"I have sand," Roman said. "You use the orange shovel."

I smiled at him in my rearview mirror while the other kids climbed out of the car. They hadn't gone to movies either, or on dates, or to sleepovers. Our lives were on hold while we worked insanely long and difficult hours. We were giving up so much with the hope of a small step forward. How did life come so easily to so many other people? Other women had husbands who helped, or at least paid child support and felt an obligation to provide for their kids. Other women had friends and big families and safety nets.

My parents were amazing and supportive, but neither of them lived close enough to be part of my everyday life, and besides, they had their own ghosts to overcome and futures to dream about. My mom was trying to find a way to retire early so she could travel and see her family in

Wisconsin more often. She had gone through extreme hardship in her life, and no matter how hard she worked, she hit roadblocks and challenges. I wanted more than anything for her to have a break. She had accomplished so much, but was always working for everyone else. It was time for her.

The kids settled into pajamas and disappeared into their rooms. I called my mom and sat out on the back porch to let her tell me that things were going to be just fine. In fact, they were going to be superb. "You have to make mini vacations out of everyday life," she said. "Remember how poor we were when you were a teenager? There were several years we almost starved to death. If it weren't for the free lunches at school, I don't think we would have made it through. But we found ways to have fun."

They had been horrible times. I was too malnourished to stay awake in class. Boys in my high school showed me pictures of anorexic women and jeered, "Look familiar, Cara?," laughing and socking one another in the arm. They might not have laughed if they saw me slipping ketchup packages into my purse to eat for my supper. Even when Mom made a big pot of soup from discount-bin pasta and dented-can vegetables, I would try not to eat much so there would be enough for her. She didn't have the free lunch I got every day. She didn't even get ketchup packages.

I played a game on weekends and during the summer that I had never told her about. I called it my two-o'clock game. If I could hold out on eating my one meal for the day until two, then I could still get to sleep at night. It was an exercise in extreme self-control, because I woke up weak with a sharp enough pain in my belly that I sometimes wondered if it would just eat a hole right through me. The easiest times were when I had a book to hide in. I didn't own any books, but we went to the library regularly and I pretended the stories were as good as food until two o'clock came.

"The kids and I have it a lot better than we did then," I said, eyes tearing. Who was I to complain? I had let myself forget how far we had both come. "We have more than enough to eat. And we have heat. Remember how cold we got? The toilet would freeze. And poor little Snoopy couldn't ever keep a bowl of water because it froze right there on the kitchen floor!"

Mom laughed. "We slept in a half dozen layers, and you tied a hood around your head at night. Remember that? Just your nose and mouth peeking out. But we still made vacations. We had little Friday-night celebrations watching the PBS fund-drive movies on that old television with lines all through it."

"*Doctor Who!*" we said at the same time.

"We went and picked up pecans together," Mom reminded me.

"I hated that. I was mortified to be crawling around on the college campus picking up buckets of nuts. I was probably pretty mean to you about it."

"We laughed about it," she said. "I wasn't thrilled to be out there either. But we had nuts to eat."

"And to give for Christmas gifts to Grandma and Grandpa," I said. "We made the best of it. We laughed a lot, didn't we."

"Don't worry so much about the details. You're doing so very, very well, and I'm proud of you."

I went inside and found Jada and Roman playing Wii bowling. The game may have started fun, but it had dissolved into arguments and stomping. "Anyone in here want to go for a walk?" I asked.

"In the dark?" Jada asked, wide-eyed.

"Sure. When I was a kid we walked at night all the time. We'll make wishes on the stars and say good morning to the night creatures."

"I'll walk!" Roman said, running for the stairs.

Hope and Drew stayed in their rooms, cherishing the quiet time alone. But Jada joined us, and so did Hershey. We imagined fairy creatures waking up in the tall grass and lazy opossums and armadillos rustling around in the forest.

"I wish for a giant frog. Big as me!" Roman shouted to the stars.

"Ewww," Jada said. "Think how big the bugs would have to be to feed him! I wish I could be in the WNBA. Or maybe travel to Africa. Or India."

"Then I wish for Disney World," Roman amended.

"I wish I had four kids and a magical house called Inkwell Manor," I said, taking my turn to shout to the Big Dipper.

"Mommy! You already have that!" Roman said.

"See? I told you wishes on stars always come true."

–18–

Hear the Words I *Fall* Mean

I knew it would be difficult to move Adam out and finalize a divorce, but I never imagined how often he would forget that these things had happened. Every night I double-checked the window and door locks, and every morning Hershey and I looked for anything bumped out of place. We walked our patrol with her shoulder pressed against my thigh, first through the interior and then along the outside perimeter. I wasn't sure what we were looking for or what we would do if we found it, but with the illogical, unpredictable shadow of insanity ruling our world, going through these motions gave me the much-needed illusion of control.

I was hyperaware, over-the-top vigilant. All while smiling peacefully enough that Hope and Drew could walk across the street to their elementary school without watching their backs, and toddler Jada wouldn't cling too tight.

It's impossible to watch every step, to keep your guard up every second. So now and then I slipped. Most of the time everything was okay. Most of the time I could take out the trash without seeing a bogeyman. Most of the time slipups didn't matter. Until the times they did.

"You all right?" The voice was low, gentle, and close. Too close.

It opened my throat like a key. "Akraham! Teckrip!" I said. And if I had a minute to think, I was sure, I could translate the ancient words into modern English. But I didn't have a minute. All my minutes might have found an end exactly halfway up my long, dusty driveway. Adam stood a step away from the gravel, where his footsteps were silent. A thick patch of dandelions bent under his right shoe, suffocating. Jada's favorite weed-flower.

I looked past him at the house. Just on the other side of that door Karma was waiting, ready to defend me. But she hadn't come with me tonight, and I couldn't beat Adam in a footrace, not when his chin was lifted off his chest and the drool cleared away. Not when his feet were lifting high enough to stomp dandelions—not when he was off his meds.

"Are you all right, Cara?" he repeated. It was the old Adam, the one I'd loved deeply before his mind slipped away. He had so much charisma that my knees felt weak from more than terror, and I was mad at him for still affecting me. There in the starlight, it was impossible to believe he was the same person who hurt me, who scared me.

"I'm okay," I said, careful not to sound too okay. Because he wouldn't want me to feel like I really did—happy to be free of him and building a life of my own. We'd been divorced several years. He would want me to be tortured by the loss of him.

"Are the kids okay? You look really beautiful. You have always been beautiful."

"The kids are good. Busy with end-of-school stuff."

"You shouldn't be out without a bra." His chest pushed forward, shoulders back, and I knew what was next, the finger poking at my sternum, shoving the point home.

"I was just taking the trash out. And it's dark. The kids didn't get the can up. You know how they are with chores. Scattered as always." I crossed my arms across my chest. The sleep shirt I had put on after my shower was thin, not something I would normally wear outside. *I don't have to explain anything. I'm not your business. Not anymore. You aren't welcome here. Go!*

Instead of driving his point home, he pinched his fingers across his eyes and held the bridge of his nose. "You heard what Dr. Christe said? Schizophrenia?" His voice choked in a genuine sob. "I'm sorry, Cara. I didn't know. I'm sorry."

Just that quick I wanted to tell him it was okay, that I was sorry, too. He looked so weak, so vulnerable and lost that I wanted to hug him. I didn't want him back, though, not even then. I was sorry—not stupid. It was a cruel twist of fate. A goddamned shame. But I still didn't want him back. "I'm sorry, too," I whispered. "Dr. Christe says there's medicine, things that—"

"That's why they did this." His voice was low and the words were almost too fast to process. "They did this thing to my brain. An implant or a beam or however the hell they do it. They did this because they wanted me to take those pills that kill everything. Do you hear me? They kill everything inside. They know how important my ideas are, and they want them without the threat of having to pay me. They know my ideas could change everything. Everything. I just have to write them down. And when I take their damn pills I can't write a damn thing. Too shaky. Too dead. I'm going to write it, though. I'm going to make enough to take care of you and the kids. I can support my wife. You know that, right? You know I can."

In the early days I had traveled right along with him on his path to madness, believed the little tales that built into something so fantastical that I realized it was impossible. Even then I'd been generous when I tried to sort fact from fiction, giving him the benefit of the doubt when a story had reasonable evidence. The day after his diagnosis of schizo-phrenia I'd even wondered briefly if it was all a trick, if he was fooling them somehow in order to save us from real bad guys who wanted the things in his brilliant mind. I wanted to believe that because it would be so much nicer than the ugliness of what had really happened, so much happier than the sad truth of schizophrenia. Watching him now, I had no doubts. He had rarely talked to me like this; he'd been a little paranoid sometimes, but usually believable, sane enough to pass mus-ter. A wave of pity hit my stomach with such force that I dropped both hands there and gagged. I took a step forward, toward the house. I needed a glass of water, something to settle my stomach and drown my guilt. Maybe he knew that and wanted to stop me, or maybe he thought I was taking a step closer to him.

He took three steps, scissoring sideways to cut in front of me. The dandelions he'd stood on leapt up. *They can breathe. They can finally breathe.* But I couldn't. I froze. His breath puffed across my face, hot on my eyes. Even though he wasn't touching me, I could feel his heat. His eyes were clear with the intensity that used to melt hearts but had mine building heat and speed.

"The kids are done with school? I'm going to kill you." He was as matter-of-fact as if he were telling me what he had for dinner. "I know they did well. They're smart."

He may have said more, but my ears were washed over with heat, and my heartbeat, and a scream that sounded real in my head without ever passing my throat. I looked at my feet, expecting to find the per-fect rock, one that would fit in my palm and against the side of his head. Cave it in. End this.

"What's wrong? I'm going to take care of you. I can take care of my wife." He stepped back, hands up by his shoulders as if to say, *I got this.*

"You're scaring me," I yelled, but it came out as a tear-coated whisper.

His jaw dropped, reminding me for a split second of what he looked like in the hospital room when his feet were too heavy to lift off the tile. He was not only surprised, but hurt, so unaware of what he had said that I looked away, evaluating if there was some way I had misheard him. I hadn't.

"I'm going to kill you."

Clear as day. Sharp as night.

"I'm going in. The kids—I've been out too long." I swallowed hard, hating the familiar tiptoeing around, weighing each word before handing it over like a peace offering.

"I don't mean to scare you. I'm sorry about—all of this. You know which words I mean."

I had started walking and couldn't stop even though I knew I should stay and say more, that I should smooth this over. Walking away was just the sort of thing to set him off. I waved over my head, flapping my hand like I'd been attacked by a plague of gnats. But I didn't look back; I couldn't turn, even though I was half convinced that he was following, stomping up the driveway, crushing dandelions along the way.

Hershey appeared next to me, a shadow materializing like a phantom. I wondered where she had been while I stood under the manic shower of Adam's words. I didn't blame her for disappearing; it was the smartest move when he came around. Maybe she would have jumped up to defend me if he had lifted his hands around my throat, or maybe even that wouldn't have penetrated her own post-traumatic reaction to the scent of him. "Good girl," I breathed. "Stay close. I won't let him hurt you." I tapped my thigh and made a soft click with my tongue.

The garage door had never taken so long to close. I imagined him rolling under it like Indiana Jones, crooked smile and all, grabbing an imaginary fedora.

When I walked into the dining room, I expected the kids to be pressed against the windows, terrified of all the things that might have happened. The downstairs was empty, and I could hear thunder over my head in Jada's room, which meant she was jumping from her bed onto her furry purple beanbag chair. Tiny white balls would be puffing out the zipper like snow.

I ran to my closet, Hershey sticking close. My .38 Special—plain-Jane instead of plastic pink—was on the top shelf. I had to climb my sweater shelves like a ladder to reach her and then had to reach behind a dusty pair of five-inch heels for the bullets. My fingers were steady when I slipped the shells into the chambers and swung the barrel closed.

Locked and loaded. A phrase from one of my dad's stories from the Honor Guard in DC. I hefted the gun, remembering his lessons on aiming and shooting so many years ago.

My hands started shaking then, jostling Karma like popcorn in a popper. Not cool. Not cool at all when I had hard decisions to make and no room for nerves. I closed my eyes and took a deep breath. The gun was cold and heavy. I had bought it thinking I could shoot anyone threatening my kids. Even him.

Adam wasn't just anyone, though, and the reasons he had for being there were understandable even if I didn't like them. It wasn't hard to imagine shooting the person leaving knives in my bed, or torturing my dog, but he wasn't that person all the time. In some moments he was still the yesterday Adam. The one who had sat with me, dreaming of our future at beaches and mountain cabins, of growing old together.

How could I ever reconcile him with the person who had looked me straight in the eye and said he was going to kill me?

I put Karma back on the top shelf without unloading her. Rest up, girl.

The kids hadn't noticed I was gone. We did our bedtime routine and everyone was asleep before I identified what bothered me most about the night encounter.

It wasn't the person or the words as much as it was who I became because of them. The kids never suspected I even went outside. But I knew that and a whole lot more. I knew great big scary things. I was planning ways I might have to kill someone if they came too close even one more time. I was telling tall tales, about how safe and happy we were, and sealing them with a false smile. I was pretending I was strong when no one had ever felt as small and weak as I did.

Of course I was doing it to protect them, both from thinking about the crazy man and from the fear the truth would bring. Then again, if they weren't afraid of him, they might let him get too close. The balance was lost somewhere between feeling safe and being safe.

I was beginning to think there was no such thing as safe anyhow. Nowhere we could hide.

That was enough reason to be a liar, I told myself that night, with the shadows growing deep around my bed and the window frames locked tight around glass that was as laughably easy to break as my courage.

–19–

Rise
I Am My Plumber

On Friday after work, Roman and I went to the Plumbing Warehouse, where a lanky man in a Where's Waldo? shirt and gauges large enough to shoot marbles through was unfortunate enough to be the one to ask, "May I help you?" He nodded at my clipboard in a patronizing way, squinted at my explanations and looked at something over my left shoulder, and finally suggested, "It would probably be easiest if you send your plumber in to make the order. Or he can even do it over the phone and you can do the pickup." He smiled and actually patted my shoulder.

I waved my plumbing permit, pointing to my signature on the dotted line. "I am my plumber." Which I had already told him, but for reasons that were more than obvious—the least of which was Roman stringing Froot Loops onto a strand of my hair—he had missed that part.

"Wayne!" he yelled, waving at someone across the warehouse and stretching his eyes wide in a now-familiar, oh-god-you-have-to-save-me-from-this-crazy-lady expression.

Wayne, it turned out, was a retired-teacher type who wasn't even mildly impressed that I was building my own house. He corrected me when I used the wrong term: "No, hon, that's a coupling, got it?" And scribbled all over my checklist. "This part here isn't important. But you keep a damn close count on these here. Got it?" Finally, he took a deep breath and said, "Look, we aren't allowed to give you a list of what you should buy, because everything is nonrefundable. You walk out the door with it, you own it. Got it?"

I nodded, hoping that wasn't the end of the lecture.

"Tell you what I can do though. I can tell you what I would buy if this were my house, and you can nod if that's what you want to do. Got it?"

I nodded more vigorously, suppressing the urge to hug him.

"You got two showers. I would want those PEX on the inside and stubbed out with copper. Don't be nodding yet." He shook a fat, dirty finger at me. "I ain't finished. I would also want an adapter for each faucet. So here you have five faucets counting kitchen, bath, and garage, and two showers. And then you have three toilets. I would get copper for all them outside the wall, too, and get adapters for each. Is that what you would do?"

I nodded.

He laughed. "Yup. You got it!"

"Oh, and what about exterior water faucets? To water your flowers and such. How many of those you got?"

I chewed the inside of my cheek, trying to remember if we had ever discussed those and pretty sure we hadn't. "Two," I said. "I have two of those planned."

Wayne told me what he would use for those, and I nodded that it was exactly what I would use, too. What a coincidence.

I loaded hula-hoop-size rolls of red and white flexible PEX pipe into the trunk. Red for hot water and white for cold. Then I added brown-paper sacks in three sizes filled with couplings, adapters, plugs, elbows, tees, hundreds of crimp rings, and two sizes of crimping tools, which looked like supersized pliers, and any number of things I no doubt would have to google before I could implement.

That plan I had made with Drew, cold water goes up and hot water comes down, may have been even more ridiculously simplified than I had first imagined.

Wayne clapped me on the back at the register. "You have any problems at all, you just call me. Got it?" He laughed heartily. "I'm just kidding. Good luck with all that. You'll do fine if you just remember everything I told you."

I thanked him and walked quickly to the car, trying to call back every single thing he'd told me. Roman crawled around from front to back, playing space mission, or maybe it was face missing, while I made a full page of notes with a somewhat accurate representation of the "plumbing wisdom by Wayne" lecture. I should have recorded it.

If my expression at the warehouse had been anything like Drew's when I gave him a rundown of the tools, fittings, crimpers, pipe supports, and adapters, I couldn't imagine how either Wayne or Waldo had kept a straight face.

We started running pipe that weekend. And despite occasional moments of confusion over which part went where, and a few really tight spots where the crimping pliers were nearly impossible to fit in the joists between the floors, the entire plumbing project went surprisingly fast. It wasn't all that difficult, and it really was just a matter of running white pipe past everything on the way up and red past it again on the way down—more or less. We crimped the copper fittings that extended out of the wall by squeezing them with an enormous pliers-like tool specially designed for pinching the fittings tight, and later when we installed the appliances we would either compression-fit or solder the final pieces together.

Hope followed us with a hammer and a tool belt filled with gray plastic half circles that already had nails threaded through them. "They look a little like hoop earrings," she said, holding a pair over her earlobes. With two hammer taps she positioned them to hold the pipe in nice straight lines that wouldn't jerk around when we turned the water on and off. More important, the pipe wouldn't sag against Sheetrock where a nail could puncture it. The PEX pipe was pretty tough, but not as nail-resistant as copper or even PVC might be. According to Wayne, I'd made a solid decision, though; all the plumbers were using PEX. And it was definitely easier for a beginning plumber, which he seemed to sense I was.

By the next Friday we were completely finished with the water lines, and I called the city inspector to sign off on them so I could hook up a faucet. When he showed up, Pete and Re-Pete were working on the roof. I had to keep pinching myself to believe it was true.

The inspector congratulated me on the plumbing and signed off. No leaks. Then he ruined it all by saying, "You really have some damage started on that subfloor from all the rain. It's past time to get a roof on this."

I waited until he was at the end of the drive to say, "Thanks, Captain Obvious," and then set out to hook up the exterior faucets. I felt defeated when Pete had to come and finish them for me, but was slightly redeemed when I hooked up the faucet in the garage the next day all by myself. We kept an oversize bowl in the sink for weeks, though, because I hadn't figured out how to hook up the drain lines. Baby steps.

By the end of May, we had a roof on the house. We were still so far behind schedule on the build that I wasn't sure it was possible to finish by the September deadline. I held out hope that future projects would be easier than I had imagined despite the fact that all the projects to date had been somewhere between ten and a thousand times harder than I imagined.

Optimists. We are the slowest of slow learners.

The next hurdle came on a Thursday night while I was trying to run iron pipe past the laundry room and onto the back porch for a barbecue grill. It was turning out to be par for the course, harder to install than I had ever imagined.

Over our late supper that night, everyone was in a good mood, so I left deadlines, finances, and worry out of the discussion. Drew didn't come down for supper, just sent a text that he wasn't feeling well and was going to sleep. He didn't want me to bring anything up to him and told me to stop asking.

I didn't think a lot about it that night. The girls and I watched a movie while Jada helped Roman build block towers that he knocked down with exceptional fanfare and explosive noises that included a lot of flying spit.

The next morning Drew sent a text that he wasn't going to school. He still didn't feel well. No, he didn't want any medicine, and no he wasn't hungry.

I was late for work and told him to text me if he needed me to pick up ginger ale or crackers at the store. He didn't text me all day.

That night, when he still refused to come out of his room, I knew something was up. After his childhood ear infections had been cleared up by tubes at age two, he had only been sick maybe twice, ever. The entire family would come down with colds or flu and none of it touched him. I mentioned it to Hope, and she got a particularly mischievous gleam in her eye. "If something is going on at school, I can find out in two minutes."

She was wrong. The bad news was so easy to find that she had it in thirty seconds. Drew was eighteen months younger than her, and two years behind in school. Still, if the juniors hadn't ended classes two weeks before the freshmen, she would have already heard gossip of this magnitude. She handed me her phone with a news article from a local station (All the News All the Time!) pulled up.

I recognized the name in the headline right away. One of Drew's friends—not his best friend, because he didn't really have one of those, but a boy he knew well enough to invite over for video games—had been killed in a violent car crash. The images of the car were chilling. And all the questions that ran through my mind in the first few seconds didn't really matter in the long run. Was he texting? Did he buckle his seat belt? Was he drinking, or high?

He was someone's little boy. Someone's brother. Someone's grandson. Someone's friend—Drew's friend. And he was dead.

It hurt that Drew was trying to handle it all by himself. Locking himself away from the people who loved him enough to help in any way they could. But I understood it, too. He was the man of the house, and he had this image that being a man meant being strong, in control, and not leaning on anyone else. As the adult head of our household, I'd finally learned that being grown-up and a true leader meant just the opposite. It meant asking for help even if that made someone else feel stronger, even if someone laughed, or mocked your plumbing terminology. The most important part of being in charge was recognizing when you weren't in control.

The older kids' dad had been so absent that I sometimes had to remind myself that his life still must affect them. He had left the air force soon after we divorced, spent years without a job while he went to college, married two more times, and then joined the army as an officer. While we were building Inkwell Manor, he was in Iraq, occasionally e-mailing the kids about bombs and the general horrors and fears from a war zone. Drew's understanding of the ordinary dangers of everyday life had to be a jumbled, tangled mess.

I knocked on his door, and when he told me he was too tired I went in anyhow. "I read about Derek," I said, sitting on the side of his bed.

He was on his stomach, head turned away from me. His shoulders started heaving with big racking sobs. I put my hand on his back, and he let me. We both bawled until our noses were too swollen to sniff anymore.

"Do you want to go to the funeral? Sometimes it helps to be around other people who feel like you do. To say good-bye."

He shook his head.

"Think about it some more. You don't have to go. People have different ways of finding their way through things like this. If the funeral isn't your way, then that's fine, but find what is your way, and do that. Okay? You have to keep moving. Keep living."

He nodded.

I had more to say but hadn't worked out how to say it. My feelings were hurt that he hadn't told me about this. Really that wasn't it exactly. It wasn't my feelings. "You know how you felt when I glossed things over and pretended they were okay, lied even to make it look like they were when it was obvious they were all going to hell in a handbasket? Well, I feel the same about this. I imagine Hope does, too. We don't hide things anymore. Understand? We deal with them together. It's the only way we'll get through this . . . and any number of things to come."

He nodded again.

"And you need to eat something. Keep moving forward. You want me to bring something up or you want to come down?" It was an old parenting trick, giving him two choices that both ended in the same result—him eating. And phrasing it in a way that he had to do more than nod or shake his head was a trick I had been honing since they became teenagers.

"I'd rather eat up here."

I smiled. His voice sounded distorted by his swollen nose and throat, but he was using it. "I'll be right back." I stopped after two steps. "I love you. And I'm sorry this happened."

He was crying again when I went out the door. I was, too. But this time they were slow tears, the sort that meant you were saying good-bye to both the lost person and the overwhelming early stage of grief.

He ate that night, but never came out of his room. On Saturday morning I asked what he wanted to do, and he asked if he could stay home. I had expected that, knowing that if he did it would be part grief and part getting out of a hard day of work.

"Tell you what. Hang out here until noon, and then I'll come back and get you. I need your help with the exterior doors. We're one hard day's work away from being able to lock Inkwell up tight." We were really more like three days away unless doors suddenly got a lot easier to install, but it was the principle that mattered.

He nodded, immediately perking up. Everyone wants to feel like there are tasks that just can't be done without them. I wanted to give him that, and in this case it was absolutely true. I couldn't build the house without him. We each had a role in the build, and his was a big one.

The electricians had started drilling holes and pulling wire, but I suspected they were pulling drags off funny cigarettes with more than half their time. They weren't particularly worried about how far behind we were, but then again they didn't appear to be particularly worried about anything. Even the fact that the house wasn't totally water-proof didn't shake them. We had a roof covered in tar paper, but there were no shingles. They were supposed to arrive that Friday, and I had hired some guys to put them on—friends of our Chico's Restaurante neighbors.

I was a little worried the shingles wouldn't show up, and a lot worried the roofers wouldn't. Pete had taught me a lot of things since we began, and the most important was the fluidity of a construction work-er's calendar and promise.

Hope, Jada, and I carried boxes of hardwood flooring upstairs and piled them in the middle of the back bedroom. Two thousand square feet of flooring takes up a lot of space and takes a lot of back muscle to move. As soon as the electricians were finished, we would have insulation and Sheetrock moving in and needed to keep the area as open as possible. But with the shop full of appliances, lights, and plumbing fixtures in addition to tools, the hardwood and tile had to be stored in the house.

Roman sat next to the growing flooring mountain and colored an entire two-by-six with a fat hunk of pink sidewalk chalk. He was focused, humming a single monotone note that drilled into our skulls until the girls and I wanted to scream.

"Ahhhhhhhhh," he continued, pausing only to pull in another breath, then letting it out with the same, steady "Ahhhhhhhhh."

I gave Drew his silence until one P.M. before I picked him up. If we had any cash to spare, I would have picked up some hamburgers, too. But things were so tight we were lucky to have bread, meat, and cheese for lunch. We actually would have been thrilled with another of Dad's turkeys, which was something we never thought we'd say in a million years.

My little pep talk and the light I had sworn I saw in Drew's eyes had both faded. He was sluggish and irritable, even after he saw how much work we'd done without him, and after he had helped finish it off. It was Roman's singing that finally pulled him out of it—well, in a roundabout way. Roman's incessant note was driving me insane, so I thought to turn on Drew's music mix. He moved a beat or two faster. And by the third song his lips were forming the words; he wasn't exactly singing along, but it was a step in the right direction. Baby steps, again. I was learning to appreciate them as much as Neil Armstrong–size leaps.

Somewhere in recent history, humans—at least those in America— had become all about feeling rather than doing. Instead of tackling our problems and sweating them out, we started sitting around and talking about them, or trying to drown them in alcohol and pills. The new methods didn't seem to be working well, from what I had seen. Ancient rites of passage always centered on action. A child had to do something physical, like face a demon in a dark forest, before becoming a man or a woman.

Drew smacked a crooked cripple into place with a framing hammer so we could try the French doors in the den again. He was taking action, battling demons, and I had no doubt that he would emerge from this trial as a man. It was every bit as useful as weeks alone in the wilderness in search of a spirit guide. Each of us was passing through into a more evolved phase with a timeless tradition of breaking down in order to build stronger.

A thin red line ran from the side of Drew's palm, down his wrist, and to his elbow. It probably wasn't much of a cut, but mixed with his sweat, the blood dripped onto the concrete slab. I had plenty of scrapes and bruises, too. We all did. Angry rainbow bruises the size and shapes of fists, as though the beatings we'd taken all these years on the inside were only now erupting to the surface, spilling out and then draining away for good.

The house felt like a live being that day, marking us, branding us like possessions, and we were marking her right back with star-shaped drops of blood and DNA swabbed on the tips of misfired nails or wood slivers. I had the idea that maybe Caroline wasn't a woman at all, but a house. I wondered what I would find if I went back to the tornado house now, and had the eerie feeling that it would be gone, completely swallowed by the earth and spit right back up as Inkwell Manor's pieces and parts. Drew swung the hammer again, beating the resistance out of an innocent piece of knotty pine. His shoulders slumped, his own resistance on the way out the door, too.

Yeah, we were building things. Every swing of the hammer made him stronger, purged his grief. At the end of the day we'd have a new door or two, and the thought made me smile. For the first time in too many years we were fearless about stepping through newly opened doors.

The shingles were not only delivered that Saturday afternoon, they were delivered directly onto the roof. Roman watched the conveyor belt like it was transporting alien beings back to their home planet. As a bonus, the roofers actually showed up the next day. The only thing that made me happier than the progress we were making was the fact that my own feet were firmly on the ground.

Pete was supposed to come by and help me work on the drain lines, but he didn't show. Drew and I managed to get the last exterior door installed. Just when I worried I was teaching him a few new words, he taught me a few. Installing windows and doors did not make our list of favorite pastimes. And with five bedrooms, closets, three bathrooms, laundry room, pantry, library, Harry Potter cupboard, garage, and four exterior doors, we had a substantial future with doors. To make matters worse, the library and back doors were complicated French doors, so they actually counted as two each—on the off chance that anyone was counting.

"As soon as the Sheetrock's in place, we can actually lock this place up!" I said, holding my hand up to feel for a breeze around the edge of the window.

"You mean if we ever figure out how to install the locks," he said, and I realized I was getting used to the exasperated tone he had fired at me for the last few days.

"Don't forget, we're also assuming no one knows how to throw a brick through a window," I added, matching his irritation and raising it three exhaustion levels. "While we're at it, let's assume no one can use a reciprocating saw to cut straight through a wall any time they damn-well please."

That took him off guard, and I regretted the small truth. We were building Inkwell Manor to feel safe, to forget that a crazed man with power tools might hack his way through our carefully measured walls and back into our life.

"I know it's slow, but we're making progress. You want to work upstairs or down?" I asked. Now that we were back to slow-moving projects, it was all work and no fun.

He wiped his face, and I pretended not to notice that he had drawn another Egyptian slave symbol on the back of his hand. He'd been doing it for at least a week. We moved through the day like we were marching in pudding.

Off like a herd of turtles, my grandma would have said.

By the next weekend, most of the sewer lines were complete. We finished running black iron pipe for the natural gas, and I had a hard time shaking the feeling that I might blow us all to the moon. A water leak would be unfortunate, but a gas leak was scarier than an ex with a thing for knives and coded messages.

On Friday, the realtor showed our old house to a young couple with three small girls. I was equally terrified that it would sell and that it wouldn't. If they bought it, we'd go from being buried under a mortgage we could no longer afford to living free and clear at Inkwell. The trouble was, we would have no place to live until the build was finished. While strangers tiptoed through our bedrooms, we drove to a nearby park and watched Roman swing—"Too high!"—until the realtor gave us the all clear. Living in a house that was up for sale made us feel displaced. We had two houses but no home. The kids retreated to their rooms after a late supper, with Roman following Jada to her room.

I welcomed the quiet sunset, hoping that Caroline would ride down on the final rays to cheer me and pass on some strength. I cleaned the kitchen under the haze of orange sun, disappointed that my imaginary friend hadn't stopped in for an imaginary pep talk. The last yellow-green of daylight streaked the horizon while I tied the trash bag closed, feeling fortunate to live in a time where trash bags were infused with mountain-fresh Febreze. "Come on, Hershey. Let's get this bag out, girl." I whacked my palm against my leg and she beat me to the door, tail thumping the wall.

It was a beautiful night, clear and so filled with starlight that I believed Caroline was with me after all. I walked around to the side of the garage to drop the trash in the can, but no one had brought it up from the road. We had a system for whose turn it was, just like the system for the dishes. A block of wood sat in the kitchen window with the older kids' names stamped on different surfaces. After they unloaded the dishwasher, they flipped the block to the next name;—forget to flip it and you were up twice. A cruder chunk of wood in the garage served the same purpose for trash. I didn't have the energy to drag one of them out and didn't really mind the walk anyhow.

Hershey trotted beside me, sniffing after a chipmunk or rabbit trail every ninth step, gravel shooting back from her paws when she launched on each new path. Freshly mowed grass and wild onions reminded me of my mom's potato soup, and the chorus of night insects boldly shouting things they never said in daylight made me smile. I was practically skipping by the time I reached the can. A fire-ant hill had started beside it, and I made a mental note to poison it before it spread. The bites annoyed the kids and left large welts on me, an allergic reaction never quite bad enough for Benadryl but driving me half mad with itching for a week or more.

I tossed the bag in and left the can at the street. Dragging it back up the gravel would interrupt night sounds, and I was in the mood to listen. I threw my hands in the air, eyes on the stars, and felt a yell bubbling in my throat. I held it in, wondering what it would say if I let it out, wondering if it would be in an ancient tongue. The things in my mind and heart had started to feel more and more foreign, but in the thrilling way of new discovery; I no longer felt like a lost, frightened soul. I had found a home inside my own skin for the first time. Things were a long way from perfect, but they were trending in a direction I knew I could live with. My mom was right. We really were going to be all right.

The next morning, Hershey wanted out the front door instead of the back, which was more likely to signal bad news than good. Labradors rarely break their obsessive patrol paths without reason. The kids had started summer vacation—well, if you could call anything about our life a vacation—so I made a to-do list for them before I opened the front door a crack. The welcome mat was a clean series of black quatrefoil blocks on a cream background. No scary messages. No signs. No real reason for me to still be looking for these things. I pulled the door open and stepped out, one foot on the mat and one on the threshold.

The long, narrow porch had a small bamboo table and two matching chairs on the far end. It had been my birthday present three years ago, a little spot to read with a lemonade. A tall, iced lemonade with a red-and-white-striped straw. I closed the door, not only the cheery front door of the house, but the door that led to scary thoughts about things left on doorsteps and last straws. I was sick and tired of spending brain cells on the past.

I stumbled my way through an interview on my lunch hour at work. To bring in extra grocery money, I was freelancing for the state paper, the *Arkansas Democrat-Gazette,* writing front-page features for their inserts. Local human-interest stories were a nice diversion from the chaos of our own story, but I had a hard time being objective with story arcs just then, not to mention how hard it was to stay awake and meet my deadlines after working past dark on the job site and rising before the sun for my programming job. I cheated by listening to the most important part of the subject's answers and then writing half the article during the interview when they carried on about less pertinent details.

We went to the job site in the afternoon and wished we could have gone in the morning instead. Late June in the South wasn't any cooler than July would be; in fact, it often felt steamier, because the summer rain clouds hadn't evaporated. My hair curled into tight spirals in the humidity. As much as I would have liked to use the heat as an excuse to work inside, we had too much to finish outdoors.

"Get the scaffolding set up. I'll be out in a minute," I said to Drew. He knew the drill when it came to putting up siding. Jada ran after him, eager to help. The only siding left was high up, but unlike me, she was fearless in high places.

Hope and I looked over an estimate one of the cabinetmakers had taped to the kitchen window. I had selected simple, unfinished cabinets and drawn the basic plan myself. The extra-tall cabinet doors would go all the way to the ceiling and have more drawers than doors on the lower half. Pan drawers, towel drawers, utensil drawers, and bread drawers. I didn't like digging in back cabinets on my knees. To offset the plain style, a decorative wooden hood over the stove would act as a centerpiece. I had ordered a custom marble-tile image of a Da Vinci sketch, a study of five characters in a comic scene, to set in the backsplash above the stove top. We needed a comedy set in stone.

It was a big kitchen, and since Hope did a lot of the cooking, she was excited. "This is the lowest estimate so far," she said, measuring her excitement against my skepticism. "Is everything the same?"

"He moved the wall oven. We'd lose the floor-to-ceiling cabinet, but placing the oven away from the refrigerator makes a lot of sense." I flipped to the computer image of the appliances. "I like it. What do you think?"

She nodded, future baking days dancing in her eyes.

"I'll call him before I start on siding." I wasn't thrilled with the kitchen, but it was good enough. Ain't no church, my dad would have said with a mock Southern twang. Honestly, I was just tired of making decisions by the armload and didn't have the energy to linger over this one.

The electricians showed up around suppertime, smiling and barely lifting their feet off the ground. They drilled holes and pulled wire with surprising efficiency. I was actually impressed with them for once, until Hope came out with Roman on one hip. "I think there's a problem with one of the pipes."

I thought right away that she must mean a water line, because there wasn't much that could go wrong with the drain lines when nothing was draining into them yet. But I'd forgotten that Tweedledum and Tweedledee were back on the job. They had drilled a hole in the four-inch sewer line running down from the kids' upstairs bathroom through a wall in my library.

"Just get one of them couplers, cut it in half, and glue it on over the hole," Tweedledee said. "Put the seams against the studs and the inspector will never notice."

The proper way to fix the hole would be to cut out the section of pipe, and replace it with smaller sections of pipe and couplers to hold it all together. It was going to be a real pain, since the bottom was set in concrete and the top was wedged against the ceiling. We had no wiggle room. And the asinine suggestion that I try to slip a spliced-together fix past the inspector wasn't going to fly with me.

"We're talking about sewage running down a wall in my library!" I said. Okay, I may have shouted it, actually. I took a deep breath. "We'll have to cut this section out. Splice in a repair, and retest for leaks." *Damn it* was left off but implied by my tone. They didn't offer to help do the work or pay for the parts, and I wasn't in the mood to discuss it. I would subtract the replacement parts from their final payment and attach the receipts.

We had electricity in the house, at least in theory, but wouldn't be able to flip the switch and use it until after the Sheetrock was up and the electrical fixtures and outlets were installed. My confidence well was shallow when it came to the likelihood that the electricians had done things right, and making repairs after they were covered up would be next to impossible.

The times when we were overwhelmed with things to do were tough, but it was always more difficult when we were waiting for other people to complete tasks. So the next few weeks had us all on edge while the cellulose insulation was blown in the walls, the final bricks were laid, and the Sheetrock was hung and finished. We did a lot of cleanup and planning inside and out, and on a hot July afternoon, we put fiberglass insulation in the ceiling of the garage so my room above would be more energy-efficient.

"It's literally a hundred and ten degrees," Hope said, checking her phone. "This is a deep layer of hell."

I didn't want to tell her that carrying the insulation rolls into the garage and setting up the ladders was the easy part. We'd bought six-inch rolls that we'd double in the twelve-inch-deep ceiling space. But the fluffy fiberglass had a paper backing on it that would create a moisture barrier between the layers if we left it there. Not good. I started ripping the paper backing off half of the rolls, marveling at first over how easy it was compared with how difficult it had seemed in my mind. Drew took my prepared rolls and started shoving them in place, layering the paper-backed layer underneath with Hope just behind him stapling the paper to the ceiling joists to hold everything up.

When I finished peeling away paper, Jada and I started our own assembly line, with her handing insulation up to me while I shoved and stapled with an electric staple gun. She also kept the cord and long pieces of insulation from tangling. Thankfully, Roman napped in the back of the shop through the worst of it.

The job would have been miserable in the dead of winter with us wearing full protective clothing. But covering every inch of skin with thick clothing in the heat would have killed us, so we bargained between heatstroke and discomfort with thinner gear than we probably should have. We were overheated and sweaty, with tiny shards of fiberglass coating us; it was the worst I had felt in my life, truly a task I wouldn't wish on an enemy. A layer of hell, indeed.

"Worse than being tarred and feathered," Drew said.

"I feel like fire ants are all over me!" Jada whined.

"I want to die," Hope added, and I silently agreed with all of them.

We traded jokes for a while, then complaints a while longer. But before we were halfway done, we were too miserable to speak. Drew's CD stopped—someone must have forgotten to hit the repeat button when they started it—and no one bothered to turn it back on. We gestured when we needed something, grunted when we smashed a finger, and rehydrated when we started blacking out from heat exhaustion. As horrible as I felt, seeing my kids so far past fatigue and discomfort that they couldn't even bicker and complain made the whole thing worse.

Roman woke up and toddled out of the shop clenching his grungy cat, Peek-a-boo, in one fist. He stood in the doorway watching us, and no one had to tell him to stay out. He could see that whatever was happening in the garage, it was not fun. I handed him a juice box from the cooler, and he sat under a tree in his Tweety Bird lawn chair, perfectly silent in honor of our obvious suffering. Hershey sat with him, whining now and then over the unhappy tension.

We stapled the last row up when the sun was a glowing ball of unrelenting heat on the horizon. There were no celebratory dances. No victory. No words. The insulation had inflicted enough pain to be the battle victor.

We rinsed our faces, arms, and legs with the hose, but it did little more than cool us. Our clothes and hair were still filled with bits of fiberglass that rained down when we moved and stuck to our damp skin.

A shower and generous handfuls of soap followed by equally generous handfuls of lotion was the only thing that would offer relief. Still silent, we packed tools away and loaded up the car.

"Crap," Drew said, pointing to a stack of concrete-reinforcement wire in the driveway. We were trapped. Blocked in. The six-by-twelve-foot grids of rusty wire had been delivered that morning and we'd forgotten all about it. Eventually, the wire would reinforce the slab outside our garage and a driveway up to the shop. The rest of our long drive would be paved after we'd moved in and I saved up the money. But the only thing that mattered just then was that the wire was blocking our way out. I took a few steps toward it, measuring the idea of driving around without hitting a tree or a muddy sinkhole. I might have taken the risk if I hadn't remembered that the Sheetrock truck would need to get up the driveway bright and early.

I went to the shop for a pair of gloves, and the kids followed, silently sorting through the milk crate of gloves for a right-and-left pair, no matter the size or mismatched colors.

Drew and Hope stood on one of the short ends and I took the other. The wire sheets tangled in each other when we lifted them two at a time, and then tangled in the long grass and shrubs when we dragged them across to the edge of our property. On the final trip, we struggled with three sheets, determined not to walk all the way back for a single piece. We hadn't eaten much all day and were at the edge of heatstroke. If the pinpricks of fiberglass hadn't been torturing us, we might have slowed down and been more careful. I might have watched the four-inch spikes of wire sticking out from my end of the sheet as carefully as I watched the grass for the copperhead snakes that we knew lived nearby. But we were tired. We were desperate. And we were less careful than we should have been.

When the spike of rusty metal stuck into my left calf, I thought for one instant that it was just a scratch and my exhaustion had focused the pain, made me overreact. But when I bent over to look, the spike was shorter than it should have been by nearly two inches.

I exhaled quickly and pulled it out, like ripping off a Band-Aid; there was no reason to wait and think it through. More than anything, I was pissed off that I had yet another thing to deal with on a day that had already had enough of me. Rich blood pumped out, matching the rhythm of my heart rather than just dripping in a steady stream. My vision tunneled. I had passed out when the older kids' dad had his wisdom teeth pulled and again when Jada's bottom teeth poked through her lip after a fall. Passing out there in the field would have been a welcome reprieve from the day.

"Mommy?" Hope's voice went wobbly, sounding a lot like Jada's.

"I need," I said, looking around for something to put over the pulsing wound and not seeing anything. "Tape. I need the roll of duct tape." I pulled off my left shoe and sock, wadded the already bloody sock over the hole in my leg, and fell backward onto my butt.

"You okay?" Hope asked, her face ashen and her hands shaking.

"It's just a little hole. Where's the—"

Drew handed me a roll of gray tape. I wrapped tape around my leg to hold the sock in place. Definitely not the most sanitary wrap, but it couldn't be helped. Jada was holding Roman and leaning against the car. All four of them looked terrified.

I took a deep breath, preparing myself to shrug it all off and reassure them. Maybe I could have pulled that off if I hadn't looked down at my leg. The sock was drenched in blood. On my exhale, I leaned over and puked in the grass, narrowly missing Drew's foot. It wasn't that the injury was all that terrible, but combined with our hellacious day, the heat, and my squeamishness, it was more than I was prepared to handle. I put a hand up, palm out, to the kids and waved like it was no big deal, but in reality it was in surrender as much as reassurance.

"Just need to keep pressure on it and get a tetanus in the morning. Good as new."

Hope drove us home and no one spoke.

Some of our words had been stolen away by exhaustion, that was true, but my mom had taught me to live by the old "if you can't say something nice" rule, and I had nothing nice to say.

We were so far beyond tired of the project that there wasn't a word to describe what we felt. And with so many things left to do, the deadline looked more impossible every day. I wanted my kids to go on dates and eat spaghetti and meatballs instead of jerky and crackers for supper. I wanted the house we were living in to sell and I wanted the new house to be a home instead of the hardest damn thing I'd ever done in my life. I wanted to go on vacation with my mom again and invite my dad down to relax.

I wanted to take my own turn at feeling broken and let someone else take a turn at cheering everyone up. But that isn't how being a mom works. So I swallowed all those thoughts, got everyone showered and fed, and carried on with the pushing-forward, the cheering-up, and the determination to work hard enough to make everything better.

Have I mentioned I'm an optimist?

—20—

Down by the River *Fall*

Even though Adam and I had been divorced for well over a year, my erratic sleep reflected how often I still worried about him coming back. I stayed up late, woke frequently, and found deep, solid sleep only in the early-morning hours before my alarm rang. It wasn't a sustainable pattern, and I told myself that every evening before I climbed into bed and did it again.

My phone was ringing, and I had the sense that it had been for a while. But it was so far away that I wasn't sure how I was supposed to get to it. I tried to climb up out of the foggy sleep determined to hold me down, and I slowly became aware that I was in my bed.

A woman had been yelling at me in my dream. She was red-faced and angry. When she opened her mouth, the ring tone of my phone sounded from deep inside her.

Yes, I'll get it. Leave me alone.

I often felt like it had been years since I'd slept a whole night without worry or fear. But that never seemed like a terrible thing, as long as there was hope that it would end sometime soon. A person can get through just about anything if they believe it isn't forever. I reached over to my nightstand and fumbled for the phone, knocking it to the ground. It stopped ringing. Fine with me. I rolled over so my back was to it, but I had only pulled in two slow breaths when it started again. The ringer was turned too low to wake the kids, but I couldn't ignore it no matter how much I wanted to.

I leaned over, grabbed it, and tucked back under the blanket like there were monsters under the bed.

It was a Little Rock number. "Hello?" I cleared my throat.

"Is this Cara? Cara Brookins?"

"Yes. Who—"

"Shit. It's her. I have her," the man said aside to someone else. "Cara, this is Officer Stracener with the Little Rock Police Department. I need you to confirm that your children are with you."

Cold rushed from the sides of my neck down my torso. "They're here. In bed. Asleep." My voice was tiny. Insignificant. The voice of a liar.

"No. I need you to confirm that each one of them is there. I need you to go check your kids. Now." He was firm. Commanding. Nerves— or fear—stretched his tone a notch too high, made it flutter at the edges.

I couldn't move. Couldn't speak. My heart galloped so fast that I half expected Officer Stracener to witness my heart attack over the phone. The last of me. I had nothing left.

"Cara? Are you checking your kids?"

"Let me talk to her. Cara?"

My mind went around in a circle before I whispered, "Sophie."

"Cara, Adam drove his car into the Arkansas River. The car's gone, but he got out and swam around, naked and yelling crazy stuff."

"River?" my lips said but my voice did not.

"We need her to check the goddamned kids!" Officer Stracener was losing his cool, but I had enough for both of us. I was sinking deep into a cool, dark place and I wasn't sure I would ever find my way out again.

Sophie said something I didn't hear. Maybe I didn't want to. Then she was loud, talking fast. "He told them you were in the trunk. He told them that, and he believed it. But you're not, so—"

So my kids might be.

A noise exactly like Hershey had made, bloody and taped like a rodeo calf on my back porch, came out of my throat. Then another, and I sucked it all back in and bit my lips to silence. I was in my doorway without any memory of standing.

Why had I put four-year-old Jada in her bed last night? Why? She had fallen asleep reading with me in my bed. Why? What was I thinking? Just because we hadn't heard from him in a while, had I really believed we were safe?

I made it to the stairs, gaining confidence when Hershey appeared next to me, sleepy-eyed. She would have alerted me if anyone had entered the house. Wouldn't she have? Or would she have cowered, too afraid of Adam to move or even growl? I crawled up the stairs like a toddler. Knee. Palm. Knee.

The phone was in my hand. Still connected. If they were talking I couldn't hear them, but they would hear the phone thumping against the stairs. Up. Up. Up. My vision tunneled, cleared, and tunneled again.

I had been afraid for my own life so many times, but I'd never even imagined he could slip my kids right out of the house and drive them to the bottom of the Arkansas River, float them out of my life for good. It was a brand-new terror born into a mind that thought it was full up with them.

At the landing, I stood, even though I wasn't steady on my feet. My mind spun in a frantic whirlwind, urging me to run as fast as I could to find my children. At the same time the too-logical side of my brain held me back, froze my body in place. There were only two possible outcomes. The kids were either there or they weren't. And that urgent side of my brain didn't understand that speed couldn't change the outcome.

Officer Stracener wasn't in a hurry to find out if my kids were in the trunk so he could rescue them; he was checking to see if they had bodies to recover. My children's bodies.

One, two, three.

I held on to the half wall at the top of the stairs, hyperaware of the rough Sheetrock texture under every fingertip. I curled my toes into the carpet and swore I felt each individual fiber. Hershey had stayed at the bottom. As badly as I wanted her with me, I didn't have the courage to open my mouth and call her.

For one last minute, a precious one, I stood there as a mom. In only seconds I could walk into one room after another and find empty beds. Cold sheets. It could be the very last minute that I was someone's mommy, and I needed to hold it.

Jada's room was closest, but I couldn't go there first. At four, she would be the easiest one to get out of the house in total silence. I started to think of ways he could have pulled the other kids out and stopped myself. They were ugly thoughts.

Drew's door was closed, and when I tried the handle it was locked. The little pseudokey over the bathroom door fit in all the doors, and I slipped it in until it clicked the lock open. My son stretched diagonally across his bed in a pair of checkered boxers, feet tangled in his sheets. The room smelled of body spray and dirty sneakers.

A sob cracked out of my chest so rapidly it hurt like it had been jerked out by a fist. I pulled the door closed and ran to Hope's room, my hair flying and arms out, so I must have resembled a ghost running across the long playroom. Hope's dark hair fanned onto her pillow like it had been arranged. The quilt was pulled neatly to her chin. I could hear her slow breathing but couldn't come anywhere near to matching the pace.

Tears had drenched my face. I could no longer breathe through my nose. The phone had gone missing at some point and I'd have to find it eventually. But not yet. One. Two. I had two children.

My head and kidneys ached from fear and adrenaline. My vision tunneled out more than in. I was cold. At some point I realized I must be going into shock. I gagged. The only way I could make it to Jada's room was by holding the doorframe and hugging the wall like Spider-Man, like a woman who had lost gravity.

What if she's gone? How will we go on? The kids—we just can't—

I couldn't hear anything from the doorway. Shouldn't I hear her?

Jada's door caught on a pile of clothes when I pushed it open. Even from the doorway I could see that her pillow was empty.

From the middle of the room I could see a lump in the middle of her bed. A dark, hopeful shape. I stood there for at least a minute, imagining it was her and everything was okay. Then I imagined Adam, and a terrible part of me wanted him to be in his car at the bottom of the river—out of my life forever. In a watery grave. I could see him there clearly, curled up in his own trunk. Gone.

I walked across the rug, dragging my feet to keep from stepping on a project or stray earring. I ran my hands over the pillow, palms flat, then down the bed, tangling my fingers in blankets. Nothing but blankets. I moved slowly at first and then faster, frantic, looking for a piece of my little girl. I jumped when my hand ran up against a stuffed toy, flipping it over with a mechanical mew. I echoed the cry and resumed my search, friction heating my palms and making a whistling noise against the sheets. When my hand found her back, I almost shook her, angry that she was pressed long and flat against the footboard, using a beach towel for a blanket.

Three. I had three.

The walk back to the stairs was dark. My tears hadn't stopped. I wasn't sure they ever would. I found my phone on the carpet at the top of the stairs. It was still connected.

Going backward with one hand and my knees, I moved down the

stairs. "Officer? Sophie?" But even I could tell my throat was squeezing my voice to a squeak. Like a little white mouse. I sat on the floor at the bottom, holding Hershey and crying against her side. "Sophie?" I said again, and this time someone heard me.

"This is Officer Bradley. Am I speaking with Cara?"

"They're all okay. My kids. They're all here."

"We got 'em! All good!" he shouted. "Kids accounted for. Get him out of here. We got the kids."

"Jesus Christ," Stracener said from a distance, and then he must have taken the phone from Bradley. "We have a Hamot officer pulling into your driveway now. He can come in and sit with you for a while. Call someone for you."

"No," I said. They hadn't sent the officer to sit with me, they had sent him to check my kids' beds because they thought I was too weak, too small to do it myself. "I don't want him to come in." I was still crying, and there was no way to pretend otherwise when my nose was completely blocked.

"Are you sure? Can I call someone to come over? You might not want to be alone."

I steadied my breath. "I'm not alone. My kids are here." Lights were drawing and redrawing a blue line across the dining-room wall. "We're just fine."

"Call if you need anything. We'll do whatever we can," he said.

I hung up, wondering if I had thanked him or only thought the words. My head was still scattered and my thoughts couldn't find a straight line to anything. The clock on the oven said it was 4:31, and I was having trouble finding oxygen. Someone had sucked it all out of the house.

The police lights switched off before the car backed out and hung a right toward town. A deep breath took the very last molecule of oxygen and used it up. I lurched for the door and pulled it open, sucking in gulps of fresh oxygen and starting to cry again.

My forehead throbbed with sharp pains on either side like someone had accidentally left a couple of steak knives in my skull. When I leaned down to rub the worst spots near my temples, I saw something on the welcome mat. Hershey sniffed at it and pulled away with a little sneeze.

One of the kids had left a glass there. But why would they do that?

I picked it up with my left hand, because I was afraid if I moved the right one from my temple my brains would shoot out. Water sloshed over the lip.

Water.

A dark figure floated in the glass. A little dead mouse. My hand shook badly enough to drop it, but somehow I held on long enough to lower it back to the welcome mat.

"Better you than me," I said, but I meant *Better you than my kids.* I couldn't just stand there thinking about all the might-have-beens. All the what-ifs. Adam had been at the house and walked right up to the front door while we slept and I'd never known it. I had the feeling he was trying to tell me I was lucky this time. He could have hurt me if he wanted, he could have made us all take a dive. But I had been lucky. We were all so lucky.

I flapped my left arm against my leg like a wounded bird. Hershey abandoned the trail she was sniffing through the yard and leapt over the glass to get inside. She leaned against my thigh and put her nose under my hand. A subtle hint that she was open to some attention.

"Good girl. Keep an eye out, and don't let him in. He has no right to be in this house. No matter what." I rubbed her head, gave her three solid pats on the ribs, and laughed when the hollow echo made me jump.

She went with me to check all the downstairs doors and windows, and then to push the dining-room chairs in front of the doors. I hadn't worked out yet what I would tell the kids. If I was going to start barricading the doors, I would have to tell them something. When I was in the kitchen sorting through the knife drawer for just the right one to keep on my nightstand, I realized how ridiculous I was being. The chairs and the knife weren't a bad idea, but they would be useless tonight. After driving his car into the river and claiming that a body or bodies were in the trunk, Adam wasn't going to be sneaking around my house for a while. He'd earned himself a trip back to the state hospital, where slipping pills into the potted plants wasn't going to be as easy as it was at Ivana's or Sophie's.

I closed the knife drawer and put the dining-room chairs back under the table. Being realistic and cautious was smart. Being paranoid and irrational was not only stupid, it was dangerous. Adam might have suggested that I was slow and stupid all these years, but I was starting to believe he was wrong.

The thudding in my temples had slowed, but it had worked like a bilge pump, draining every last bit of energy from my limbs. I wanted to go upstairs to get Jada, to carry her back to my bed and sleep with one hand on her tummy. But my fear wasn't the sort of energy she needed to feel. Besides, I could barely lift my feet to move across the den toward my room. When I reached the bed I rolled into it, my arms and legs leaden weights.

I never would have imagined I could sleep after the terror of thinking I had lost the only things that mattered. But my body separated into two parts, half drifting into the early-morning sky and half sinking deep into the earth. My dreams started out fractured and chaotic but settled into a rhythm that woke me shortly after sunrise as though it were music.

I had lost some of my urgency and gained an appreciation for tiny moments. The way my breath moved slow and calm in and out of my lungs felt good. The sheets felt luxuriously smooth. Even my pillow-case's fake mountain-fresh scent that came from a softener bottle made me smile.

—21—

Rise
Glue Me Back Together

I slept that night with my punctured leg propped and iced after I'd soaked it in peroxide, then alcohol, then applied antibiotic cream, then taped a split-open aloe vera leaf to it. My whole body tingled from the fiberglass insulation, but the worst of it had washed away in the shower. If I hadn't been too dehydrated to make tears, I would have cried myself to sleep.

Benjamin was there as soon as I made the conscious effort to relax my shoulders and imagine a disk of light passing through me. He was leaning over me, his face clear. I studied him, wanting his pity to validate how pitiful I felt. Per usual, his expression was more happy than sad, more peace than pity. His eyes smiled and his lips curved barely past a neutral expression. It wasn't mocking, like I had thought for the first few seconds. He was encouraging in a way that told me I could do everything I set out to do and then some.

I wished he'd say the words, speak out loud that he was proud of me. How long had it been since I had heard words like that from anyone but my parents? Years. He didn't speak, and I realized he probably never would. The look in his eyes would have to be enough. I exhaled, at peace, and slept right through my morning alarm.

The kids would be in the way at the job site, with the Sheetrock guys spraying the finish texture inside and hanging the sheets in the garage ceiling over our insulation. I left them at the house with a list of simple chores and went to my doctor for a tetanus shot. Dr. Sam—short for Samantha—gave me a list of things to watch for with the puncture wound. It had a high risk of infection, but she thought it looked clean considering the conditions it had happened under. I was thankful I didn't need stitches.

I wished I could go home for a nap, but had to go in to the office instead. My commute was about twenty-five minutes, and that was the only time I ever found myself alone. I realized on that drive that I was feeling restless and a little vengeful, so I started thinking about Caroline again. She had been lying low lately, and I missed her. There were still things I needed to learn from her strength.

When I got home, the Sheetrock foreman called to say the job was done and ready for me to check out, which was code for "Come over and write me a check."

The kids were as anxious to see the finished walls as I was, so we loaded into the car with Hershey and drove over.

"I can't believe how many rooms there are!" Jada said, dancing through the upstairs. "Just a few days ago, I could walk through that wall!" She bumped up against the wall separating her room from one of the upstairs bathrooms.

The first thing I noticed was how much quieter it was. Work in one room didn't echo through the entire house and ricochet through my skull like it had for months. We all went to our own rooms, except Roman, who bounced among all of them like a pinball. I lay down in the spot where my bed would be and stared at the ceiling. Even though we were a long way from finished, even though my calf ached, I couldn't stop smiling. We were actually doing it. We were building our own house, and it looked every bit as good as what a real construction crew could have built.

Red. I would put red curtains in my room and a fuzzy rug beside my bed to curl my toes in. "We're a kick-ass family," I whispered to Caroline, and I felt her smile along with me. She'd been hanging out in the shadows all along.

It was the first of August, which made the countdown to our September 13 deadline impossibly close. The rest of our to-do list was on us, and it was more like three months long if everything went perfectly. Impossible. But we'd done impossible before, albeit not when we were quite so exhausted. The stolen minutes to look at the ceiling were a guilty pleasure we couldn't afford. I sat up. "Drew? You ready to put in a couple doors?"

He didn't answer, so I stalled for him, reviewing the list on my phone. Doors, trim, caulk, paint, hardwood flooring, concrete flooring, tile, showers, bathtubs, toilets, cabinets installed, stain and finish cabinets, make concrete countertops, install sinks and plumbing fixtures, lights, switches, outlets, stairs, rails, exterior porch rails, back steps and rail, garage doors, concrete slab, library shelves. I rearranged the items in what I guessed was the right order.

It really wasn't possible. Not even for an experienced construction crew working overtime. Our budget was too tight to hire workers, because I had no intention of using all the money the bank had approved. If I did, I wouldn't be able to afford the final mortgage of Inkwell. This was a low-budget build. I had to make it work.

I found Drew downstairs. He had carried in three doors by himself and propped them against the wall in the dining room. While it would have been nice to believe he realized how overwhelming our list was, I knew his enthusiasm was because he thought we were almost finished. As hard as we'd been pushing for almost eight months, the final six weeks were going to be even more difficult, and we were going in feeling fully spent. I didn't say any of this to the kids. Whatever well they could find to pull enthusiasm from, I wouldn't dampen it. Not yet.

The girls were cleaning the upstairs, getting the floor ready for the hardwood, which was in two-inch tongue-and-groove strips that would be glued to the subfloor. Roman was in his room, zooming Matchbox cars—real ones rather than painted rocks—around and around the stack of hardwood flooring. Drew and I installed the laundry-room and pantry doors faster than we had any of the exterior doors, but the downstairs bathroom went wrong and then more wrong before we got it to close evenly. It was dark by the time we finished, and we were working with a shop light that put off a lot of heat. "Enough doors for tonight," I said, expecting Drew to want to head back to the house.

"Those last sheets of plywood are blocking the upstairs doors. What are we doing with those?" he asked.

It was good to think of our building supplies as the last ones. The last two-by-sixes, the last plywood, the last nails, screws, or Liquid Nails. "I thought we'd use them in the attic for storage platforms."

"Let's carry them up before we leave, so the doors are ready to go when we come back."

My calf was throbbing, but I didn't want to stand in the way of his momentum. We needed every extra push we could get. All the months of building had made for some impressive muscles. Drew had turned from a pasty-white, thin, geeky boy into a tan, muscled young man. Before the Sheetrock went up, he could jump up and grab the ceiling joists and pull himself up through them effortlessly. My muscles hadn't built quite as much as his, but I definitely had muscles I hadn't believed I owned. Carrying the four-by-eight sheets of plywood upstairs took little effort.

The attic door hadn't been installed, so there was just a hole in the ceiling in Roman's room. We carried ladders up and positioned them as well as we could. Hope helped us stabilize everything while we hoisted the sheets up one at a time with Drew all the way in the attic and me perching at the top of the ladder to push the end of the sheet up.

Everything went smoothly until the final sheet, which wedged against a crossbeam on a rafter and wouldn't budge. We would have just left it for another day, but it had Drew blocked in the attic space unless he slithered around the side on his hands and knees. The blown-cellulose insulation was easier on skin than the fiberglass kind, but we both decided we might as well just finish the job for good. "Hold on," I told him, "I'll climb up and help from up there. I can get more leverage."

We tried a half dozen maneuvers to loosen the stuck piece, but failed. "Brute force," Drew said. "We're just going to have to push it out the way it came in. You push down on your side to pivot it, and I'll push up and try to bend it a little at the same time. It'll pop right out."

The reasoning was sound. I pushed down with everything I had. He pushed up. I felt the wood bend under his pressure, but I never felt the instant it gave way. We hadn't planned that far ahead. The top spun around and slammed into my head, just above my left eye. Following the basic rules of physics, my head slammed into the rafter behind me. The pain was impressive, and so was the blood. I couldn't tell exactly where it was coming from at first, because my entire head throbbed from the hit.

Drew wiggled the plywood down into place, yelling while he did it. "Hope! Mommy's hurt! I need your help!"

Hope came up the ladder while I turned to walk toward it. Rafters were spinning, but I was pretty sure it was just an immediate response to the hit, not a symptom of a serious head injury. Blood dripped onto the plywood and the tops of the ceiling joists we'd worked so hard to straighten after leaving them out in the rain. It soaked into the insulation, dropping like bread crumbs to mark my path to the ladder, down it, and to my bedroom, where I sat on the floor.

"Get me some ice and a washcloth," I said, as though those were things we would actually have. Jada started taking her sock off but I waved for her to stop. Hope brought a roll of paper towels, and I shook the Sheetrock dust off them before pressing a handful to my left eyebrow, which had become the focal point of the head pain.

"You need to go to the doctor," she said.

Drew swung down from the attic opening without using the ladder. "Definitely. That's a lot of blood," he said. "How bad is it?"

"Head wounds bleed a lot. It might not be that bad. I need a mirror." I didn't want to go to the doctor. I was too tired to sit in an ER. Not only that, I hated the idea of stitches. Yuck.

Drew disappeared and we sat quietly, mopping up blood. When he came back, he was carrying a four-foot-long wall mirror for my bathroom. I laughed. "I'm not getting ready for a cocktail party!"

"All I could find." He laughed, too, and propped the mirror in front of where I sat cross-legged in a little cloud of crumpled red paper towels.

It took me a minute to work up the courage to lift the pressure off and look. A long cut under my left eyebrow gaped open and started bleeding again. But it wasn't the cut that caught my attention, it was my hand. The entire back of my left hand and my middle and ring fingers were purple and bruised. The fingers were obviously swollen. How I hadn't noticed that injury, I'd never know. I flexed the hand and winced. The fingers wouldn't bend all the way. Typing was my livelihood. Whether the eyebrow cut needed stitching or not, my hand needed an X-ray. Damn it. I didn't have time for injuries.

"Ewww," Drew said, looking away. "It's going to need stitches for sure." He hadn't noticed my hand and I kept quiet.

"I probably should have it looked at. Let's get everyone home and Hope can drive me to the hospital. No hurry. It's just a precaution." I stood up, marveling at how little my calf hurt compared with my head and hand.

Roman and Jada didn't even know I'd been hurt until we called them to leave. Jada had lost her shoes somewhere in the house, and we finally gave up and left them there. When we got back to the house, Roman cried, wanting to go with me, but Drew finally lured him away with popcorn and a bad ninja movie. "Cookies, too?" Roman asked, milking the bribe for all he could.

Hope packed my hand in ice while I held a second pack on my head. It was strange to have my kids taking care of me. And it was also frustrating to have accomplished so much with the house and feel weak and broken instead of strong. I thought of runners at the end of a marathon. They looked a lot more beaten than bright-eyed and bushy-tailed. But this was not what I had imagined when I was standing outside the tornado-broken house, and it wasn't what I felt that Caroline expected of me.

I wanted winning to hurt a lot less.

In the waiting room, I read a book on my Kindle, and Hope pinned room-decorating ideas on Pinterest. The usual cast of crying babies and tired elderly sat around us, worrying through their own pain with little interest in their neighbors. Hope had brought a bag of almonds, and a bottle of water for each of us. If I didn't feel like an ice pick was protruding from my brow, I would have enjoyed the reading break.

When I was finally called into the back, everything went as expected at first. They took me to Radiology for an X-ray of my hand and surprised me by taking one of my face in case of a fracture to the orbital socket. I hadn't thought of that. They followed the painless radiation blasts with a very painful wound irrigation. The male nurse was a newbie and managed to drench my shoulder, back, and then the entire bed with saline solution and had to change the sheets and bring towels to mop my clothes dry. By the time I resettled, we were moved from our curtained room to an examining room with a door. I worried that it meant my hand was broken. I could not build the rest of the house with a cast on. Instantly, I was depressed.

A sturdy woman with bright red glasses and white hair so thin she was almost bald came in and sat down beside the bed. Hope ignored her, still decorating the house through Pinterest.

"I'm Pamela," she said, patting my leg. "And I just wanted to come in and chat with you for a while, hon."

I nodded, wondering who had told her I was a writer. It wasn't as though I was well known enough to have fans seeking me out, but every time someone learned I wrote novels, they either had a novel they wanted to write, or they wanted me to write the story of their life into one of my novels. I closed my eyes, trying to summon the energy to show interest in her story and give her solid information about a career versus a hobby as an author.

"Good news is the hand isn't broken, and neither is your skull. Just banged up. Now tell me about this cut here, and how you got it. Okay, hon?" She patted my leg again. "And what did you hit with that hand? It's really banged up, now, isn't it."

I told the story again, wishing she would write it down so I didn't have to repeat myself. She had asked a half dozen more questions and pointed at the network of nasty bruises and scrapes covering my legs and arms before I figured out what was going on. I laughed, first a little chuckle and then for real. Hope and Pamela sat up straight, eyes wide and on me, then darting to the door, wondering if they should go for help, call someone to scan my brain.

I waved them down. "It's just ironic. You think this is evidence of domestic violence, right? And after all those years of sporting my husband's bruises on my neck and hips, when not a single person asked about them, now I get hurt in an attic and alarm bells sound."

Pamela smiled, tight-lipped and noncommittal.

Hope looked back at her phone screen.

The doctor rapped his knuckles on the door, then came in before we invited him. "How's everything going here? Getting things sorted?" He had a British accent, and I wondered how he ended up in a Little Rock ER. He leaned in close to look at my cut, swiveling a magnifying glass on a pole between us for a better view.

Pamela relayed the attic story, doubtful but coming around, and I promised it was true. "Trust me, I know domestic violence. I'm free of that now." Maybe it wasn't entirely true. Matt's hands weren't around my throat on the average Tuesday night, and we hadn't seen Adam in years, but fear has a long reach. They were still hurting me through the dents and craters they'd left in my self-esteem. The doctor was more interested in my house-building project than a domestic-violence threat. We chatted about energy-efficient building and passive solar. Then he suggested that it was time to start stitching up my face, and I balked.

"What are my options?" I asked, eyeing the door and mapping the best getaway path.

"You made a hole in your head, and we have to close it. Not a lot of great options for that. At the very least I have to glue it." He leaned in for another look. "Longer than I'd like for glue though. If you split it back open it's more likely to scar."

He pinched the gap together a few times. I closed my eyes and kept my breathing even, pretending the razor knives of pain were no big deal and hoping that would help make the wound look small enough to be glued back together like a chipped lamp.

"If you think you can stay out of attics for a while, we can give the glue a try."

The counselor left and sent in a nurse with a tray. I imagined it holding nothing but a big tube of epoxy. We continued talking about the various stages of building a house and more energy-efficient options. I wasn't sure if he was genuinely interested in construction or merely trying to verify that my beating had come at my own hands.

Hope never looked up from her phone, partly because she was lost in Pinterest land, but also because she was nearly as squeamish as I was. A peek at my sliced-open eyebrow through a magnifying glass would have undone her.

". . . I believe those laws are in place for a very good reason, and I don't want to make you uncomfortable. Doctors and patients aren't supposed to have personal contact. It's a professional relationship. I believe that, and I support those laws. I really do," the doctor was saying.

What was his name again? And what in the world was he talking about? Of course I was uncomfortable; he had a buffet-style warming lamp inches from my head and was pinching a deep gash in my head. Laws about personal contact? Something was wrong. A snake of warning slithered down my spine. This was something else. He wasn't talking about houses, abuse, or wounds anymore. I must have squirmed along with that snake.

"Whoa, now. This is going to sting, but it's vital that you stay absolutely still for about three minutes. I've got to hold this glue in place while it sets. You can't move."

I almost nodded, because the warning snake had stolen my tongue, but I caught myself and held still, steadying my breathing and trying to slow my heart. His hand was pressed over my left eye, holding it closed. I wanted to close the right eye to block out his distorted face through the magnifying glass. It had turned him into something surreal and nightmarish.

He leaned in again, worsening the effect. "Now let me know if this makes you uncomfortable," he whispered. "I'm going to put something in your hand now. I'm letting you know so it doesn't surprise you. Stay absolutely still."

I did stay still, but due to fear paralysis rather than obedience or curiosity. I'd seen movies about perverted things that happened in doctors' offices and nurses who stood by silently. What in the hell was he about to put in my hand? It wasn't just the nurse, either. The door was open about a foot, and my daughter was in the room.

What is happening?

I felt a scream clawing up my throat. Caroline would scream, but even when a bead of sweat dripped down my temple, leaving a tickle trail, I knew I wouldn't scream. I knew I would stay frozen in shock and fear.

He shifted his shoulders sideways, expertly keeping the hand holding my face together and perfectly still. My left hand was on the bed beside me, palm up, with an ice pack on the bruised knuckles. The rough edges of a tongue depressor slid across my fingers and they closed around it. A flood of embarrassed heat flooded through me.

"Ignore that if it makes you uncomfortable," he whispered. "I'd love to talk more about the house though. If I build my retirement cabin, I want to go in with as much information as I can. Do it right."

My hand throbbed from the grip I had on the tongue depressor, and I wondered if it was one of the grape-flavored ones they used to give my kids when they were cranky. My mind was so tired and bruised that I had slipped into a state of deep distrust that turned this curious doctor's gentle outreach into something ugly and terrifying. Adam had made some headway in his effort to break my mind along with his own.

I relaxed, this time for real, and had time for two deep breaths before the doctor pulled back and smiled at his handiwork. "I'll put a little tape on this. Try to keep a neutral expression for a while. No extreme laughter. No crying. Doctor's orders."

I smiled, but only on the right, and closed both eyes. Taking control of my mind was not an overnight victory. Two steps forward, one step back.

"Stay still for a few minutes. The discharge nurse will be back with paperwork. It was really a pleasure meeting you." He put out his hand and shook my good one. "Be careful, now. I don't want to glue you back together again."

"Thank you. Next time let's bump into each other in the plumbing aisle, or selecting carbide drill bits or something."

He waved at the door, never seeming to notice the roller coaster of confusion and fear I had just traveled over a tongue depressor. As soon as he was gone, I looked at it and found his personal e-mail address in blue ink, scribbled out once and then rewritten below. Of course I would e-mail him some tips about house building when I had a chance, and I would also keep the stick as a reminder that it was okay to relax and trust. Not everyone had something dark and nefarious in mind. Some people reached out for friendship (grape-flavored friendship in this case)—something I had forgotten how to do years ago.

Mommy guilt is a powerful monster. I had worried from the start of the project that the kids would wake up one day and refuse to lift a hammer ever again. They weren't two-year-olds (well, except for the two-year-old), so there was little I could do to force them if they really decided to rebel. The real problem was, they hadn't.

We were all in as a team from the start. We'd had days when one of them would feel discouraged or so exhausted they cried from muscle pain, but there was never a day when they just up and quit. We catered the day's music to the downhearted and gave them the easy tasks or the best job on the site—playing with Roman. It never took long for spirits to rise. I respected and admired their strength and determination. But paradox of paradoxes, that's exactly what bothered me.

They were missing so many of the everyday high-school and middle-school experiences that I had sworn over their cradles they would have. Poverty had robbed me of many things as a teenager, and I hated that my decisions had put my own kids on the outside of normal.

Jada managed to stay on the basketball team through the school year because it was one of her classes at school instead of multiple after-school practices. But she had fallen behind and wasn't planning to be on the team in the fall. I wondered if part of the reason was the summer ball practice she was missing.

Drew had dropped out of band and didn't have a single extracurricular activity. Thanks to social media and his school classes, he maintained a few good friendships. But he was missing outings to movies and paintball fights.

Hope was old enough that our work was affecting her future in a more profound way. She had become involved in local politics and was offered a position at the beginning of summer as an intern at the Democratic Party of Arkansas under Bill Gwatney. She was planning to become an attorney, to change the way domestic-violence victims were treated in court, so the internship was an important foundation for her career. I wavered for only a minute before I told her to take the job. And she was diligent about working double time cooking and cleaning at the house we lived in and building on the job site whenever she wasn't at her internship. It made things more complicated, but it was the right thing to do, deadlines be damned.

She decided to attend the Democratic National Convention in Denver, with the hope that her hero, Hillary Clinton, would be the Democratic nominee for president. It was going to be an expensive trip, so she set up jobs cleaning several houses in order to raise the money. She would miss the first couple of days of her senior year because of the trip, but it would be more educational than anything she could pick up in a textbook.

By August, her schedule was taking a toll on all of us. She was exhausted by the extra work, and we were so far behind schedule that we desperately needed her help.

"I think I'm going to quit the DPA," she told me late one night while we were gluing the first narrow slats of cherry hardwood across my bedroom. "I got an offer to work on a local campaign that will be fewer hours until we finish the house."

"That's a bad idea," I told her. "You gave the DPA a commitment. You shouldn't go back on that. It's your word."

She argued the pros and cons of each job, and I listened without giving more advice. She knew where I stood, but she also knew that my policy was for each of the kids to manage their own lives from the time they turned thirteen. I was there to guide them, of course, but I let them make their own life decisions. My own grandmother had been on her own by thirteen during the Great Depression, and through most of human history it was considered near adulthood. Obviously, they weren't fully on their own, but after they hit thirteen they did their own laundry and their share of the household work. With all that responsibility, it seemed only fair that they also became responsible for their own class selection and planning for their futures. Five years of cushioned decision making before they were fully on their own was the best way I knew to prepare them for the real world.

Hope decided to quit the job, and I supported her. Because that's the other part of my policy. After I gently give my opinion, I'm behind them all the way no matter which way they go.

The Wednesday after she quit, I was at the office and my phone went nuts with e-mails and text messages from friends.

Have you heard from Hope yet?

Is Hope at the DPA?

Where is Hope?

Oh my God. Is Hope there?

Let me know if Hope needs anything.

I imagined car accidents and all manner of horrible things. Hope didn't answer her phone. The DPA was only blocks from my office and I had heard sirens screaming by, but as far as I knew, she wasn't supposed to be there. She had quit. Would she have gone back for any reason?

By the time I finally reached her, I had scanned the local news and heard the worst of it.

Bill Gwatney, the chairman of the DPA—and Hope's boss only days before—had been assassinated. He was forty-eight.

"I just respected him so much," she wept over the phone. "He was a mentor. He promised he would be there for me when I went through school and was looking for a job in politics. And he was always just so positive and supportive."

She was a wreck, and so was I.

"If I had listened to you and stuck through the last week, I would have been right at the front desk. I would have been the one to let him in. I would have seen Bill shot again and again. What if I had tried to stop it? I mean, I don't know what I would have done."

It was close. Too close.

"Anytime you want to quit a job, you do it. Don't listen to me," I told her, frantic to push the images from my head. We hadn't heard who had done it yet, or why. I had a terrible thought that it could be Adam. He was crazy enough that he could do something exactly like this.

We hadn't heard from Adam in quite a while, and Matt was largely out of our lives while he got his life together. Yet here was another insane man reaching into our lives and taking something away. Just when we thought the waters were safe, we were reminded that life is never so neat and simple.

Within hours the gunman was run down and shot by the police. No motive was ever discovered. He had written profanities on the wall at a Target where he worked and walked out of the job earlier that day. They had found a Post-it note at his home with Bill Gwatney's name and a phone number but no other connection. It wasn't Adam.

Friday night I went with her to a vigil on the steps of the courthouse where Bill had been a state senator for ten years. The atmosphere at the courthouse was nerve-racking. Everyone was afraid, wondering if someone would shoot into the crowd. Wondering what terrible thing would happen next. Hope's friends who had been in the building or in the same room with Bill needed to talk. They needed to share the horrible details. No matter how badly I wanted to plug her ears and run away, I stood with Hope and we listened.

She was too numb to cry on the way home. "I'm going to cancel my trip to Denver. He was supposed to be part of our group. He was a superdelegate. It will just be so depressing to do that now. We were supposed to leave in a couple days."

I didn't argue with her. I was afraid to offer any advice. "Go with your gut," I said, confident that her gut was luckier than my own.

On Monday we drove to the funeral. It was a huge affair, with the Clintons, General Wesley Clark, Governor Beebe, and dozens of local politicians from both parties attending. Two blocks from the church, people lined the sidewalk holding signs. It wasn't until we stopped at a traffic light that I realized exactly what we had run into: the Westboro Baptist Church demonstrators. The signs had photos of Bill with flames around his head that read "Burn in Hell Gwatney," and dozens of other hate-filled messages, and scriptures suggesting that God killed Bill as a punishment for our country tolerating homosexuality. Hope started yelling and unbuckled her seat belt. She had every intention of going after them. She hadn't slept more than a few hours in the past week and had no filters or patience left for cruelty.

I locked her door and put my arm across her, trying to hold her in the car. I looked ahead, willing the light to change so we could get away from the hateful chants, and then I saw something unexpected on the opposite side of the street. It was a long line of Harley-Davidson motorcycles. Long-haired, bearded bikers in leathers were also hold-ing signs—peace signs. "Look across the street!" I yelled. "Just focus on the bikers. Look at their signs!"

Hope relaxed, the light turned green, and I rolled down my win-dow so that we could both wave at the Patriot Guard motorcycle group who frequently counter the Westboro demonstrators. "This isn't what I expect you to do every time you see a group of guys on Harleys," I said.

By the next day, everything had changed again. "I'm going to Den-ver," Hope told me, chin up and tears dry. "I just heard that Rebecca, Bill's wife, is going along with the Clintons. If she can go then I can do it, too."

So I piled her in a van with a group of law students, all quite a bit older than her, and they headed off to Denver. It was exactly the heal-ing trip she needed.

She called me from Denver while I was on my hands and knees in her closet, gluing and pounding narrow strips of hardwood in place at eleven P.M., still fighting to make our deadline. She had just heard Hill-ary Clinton's speech and she was bawling while she quoted her. "'My mother was born before women could vote. My daughter got to vote for her mother for president. This is the story of America, of women and men who defy the odds and never give up.'"

I was crying, too. This was our story. Women like Caroline. Women like us.

My oldest daughter had seen a lot of life's bad things, but she had seen good things, too. She returned stronger and braver, more deter-mined to make changes in the world. She brought us each one of the small flags they waved as Obama spoke, and she brought a special gift for Roman. It was a twelve-inch plush doll of Obama. She had taken Roman with her to hold signs and hand out stickers near polling offices, so the names of politics were familiar to him, but his love for his doll surprised us all.

"It's Obama!" he squealed, hugging his doll close. "I have Obama!"

The doll became his security toy, and for months when he woke in the middle of the night, instead of hearing a cry for water or a blankie over the monitor, I heard him whimper, "Obama! Where's Obama? I want Obama!"

Life is stranger than we could possibly predict. And while we all leapt back in to work twenty-hour days to finish Inkwell Manor, we found new strengths, new weaknesses, and thousands more reasons to call ourselves fortunate.

−22−

Aiming True

Adam's red Honda was no more than half a car length behind me, matching my speed. If I had seen him seconds earlier, I could have kept going, driven to town like we had last time, bought some time while I called the police. But I had missed all the warning signs, because I was preoccupied with being happy, with moving on, and finally dating this guy named Matt who made me feel safe and felt like he might be a true forever-after.

Drew saw him, too, and I wondered what made him look over his shoulder. Hope spotted him only a second or two after us.

"Is he wearing . . ." Hope tried to turn all the way around in the passenger seat and I pushed her back down. "Horns. He's wearing red horns," she said, settling back in her seat and not wanting to see more.

"Hell."

"You're not supposed to say that. It's a bad word," Jada said. "Hell."

I sped up, turning sharply at the top of the driveway to angle across the front lawn instead of into the garage. He followed, and I pushed the garage-door button. I had to choose between getting into the house or running, and just then the house seemed like the better bet. He followed me, but the turn caught him off guard and I had the advantage. I whipped around in a circle, slipped neatly between the post for the basketball goal and the lawn-mower shed, and stopped in the garage with my finger mashing the door button and the nose of the car denting the shelf unit against the far wall. The door moved down, slow and careful. It was only halfway down when his car stopped in front of it.

"In the house!" I yelled at the kids. "Get upstairs now!" I should have followed them, locked us all tight in a room with the door barricaded. It wouldn't be the first time we hid from him like that. But Adam had jumped out of his car and I caught a flash of his legs—red tights, or leggings. Red like a demon.

The door sealed down tight before he got to it. I knew perfectly well it wasn't enough to keep us safe, but it was another minute bought and paid for. I ran inside and passed the bottom of the stairs just as the kids reached the top.

"Jada, did you say you saw a demon outside this morning? A devil? What were you playing?"

Jada chewed her lip. "I thought I had imagined it. There was just a peek. I didn't think it could be real." She had been little the last time she'd seen Adam. She wouldn't even recognize him if he were in everyday clothes let alone a costume from hell.

"Go in Hope's room," I said, running to my closet. "Push the dresser in front of the door and don't come out."

Drew hesitated, took two steps back down the stairs.

"Get your knife, Drew. Go in that room and keep them safe. I'm getting my gun."

He didn't seem surprised that I had one. I wished he had.

I loaded Karma and filled my pockets with shells. This time there was no doubt in my mind that I could shoot him. If he came in the house, I could shoot him to keep my kids safe. Not only shoot him, I knew, but kill him if I had to. It surprised me. When I bought the gun I had imagined scaring him with it. But I hadn't been imagining him in a devil costume that day.

I walked slowly out of my room and across the den, watching out the windows for the demon. In the dining room, I grabbed my phone and Hope's from the table. On hers I called 911 and dialed Ivana on mine immediately after.

"My ex-husband is outside trying to get in my house," I told the dispatcher. "I have a restraining order, and he's told me he's going to kill me."

"Is anyone else in the house?" she asked, sounding bored.

There was no way to explain his insanity to her without sounding insane myself. "My three kids are here. He has schizophrenia." It was the first time I had said that to anyone but my mom. It sounded scarier out loud.

"Stay on the line while I dispatch a car. Officers will be there as soon as they can." She confirmed my name and his, then repeated my address twice.

"He's at the dining-room window, looking in at me," I whispered, walking sideways with my back tight to the wall until I could turn the corner to the den.

"Where are your children?" she asked.

"Hiding." I took a deep breath. "I have a gun. Tell the officers I have a gun. It's loaded."

I heard her calling it in, sending help my way. She wasn't bored anymore, and I could tell from how fast she was talking that she believed like I did that no one could get to me in time.

Tap. Tap. Tap.

I looked around the doorway into the dining room. He was jabbing the tip of a foot-long, curved knife against the window. That knife could break the window with no real effort, but he wasn't breaking anything, just tapping, just teasing, just wrapping his fingers around my throat and holding me under the water. Deep in the river. Anytime he wanted to, he could. He could kill me . . . but not only me.

He moved to the front door, tried the knob, and then moved on to the office window.

Tap. Tap-a-tap. Tap.

Around and around the house he went, tapping and teasing. I had seen the horns, curved beast horns that looked more demon than devil. They looked like real antler-type material, and I couldn't imagine where he'd bought them. He was wearing a black shirt, a button-down that had once made him look suave instead of satanic, and red leggings that might have been Ivana's.

I remembered I'd dialed her and lifted that phone to my ear. The 911 phone was on the sofa. "Ivana? Are you there?"

"Yes, I'm here. I wish you wouldn't have called the police. I asked you not to. And good God, Cara. You have a gun? Do you really? I'm in Little Rock. I'm on my way, but I'm in Little Rock." Her voice rose and cracked. She was crying.

"He's tapping on my windows with a knife, Ivana. And he's dressed like a demon, wearing tights and horns. If I have to shoot him, I will."

She let out a little cry, like a puppy whimper. "Shoot him in the leg. Please, Cara. If you have to, just shoot him in the leg."

I hung up the phone. Not because of what she said, but because of the images in my head. I knew beyond any doubt that I wouldn't shoot him in the leg. I would shoot him over and over in every vital organ. I would put more bullets in the gun and shoot him again. I wouldn't stop shooting him until someone made me.

Something bumped my elbow, made me jump, and I swung around to see Hope staring up at me. Her eyes were haunted and dark, stretched wide with shock. I had no idea how long she had been there, what she had heard. Maybe she had been there all along, ignoring my directive to hide with Drew and Jada.

"Don't," she whispered. "Please don't shoot him." Her words fell flat, deflated before I even tried to punch them down. "Just don't," she said. No passion, no power. She was empty of all those things, and I wondered if the overload of trauma and insanity would leave her cup forever perforated, leaking trust and security. Or if someday she would be able to hold good things again without the terror that everything could fall apart at any second, without wondering if Mommy would have to hold a man at gunpoint and weigh the consequences of not shooting.

The tapping moved to my bedroom window. I didn't go in there to watch him through the glass. The shades were pulled. It was dark in there. If he made it into the house, I wanted to face him in the light. I stayed in the den, back against the side of the staircase, Hope at my elbow whispering things I didn't have the ears to process.

"This has to end." It barely sounded like my voice. It held less power than Hope's.

The 911 phone was talking to me, so I picked it up and turned to the back door. He stood there watching us through the glass French doors. The knife tip was as red as his leggings. With almost no effort he could break that glass and step right through. I pointed the gun at him, made sure he saw it. He held up the knife. A challenge. A draw.

I didn't move. It wasn't like there was any place to hide. Not really. No place to go. "Are they here yet?" I asked the 911 dispatcher.

"Thought I'd lost you," she said. "I have two cars on the way, but they were across town. It's going to be a little while yet. Hold on. Stay calm."

I closed my eyes, wanting to keep them that way for a long time. I didn't want to see Adam, and I didn't want to see what I might have to do.

"Go upstairs," I said. But I never turned to see if Hope listened or stayed to be my whispering conscience. If I listened to her, we would both regret it one day. The next time he came looking for his lost mind in our house, we would regret keeping the bullets clean and whole.

He tapped the window again, and I realized it was Morse code, but I refused to translate the dots and dashes. I opened my eyes and put the phone down. I didn't need the nervous lady anymore. She had done her best to help me and failed.

I took a long step toward the door and felt strength rising up through the heels of my feet, coursing through my veins with the power of every woman who had ever stood like I stood, with no one else to lean on, no one to help. I felt their power all the way to the top of my head and the tips of my fingers. Yes, even the finger that was curved around the chipped, black trigger of Karma.

For a second, or maybe longer, I thought about shooting him through the door. How much trouble would I get in, and could I get out of it? My kids would be safe. No matter what happened to me, they would be safe. Was it worth it? He was too heavy for me to drag inside without making that obvious, so that was out of the question.

Tap. Tap. Tap. Tap-a-tap. Tap.

I looked at the deadbolt—not to see if it was locked, I knew it was, but because I was thinking about unlocking it, letting him in so the story would be right for the police.

I wasn't panicked; I was calm and rational. I was clearheaded enough to know that I didn't want to do this again, not ever. There was only one way I could guarantee that, and that was if he was dead. I didn't want to kill him, I just wanted it to end, and there was no other answer. Time moved immeasurably slowly. I imagined what it would look like if I shot him, first in the chest, three times, then in the head if I could manage it before he fell to the floor. I could see what that would look like on the tile, on the painted door.

Tap-a-tap. Tap-tap. Tap.

Then what? What if all the bullets I had in the gun and in my pockets didn't kill him? How far could I go? I walked to the kitchen and got a butcher knife from the drawer, the one he had used to chop veggies chef-style when he'd gone through his cooking obsession. I laid it on the counter. Plan B.

I could still see him from the kitchen, lips moving and knife tapping messages to me, or to someone, maybe to the house itself for all I knew. His left horn had fallen a couple of inches, making him look a little pitiful. I realized then that he was wearing lipstick. Bright red lipstick from Ivana's collection. She wouldn't be happy about that.

I wasn't happy about it either. Most of all, I wasn't happy with what he had made me face about myself. Ever since Hope was born, I could have guessed that I would kill for my kids if I had to, if I was backed into a corner. But I never imagined I would step over that line and want to kill, wish I could get away with it. Sure, I could tell myself it was still for a noble cause, not a cruel, cold-blooded desire without a grander purpose, but that didn't make me feel all that much better.

The only thing that could was choosing not to do it.

The sun was setting behind him, a molten hell nowhere near as hot as the hell inside his own mind. *I'm sorry, Cara,* he had said about the schizophrenia. It wasn't something he chose. And it was, without a doubt, the saddest thing I had watched in my life. A man stripped of logic and his family, left with only enough of his mind to know what he lost and that he still loved those missing things. Sad beyond words.

But that didn't mean I wouldn't still shoot him if he got through my door.

He moved around to the kitchen window where Hope had seen him so many nights since the divorce. I wondered if that was where Jada had seen him this morning. Minutes later, he appeared in the dining-room window, back to his starting point. Ring-around-the-rosy.

He was trying the front door, turning the knob and shouldering against it, when blue lights flashed up the driveway, moving slower than I thought they should. Four officers approached while his knife tapped a final, frantic message in code. Karma felt warm in my hand, pointed at the floor, but ready, just in case. You never know what might happen. Anything was possible in this crazy world. Anything.

Through the long leaded-glass windows in the front door, I didn't see him resist or threaten, but he may have. Maybe I wanted him to so they could take care of the problem for me, but I didn't think hard on that. It was going too far, stepping across a dangerous line in my mind that I'd already rejected. They pushed him to the ground, shouting and making a lot of noise I couldn't interpret. I imagined my mom there with me, holding me together. Without her, all my pieces would have surely flown apart and left the house through the smudged windows.

I saw him dragged away—it took all four of them—and heard their radios make buzzes, beeps, and fuzzy voices, and I waited for a gunshot that never came.

When an officer knocked on the door, shouting his name and mine, time found its weight again and jolted my heart forward so hard it hurt. I looked around for Hope, but she was gone, and I wondered if she had ever really been there or if shock had painted her at my side. My face felt like it was only made of eyes when I opened the door, Karma loaded, finger on the trigger, barrel pointed at the floor. I couldn't feel the gun in my hand. Couldn't even tell I had a hand. How had my eyes grown so large?

A redheaded officer took the gun and unloaded it, lips moving but no words coming out. Or maybe they were, but I wasn't ears, I was only eyes. The calm I had been so sure was with me to stay flew right out the door and chased the blue lights of the first cruiser down my driveway.

I felt paralyzed right up until the officer tried to put his arm around me. The touch burned against my raw nerves, and I jumped back from

him, every cell alert and coursing with adrenaline. I ran up the stairs to
Hope's room with Hershey on my heels. Something between a knock
and a claw brought Drew's face into the crack of the door, up near the
top because he was crouched on the dresser they had pushed in front
of it.

"Kids upstairs," Officer Red said into his radio, and then "Jesus!"
when I swung around, eyes wild and teeth bared like I could rip his
throat out with them. I hadn't even noticed him following me.

Don't sneak up on a mama bear. Stay back. Stay where I can see you.

That's just what Officer Red did, slipping back toward the stairs
while I told the kids it was safe to come out.

Drew was slow to believe me. A police officer's uniform might have
reassured most kids, but mine had seen too much. No badge or restraining order had stopped a man from coming after us in demon horns.
Hope and Jada talked Drew into pushing back the dresser and opening
the door. He came out first, knife in hand. I could see that he was ready
to use it, and I knew firsthand how difficult it was to come to terms
with what you were capable of doing to another person to keep your
family safe. And I knew that hugs and words couldn't erase that knowledge or give him back a measure of innocence.

"You're sure he's gone?" he asked. Looking out one window and
then another with no idea that he was circling the house from the inside
in the same way Adam had from the outside.

I grabbed his arm and held him still. "Stop it. Listen to me."

He did.

"They took him away in a police car. Probably to the state hospital?" I looked at the officer for confirmation, and he nodded. He had a
thin red beard to match his hair. I hadn't noticed before. I searched out
his name tag. I couldn't call him Red out loud. Hamm. *You've got to be
kidding me.* Officer Hamm. No doubt the victim of an endless stream of
pig jokes.

Drew snickered. He had seen it, too.

Jada tugged on my hand, needing reassurance. I hugged her hard enough to nearly crush her. "Too close!" she whined.

Yes, I thought, *that was too close. Much too close for comfort.*

"I'll need to get a statement from you," Hamm said, staring at me a beat too long.

I still had the impression that my eyes filled most of my face. The better to see you with. My ears were foggy, like everyone was speaking into a tin can, and my voice had gone small, overshadowed by my eyes. My head had started to pound and my back ached from the adrenal-gland workout. I looked away from Hamm and back at the kids, whose eyes were stretched and hollow, too. I walked past Hamm to the stairs, waving the kids after me.

When you fall off a horse, you get back on.

When your house becomes the scene of a horror movie, you reclaim it.

I walked into my room, the bathroom, and then through every room downstairs and the garage with the kids and Hershey following like ducklings. No one spoke.

Hamm stood at the bottom of the stairs, which was nearly the dead center of the downstairs, and watched. From his raised eyebrows and the hands propped on his well-padded hips, I could tell he wanted to spin his index finger near his temple. Loco lady. Crazy as the man was. Slap-ass nuts.

His partner, a gray-haired man who hadn't spoken a word that I noticed, stayed back by the door, giving us space as though he knew exactly what we were up to. It was the house equivalent of counting fingers and toes. When we had made the rounds, it was him I stopped in front of.

"Do you need the kids for anything?" I asked.

"Probably not." He finished scribbling something on a long notepad before he looked up with a tight-lipped pseudosmile of pity.

I'm not sure if my building anger was healthy, but I was not going to stand for pity. I turned to the kids, determined not to minimize the effect this had had on them. "If you want to add anything to the police report, stay down here; otherwise, go upstairs into Jada's room and play a game. You can take ice-cream sandwiches—and napkins—with you." I turned and leaned over to make eye contact with Hamm. "Ice cream, Officer?"

"Um, no thanks. I'm good." He wiped a hand over his beard.

Jada ran for the freezer. "Ice cream in my room!" she sang. Drew and Hope stayed put.

We all sat at the table while my oldest kids made lists of the things that had frightened them, pissed them off, or hurt their hearts. They were lists no parent wants their kid to imagine, let alone live. I was surprised by how many things I had failed to hide. They hadn't talked to me about these things, which I'll admit made me sad, but they had obviously talked to one another, which made up for some measure of it. And knowing the load of secrets I had harbored, I couldn't point any fingers.

When they had both finished, they went upstairs without any ice cream. I was surprised at first that they didn't want to stay and hear what I had to say, but if I could choose to walk away and unknow all the things I had seen in the past years, I would do the same . . . except I would definitely take the ice cream with me.

Hamm and his partner, Bacon—just kidding, the older partner was Hancock—took notes, and asked effective enough questions to prove they had done this sort of thing before. Even so, the large number of bizarre stories I had for them appeared to tip the scale toward worst-case scenario of their careers.

"We were pretty far away when we got the call. It took a long time for us to get to you," Hancock said. "It happens that way sometimes. Keep your gun ready, but away from the kids. If this were to happen again, if he were to get in the house, you should be prepared to shoot him."

For the space of a single inhale and exhale, I wondered if I should have done it, unlocked the door and let him in to end it. This wasn't over. Not now, and not ever. He would keep coming back. He would come to any other place I moved. He wouldn't stop until something terrible enough happened that they locked him away for good. Until then, with his mental illness as a bargaining chip, they would always let him go. A few days or a week to stabilize him on his meds, and he would be free again.

Free.

That was a thing we would never be.

Hamm rattled off a list of charges. I waved dismissively. It didn't matter what they charged him with. Yes, I would press charges, but it would only create short delays, days where we could breathe easy, not years.

By ten thirty P.M., they were gone and the house was ours again. Jada was asleep. I put Karma back in my closet, this time showing Drew and Hope where to find her. "He'll be back at the state hospital for a few days, maybe longer. You guys okay?"

They nodded and meant it.

"Get some sleep." I hugged Hope hard, and then Drew. He held on longer than I expected but not as long as I would have liked. These experiences were changing them, damaging them in ways a lifetime of good fortune couldn't undo. People have endured worse, I told myself. Concentration camps, wars, torture. But having to sink so low in the scale of human atrocities to find a life more frightening than our own was a small consolation.

−23−

Rise
Scramble to the Finish

The cut over my eye quickly became a thin, unimpressive red line, but the bruises were dramatic and ugly, extending from the middle of my forehead to just under my cheekbone. I worked hard to keep a poker face for the first few days, which the kids took as a personal challenge to send me into hysterical laughter at every turn. It was better than the alternative, so I played the game, half terrified I'd split everything open with each outburst.

My hand was slow to heal, but functional enough for me to keep pushing forward with the work. Once the doors were installed, the girls punched the nails and filled the nail holes. Hope started caulking the seams and then prepping to paint, trim first and then the walls and ceiling. Even though we had lots of decorating ideas that involved color, we opted for a single color called Vanilla Brandy for walls and ceiling throughout the house. The trim would all be Parchment Paper, a creamy white that I really loved, and not only because of the name. Rolling through the entire house with a single color saved hours of cleaning paint trays, brushes, and rollers. We could get creative later on—assuming we ever had the energy.

My optimism pulsed with a steady glow.

In mid-August, the cabinetmaker installed the unfinished cabinets in the bathrooms and kitchen. They weren't everything I had dreamed, but they were functional. We began staining them, which took a lot more time and probably killed a lot more brain cells than I could spare. Hope was the fastest painter and stainer, but she emerged fully coated from nose to toe in whatever substance she was applying. The rest of us couldn't figure out how she managed full-body application, but didn't complain about her method, since it yielded speedy results.

Just when we thought we couldn't handle the scent of stain for another second, Pete helped install the oak stair treads and railing, and the cabinet guy finished the rough build of my bookshelves in the library. Gallons of stain and polyurethane loomed in our future.

I abandoned the kids to the stain and paint while I started the tile work in the bathrooms. My bathroom had several diagonal walls and the counter was set diagonally, which made for a nightmare of trips up and down the stairs for wet-saw cuts. My five-by-five shower also had to be tiled from floor to ceiling. In our spare time we built the frames for concrete countertops, which proved to be a lot more difficult than it had looked on YouTube. My mom spent an entire weekend perfecting the frames so that they could be easily removed after the pour. She sealed every seam with caulk and bright red duct tape. Without her extreme attention to detail, half of my frames would have been permanently embedded in the countertops.

All the finish work was slow and took ten times longer than we expected, but nothing was worse than the wood floors upstairs. We had been working on them for over a month. Around two thousand square feet of hardwood flooring had to be laid through the bedrooms and closets, all in two-inch-wide strips. Some days, sixteen hours of spreading glue and hammering the tongue-and-groove pieces together with a rubber mallet moved us only a couple of feet across the expanse of the house. Roman was given the job of pushing the long, emptied flooring boxes out my bedroom window, which was open only eight inches so he couldn't tumble out with them. "Look out below!" he yelled, sliding each box out and giggling when it sailed down to the growing heap.

By the end of August, it was looking like a real home. It was nowhere near finished, but we could definitely see a light at the end of our very long, dark tunnel.

The electricians had installed half a dozen lights and then vanished. They had had a falling-out and refused to come to the house at the same time, which reduced their sloth-like pace by half or more. We were anxious to have outlets and working lights so that we could ditch the long extension cords out to the temp pole for our tools and spotlights. I knew how to install them myself, but not only was that against code, it would take up valuable time already allocated for the impossibly long finish list. Besides, our contract affording them ten grand to complete the task made me hesitant to take on the responsibility, even though time was running short for our electrical inspections.

When Tweedledee and Tweedledum finally had enough fixtures and switches in place to run tests, we discovered that all our fears were on target. They really had been too high to get things right. They had lost the wires for my undercabinet lights behind the Sheetrock and never found them. The expensive speakers I bought to go over the den sofa suffered the same fate, useless with the wires somewhere in a twenty-foot wall packed with six inches of blown-cellulose insulation. Neither of the professionals had a clue where to start searching. The exterior outlets popped a fuse every time we tried to use them, and only a single phone line worked in the entire house, even though every room had at least one wired phone jack.

I called them continuously to come back and fix things, but their idea of fixing things was to smoke a little while they thought things over. They couldn't get my cameras or the flat-screen monitor by the front door to work, but eventually sent a friend over to read the instruction manual.

Despite our frustration over the things outside our control, we kept reasonably upbeat about each new task. It still seemed impossible to finish for the bank inspection and the final city inspection to get our certificate of occupancy, especially after the kids had started back with school and homework, which stole away our working hours.

It was possible to get an extension from the bank, but it could result in extra fees and interest that I couldn't afford. And, more important, we couldn't handle another month or another week of building. Nine months of working nineteen-hour days had sapped every last ounce of our physical and emotional strength. The deadline was a countdown to the end of an impossibly difficult job as much as it was a ticking time bomb.

At five o'clock on the first Friday of September, with only a week left to go, I came back to the house we lived in too exhausted to speak. The kids had taken a couple of hours off after school to do homework, and I had come back to get them. But once I got there I didn't think I could muster the energy to drive back to Inkwell, let alone accomplish anything.

I had been sleeping between eight and ten hours a week for three weeks, with an occasional twenty-minute catnap on a pallet in Hope's closet at Inkwell. Even working those hours, it seemed impossible. We hadn't poured our concrete countertops yet, let alone finished them. And until that was done, we couldn't install sinks, faucets, or the stove top. Those tasks alone added up to more than a week of work, but we still had to make railings for the front and back steps in order to pass code, and we had to install toilets and the final electrical fixtures. The stairs needed a final coat of polyurethane, and the concrete floors downstairs had to be coated with xylene. The outdoor faucets had to be installed, and so did the garage doors and the concrete slab.

"I'm going to lay down, just give me twenty minutes, I'll set an alarm." I wasn't sure if I had spoken the words aloud or merely thought them. The mattress swallowed me up, pulling me down to the deepest sleep I'd known in months. Benjamin wasn't there. I rarely thought about him or Caroline anymore. In some ways, I felt I had outgrown them. He had been there to bring me peace and she had shared strength, two things I felt like I had finally found within myself. The kids and I were no longer the strangers we'd been on those first days of piling concrete block and mixing mortar. We worked as a team, a well-oiled machine. We laughed and practically read one another's minds. The magic we had all found in the tornado-damaged house, the inspiration that started with Caroline, had been reborn in Inkwell Manor.

"Just one more week," I whispered, smiling my way into the dreamless catnap.

"A ghost out the window!" Roman screamed. Jada laughed and Hershey barked, her nails clicking across the floor. Another game of chase.

"Twenty minutes," I mumbled. "Can't I just have twenty minutes?" Without opening my eyes, I felt for my phone. Even after I found it and held it in front of my face, it took me another full minute to get my eyes open. Another scream, this time with both Jada and Roman crying, which set Hershey off barking and whining, all while I tried to work out the numbers on my phone screen. It was seven. Two hours? Why didn't the kids wake me? I had an e-mail from the newspaper with another article request for the freelance job, but that had been sent at six in the morning.

I checked my clock again. It was seven in the morning. I had slept for fourteen hours. Two weeks' worth of sleep at once. It's a wonder I survived it.

I pushed to my elbows. Drew stood in my doorway, his silhouette so much larger than it had been before the build. "Ready to get some work done?" he asked.

"Why didn't you wake me? We have so much to do. I can't afford that much time off!" I was angry, but more than that I was scared that the last hope of meeting our deadline had just been stolen by the sandman.

Drew laughed. "We tried to wake you after twenty minutes. Then after an hour. We took turns trying every thirty minutes until eleven. You were practically unconscious. You needed it."

I stood, stretched, and smiled. Aches that I was half expecting to feel for the rest of my life were gone. "I'm starving."

"Hope and Roman are cooking something. I made coffee." He grinned. "Not that you'll need it."

We got three days' worth of work done over the next ten hours. The mood was light, and our work was so synchronized that we appeared psychic. Hope had a paper to work on, and by six o'clock Roman was tired enough to cry over every bump and bug bite. "I'll take you guys to the house, then I'm coming back to seal the concrete floors. It will be better if you guys are gone for that anyhow. Fumes are supposed to be toxic."

Jada sang the alphabet backward for half the ride home. I was proud of Hope for not strangling her. We were happy. For the first time in a very long time we were just plain happy. The idea sent a chill down my spine. Happy people get lazy. They forget to be on guard.

I took a deep breath. We didn't have to be on guard so much anymore. Matt had chilled out a lot, and while Adam might show up at the back door one day, we weren't the same people we had been the last time he came around. We were strong in ways that had nothing to do with the biceps we showed off to one another when we had the energy to flex our new muscles for fun. We could relax. We were all going to be okay. And we were so close to the end of this project that we could taste it. The kids could get regular teenage jobs and go on dates. They could have friends over to hang out instead of hanging plywood and hoisting bathtubs. I could spend time with my mom again.

The kids dragged through their bedtime routines and I hugged them all. Roman was asleep before I was out the door. I cried on the drive to Inkwell—not full-out weeping, but a handful of tears for the burden I could see lifting from my children. Pulling up in the sandy, washed-out driveway of Inkwell Manor made me smile, though, just like it always did. I stopped at the end of the drive, car idling. The house was something of a marvel, even by moonlight, as surreal and impossible as a colossal pyramid. We had actually built it ourselves. That wasn't all, though; it had built us, too, individually and as a family, until we had become a vital part of one another.

I pulled up to the garage, which still didn't have doors. And because the slab hadn't been poured outside it yet, there was no way to drive inside over the high concrete edge. Still, it felt more welcoming than the other house, safer.

The xylene finish for the downstairs concrete flooring was in a five-gallon metal pail in the garage. I had mopped and swept the floor before we left earlier that day, so it was fully prepped. Just to be sure, I swept again. The stain I had sprayed on with a garden weed sprayer, the green kind that you pump up to create air pressure, was called Cola Brown. The end result wasn't what I had hoped, but only because of my amateur technique and inferior equipment. I had high—optimistic and unrealistic—hopes that the finish would hide rather than magnify my mistakes.

I opened all the windows and doors, upstairs and down, because ventilation was essential with the toxic chemical. The instructions strongly recommended protective breathing gear, which I did not have. There was no wind to blow dust inside, so I bargained that the ventilation would be adequate.

Staying true to my commitment to center the house's purpose around my writing, I started in the library. The shiny finish brought out the natural variations in the concrete. I lost myself in the work, admiring the floor as I rolled a thick paint roller with a long handle forward and back, reloaded in a square pail, and went again, closing windows and doors as I passed them so they wouldn't be open all night. By the time I reached the dining room, only the front door was open, and it was the one I would back out of when I finished.

But in the corner of the room farthest from the door, I realized I was in trouble. I touched my lips and couldn't feel them. In fact, I could feel none of my face below my eyes. How long had that been going on? It seemed to have happened all at once. I took a step toward the door and realized I couldn't feel much below my waist either, not enough to walk, anyhow. I dropped the roller in the bucket and fell to my hands and knees, crawling toward the door. By the time I reached it, I was on my belly doing the same combat crawl Hope had done until she learned to walk. Slithering like a snake, I made it to the front porch and as far away from the door as I could get without rolling down the porch steps.

For a few minutes, I wondered if the paralysis could be permanent, or if the fumes had caused brain damage. Wouldn't it be ironic to build a house called Inkwell Manor with an enormous library and never be able to write again? The bullfrogs around the pond next door didn't seem overly concerned with the pins and needles in my face and scalp, so I closed my eyes and listened.

At least two hours had passed when I woke up. Whether I had been napping or unconscious I didn't know, but I felt normal except for extreme thirst and a headache. With my shirt pulled up over my mouth and nose, I ventured back into the house, and I rolled on finish in the dining room and foyer at record speed until I was standing back out on the porch to do the last few feet.

Thank goodness the kids hadn't been around to inhale any of that crap.

I left the roller and bucket to be thrown out, my head aching too badly to clean them with more caustic chemicals. When I was back at the house with the kids and rubbing Hershey's head before I climbed into bed, I realized I had no memory of the drive there.

Chalk xylene application up as a huge mistake. I would never come near the stuff again.

My dreams were of Caroline, or of me as her. Maybe we had become the same creature. It was a thought I didn't like very much. Some part of her was more than just strong, it was vengeful, and that frightened me.

But did it really? Did it frighten me more than he did?

Not anymore.

The next week passed in a fog of work followed by more work and far too little sleep. We were all in a cloud of exhaustion on the night before the final inspection. It was a cool September night, which we welcomed after working so long in the heat. Our major task was installing all the plumbing fixtures and toilets. We had plenty of smaller tasks to finish and a lot of cleanup. Every day a fresh layer of sawdust, concrete dust, and Donna Fill coated everything.

Faucet installation would normally be simple, but we were installing our faucets in four-inch-thick concrete countertops. I had made inset circles out of larger pipes so that the thickness immediately around the faucet handles and spigot would be closer to that of a granite countertop, but they should have been slightly larger in diameter. I ended up flat on my back under the bathroom sinks with a hammer and large flathead screwdriver, chiseling away concrete in tiny chips, terrified that I would hit too hard and shatter the counter. There was no way to patch it: A break would mean starting over. A break would mean we didn't pass inspection.

Safety glasses kept my eyes clear, but I had dust and chunks of concrete in my hair, mouth, nose, and ears. By the time we finally got the faucets in, it was ten P.M. and we still had the drain lines and toilets to install. The stove top had gone in the night before, so we broke it in making a giant pot of ramen noodles, nobody's favorite but they were quick and easy. The only other food we had in the house was hot cocoa, so I warmed a pot for dessert and we drank it from plastic cups.

Roman went to sleep on a pallet upstairs, and the rest of us went back to work. At two thirty A.M., Drew carried in the last toilet. "This is it!" he said, an enormous grin shining under exhausted eyes. Then he pulled the box off the toilet and said, "Crap! This totally sucks!"

"What?" I asked, my face draining as pale as his before I even knew what was wrong. We were too close to run across a problem now. One more step. Only one.

"The entire base of this toilet is cracked. We have to return it." He balled up a wad of bubble wrap and threw it at the wall.

I held in a laugh. As violent acts of temper went, bubble wrap was pretty lame. Or maybe the laugh trying to steal out was actually hysteria. It seemed impossible that the very last task for the night had gone wrong. "The hardware stores won't open until seven," I said, wiping a hand over my face. "There's nothing we can do."

"Can you have them come later tomorrow? Instead of seven A.M.?" Hope asked, a paintbrush in her fist and a fresh coat of paint covering the entire front of her shirt, her left arm, and both thighs. "If you call them?"

I shook my head. "We're first on the schedule."

"Surely they'll understand. The other toilets work. They can see we know how to install them, and that we'll get this one right, too," she argued.

Both Drew and I shook our heads. "That isn't how inspections work," Drew said. "They have to check off every item."

We had to pass. We were not going to delay it by a week or a day. We couldn't. Emotionally, we couldn't handle another minute under a ticking clock. "We have to make sure he doesn't flush this one," I said, opening the box with the wax ring and handing Drew the flex pipe. "Let's install it as though everything is fine. Just leave the water off so the bowl doesn't fill and leak. I have an idea."

Drew installed the toilet while I went out to the shop for the tissue holder and the towel rod. They didn't have to be installed for the house to pass inspection, so they had been knocked off the essentials list, to be finished at a later date. He was hand-tightening the bolts for the tank when I walked back in.

"We're going to close the lid and cover it and the back of the tank with screws and parts from these," I said. "No one would want to move all that stuff to check it. We'll make sure he does upstairs first, so he's flushed a couple toilets. Then we'll keep talking to him, distracting him, so he can't even remember if he has flushed this one."

"What about the baseboard in Drew's room?" Hope asked. "We don't have any more finishing nails and the last two pieces aren't up."

"I don't even know if they have to be." I looked at the ceiling, hands on my hips. I was dizzy and nauseous from exhaustion, and we had to be back for the inspection in only a few hours. "We'll station Jada in that room. I'll take you all to school late, after the inspection. She can stand in the corner and hold the trim up with her feet."

We had more secrets, like that the sinks weren't attached to the countertops and would slide around if anyone bumped them. But nothing major was wrong with the house that we knew of. If we could slip these minor issues past the bank and city inspectors, we would be set with a certificate of occupancy for our own home. Not just any home, but one we built with our own hands. If the cells in my cheeks weren't too depleted to respond, I would have smiled. "Let's go back to the house and get a couple hours of sleep."

The little tricks and big distractions worked. The inspectors were both surprised and overjoyed to hand over my final paperwork. "This has been a fascinating project right from the start," the bank guy said, and the city guy nodded in agreement.

I pretended that they didn't mean the same fascination that kept bystanders staring at a train wreck. But we'd surprised them with success instead, and that made me pretty damn proud.

We did the impossible. We can do anything. Live? Does this mean we are strong and resourceful enough to stay alive?

After school, no one asked if we were going to Inkwell Manor; they just settled in with homework and television. Drew played a video game. In fact, we didn't set foot on Inkwell property for the next seven days. We still loved it, we still felt more at home there than in our big house filled with bad memories, but we needed to catch our breath before we packed and moved. For the last month of the build, we had loaded up the cars with assortments of household goods and filled the shop and the center of the dining room with boxes and bags. But the bulk of our things would take a truck and a lot of work to get over there.

On the seventh night, after a fajita supper, everyone disappeared into corners of the house to work on projects or hobbies. I missed them now that our joint project was finished, but I also knew that it was healthy for us to have our own interests. We would never lose the bond that the build had created. I felt selfish calling them all to a sofa meeting, but it was time.

"I know we're waiting for the house to sell before we do a full move to Inkwell, but we eventually have to go over there and finish things up."

They let out a collective groan.

"It won't be like before. We don't have a time schedule. But the things we didn't have to have finished for our inspection still need to be finished before we can live there. We need shelves in the pantry and all the closets and clothes rods. The last toilet needs to go in, too. It's all small stuff, but it will make moving in a lot easier."

They agreed, and we made a schedule. It was slower than I would have liked, but we were truly out of energy and enthusiasm. And we were all a little depressed that the house hadn't sold yet and we couldn't move in and celebrate. It felt a little like we had done all that work for no reward. It was a financial hardship to maintain both households, too. But the realtor insisted that an empty house would be even more difficult to sell.

It was several months of full nights of sleep and regular meals before our bruises healed and our muscles stopped aching. We finished most of the extra projects at Inkwell and moved more things over there. It wasn't until the end of March that we sold the house.

We gathered again for a sofa meeting.

"Are you guys ready to move for real?" I had no idea what I would do if they said no.

Jada leaned in to Hope and pulled her knees up to her chin. They were both watching their feet.

"Spending the night there is going to be so awesome," Drew said. "After all those months of imagining it."

"The actual moving part isn't any fun, but it's a lot less work than building a house. Let's start packing tonight."

They didn't only pack almost everything we owned into the impressive stack of boxes we'd been collecting for months, they also started disassembling furniture and piling it in the garage. They worked together, barely needing language to communicate. It was an impressive thing to watch.

The next afternoon we started carrying things over in a trailer I had picked up from craigslist. We had planned to rent a truck, but they kept insisting that we just take another load or two by trailer.

"We've moved almost all the furniture," I said at around nine that night. I had just hung up the phone with my mom. She was planning to come help us unpack on the weekend but had started to feel bad again. She'd had pneumonia over the winter and had stayed with me for several weeks while she healed. I had worried about her, but she was tough and never complained. "Should we call it a night?" I suggested meekly to the kids.

"The only thing we have left are the beds," Drew said. "Why don't we just take the mattresses over now and sleep there tonight. We can get them all in one load if we leave the box springs."

I was exhausted, but after months of dragging their feet over the move the kids were practically frantic to sleep at Inkwell. They pushed forward with no complaints. It was just like the build had been: Keep placing one foot in front of the other until the task is complete.

We had filled my library and the dining room with the bulk of the boxes, because they were closest to the front door and I couldn't walk any farther than that. For the most part we had no idea what was in the boxes. At the beginning we had labeled them carefully, but then we had unpacked the boxes and reused them for so many more trips that every label was a jumbled mess.

"We'll sort it out later," Hope said when I pulled kitchen utensils, DVDs, and socks out of a box. "Let's just get the mattresses in."

Their euphoria was contagious. I was starting to feel that our long-delayed celebration was happening. A smile spread across my face and didn't go away. Drew put on a dance mix, and we sang loud enough to be a disturbance. Even though it was way past his bedtime, Roman ran and leapt, and danced along with us. We were free and happy in a way we never would have been in another house. This was our personal space in every sense of the word.

"We need your help, Mommy!" Hope yelled from the dining room. They had my king-size mattress wedged on the stairs. The diagonal wall over the stairs may have met code, but it could have used a couple more inches for moving a pillow-top king mattress. We had to bend it and push with all our might to get it through.

I e-mailed my boss that I was taking the next day off to finish moving. I needed the time to enjoy settling everything into the place we'd made for it.

So on our first night at Inkwell Manor, we slept on crooked mattresses that blocked doorways and were half-made with mismatched sheets. My head was facing south instead of north like it had at the other house. The 180-degree life shift was welcome, but disorienting, too.

I had trouble falling asleep, and blamed it on a short to-do list. The mile-long-list review had worked like sheep counting for the past year. What would I do without it? Other than some cleanup at the other house, the long-awaited result was complete.

When I finally slept, it was more like work than a restful thing. Caroline appeared over and over, always angry, always yelling, always at me. She had never directed any of her fierce temper at me before; it had always felt more like it wicked up through me with someone else as the target. When I checked my phone clock at three A.M., I realized I was afraid of her.

We had built the home inspired by her tornado house. We had rebuilt our family. Most important, we had survived mountains of craziness. All at once I was glad that her nail was out in the shop and not in our house. I couldn't shake the eerie feeling that she wanted something more from us.

I slept again, but she was there waiting for me, almost nose-to-nose with me in anger, and I had nowhere to go to escape. She was wrapped in orange and yellow instead of her signature red, cheeks glowing, lips moving in an ancient tongue I couldn't interpret.

Finally, in the wee hours of the morning, Benjamin appeared in front of her like a shield. He sat as calmly as ever, but stared intently at me. I felt small and weak, like they were ganging up on me after being my inspiration for a year and a half. *What? What do you want me to do? I wanted to scream at them. We're done! We built it! It's wrapped around us, protecting us. What more do you want from me?*

All at once, Caroline leapt over Benjamin and hovered over me, orange dress and wild hair fanning out in waves, her body parallel to mine and about six feet above me. She looked more like a demon than the matriarch and supporter I had imagined her to be.

I looked back at Benjamin, needing his calm protection. But his eyes had gone wide and angry, too. He opened his mouth and I flinched, expecting a plague of locusts to stream out and suffocate me.

"Rise!" he shouted.

It was the only word I'd ever heard him speak, so I did. Faster than I could blink my eyes open, I stood, stumbling beside my mattress, feet tangled in my sheets. Even after I worked my eyes open, the world was cloudy. It was six o'clock. A foggy spring day that would be my late grandpa's eighty-ninth birthday.

The house was quiet, so I started pancakes for the kids. They weren't big breakfast eaters, but a quick bowl of cereal or a breakfast bar wasn't an option when they were probably buried in a box of garden trowels. I had moved around a lot in my life, but I had never been so disorganized and frantic with it. It didn't worry me, though, because of all the moves I had ever made, this one felt the most right.

The only thing still bothering me was the nightmare about Caroline and Benjamin. They had been a strange gathering of forces that helped me through when I needed them. But now I worried that my restless mind had turned them into something different. I knew how easily a person could slip into insanity. The kids and I had created a peaceful place to live, and now it was time to settle in and find peace in my own mind.

I was ready to take on the task. I was sure of it.

-24-

Fall and Rise

You Built Your Own
Damn House

You'd think that by then I would have known better than to be sure of anything.

But I'm an optimist.

Drew and Jada went off to school after begging unsuccessfully to stay home and help unpack. "We'll have plenty of time to get things settled. Go learn something," I told them.

Hope had left her senior year a semester early to work as an intern to the executive director at the Clinton Foundation, and by a stroke of luck, she had a few days off.

Roman and I were lounging on a twin-size mattress on his bedroom floor. We needed a few lazy minutes of play before we attacked the boxes in earnest.

Finally, reluctantly, I got up to check the e-mail on my phone in case anything had come in from the office. I had missed dozens of calls from my mom.

I dialed, heart racing, wondering if something had happened to her sister in Wisconsin who had been waiting for a kidney transplant. Mom was planning to start the testing to see if she could be a donor.

But instead of Mom, my brother John answered. He had lived with her off and on most of his life, never able to hold a steady job with his disabilities.

"Why don't you ever answer your damn phone?" he said before I got a word out. "Mom's sick. Really bad. I'm pretty sure she's dying. But she won't go to the hospital. I called a friend to take her but she said she can't—"

"Call 911. Now!" I told him. I was already crying, already wondering why I had ignored the bad dreams.

"She won't go. She says not to." His voice was shaking. He was scared.

"Call them right now or I'm going to. Tell her she doesn't have a choice."

He hung up to call 911 and then called me back, saying she was getting worse.

I got dressed, threw a bag with extra clothes in the car, and started driving. She lived seventy-five miles north of me. I called one of her sisters and told her what had happened. She called me back for an update twenty minutes later, but I hadn't heard anything more from my brother.

I was still thirty minutes away when my phone rang with a blocked number.

"Is this Cara?" a man asked me. A stranger.

I nodded. I didn't want to speak to him. I made foreign noises with no idea if they were real words.

"This is the doctor at the ER who attended to your mom when she arrived. I'm sorry to tell you that we've done everything we can, but she didn't make it."

"No," I squeaked through the tears. "You have to keep trying. Can't you do something? There has to be something."

"Where are you? Is anyone with you?"

"I'm driving. I'm trying to get there. I'm almost there. Please."

Mom was fifty-nine. She was the strongest woman I've ever known. She was physically strong, and emotionally strong. But what had been diagnosed as pneumonia was a blood clot in her lung. It shouldn't have happened. She should have watched my children grow and held her great-grandchildren. She should have stayed with us in the house that she helped us build. She should have retired early and driven across the country on the adventures she'd always dreamed of.

I held her still body and kissed her good-bye. I whispered, or maybe I shouted, "I don't know how to do this."

And then I drove to her house feeling weaker than I had ever felt in my life.

Nothing could save me from the biggest threat I had ever faced, not a big house, not our new muscles or mind-set, not even my beat-up old gun, Karma.

When I woke up this morning I had a mom, and now I don't.

We finished moving and unpacking. Everything found its place. I got my brother John situated about ten miles from me where I could take care of him. My dad and John had stopped talking years ago, so I knew I was on my own with him. He couldn't drive or hold a job. He couldn't save and plan for the future—not even next week but he could take care of his own day-to-day needs. And he was family. Family takes care of family.

It was months of work to get everything sorted and moved. To sell my mom's house, we did home repairs and remodeling on it, as well as to the one we moved John into. There were endless weekends and evenings on our hands and knees installing flooring, painting walls, and repairing siding.

There was no celebration for the completion of Inkwell Manor.

Not yet.

Not until we settled into our new roles over the holidays and I found days where I could remember without weeping. Not until we came to terms with the way life doesn't deal things out just the way you expect or want them. She doesn't even deal them fair all the time.

But the celebration did come.

It didn't happen as a dance party or a lot of patting ourselves on the back. It happened slowly, as we all stretched into our new sense of self and found that we had become a little fearless.

When summer came and Mom's plants were beautiful and full in my gardens, I thought about Caroline for the first time since the day Mom died. I still tried to meditate when I remembered to, and Benjamin was usually there, still and calm. I believed he always would be.

I walked to our shop, set up a ladder, and pulled the nail—Caroline's nail—from above the door. The curved scrap of metal clanged onto the concrete floor.

Then I walked toward my house—my home—with the nail, still warm, clutched tight.

I opened the back door and could hear the kids upstairs, listening to music, talking, living.

On top of a chest that belonged to my great-grandmother was a carefully wrapped antique photo my dad had brought to me that spring. The round frame had a bubble of glass over the front, and under it was my grandmother at about six years old. Her own grandmother was beside her, smiling as peacefully as Benjamin.

Oh, but her eyes! I knew them well. They were Caroline's eyes.

I pounded the warm nail into the wall in my den and hung the photo, then stood back three steps to be sure it was straight.

"I was never alone," I said to those women, and to all the others who had survived before me.

The kids thundered down the stairs and I smiled over my shoulder at them. We had ugly days ahead, everyone does, but we had more good days than bad, more smiles than tears.

And we would never be alone.

About six months after Mom died, I started feeling sorry for myself, wondering if the months of exhausting work had been worth it. If the kids and I could reclaim the lost dates, friends, movies, and countless hours of sleep we had given to Inkwell Manor, if we could take it all back and buy a small cottage with double sets of bunk beds, would we be in a better—or at least an equivalent—place?

What if I could go back and spend those hours with my mom instead?

One Thursday after school, Jada and Drew were raiding the pantry together and I was in the library, listening. Jada was having trouble with middle-school mean girls, and Drew was half listening and halfheartedly giving out mediocre advice.

Then Jada said something that caught her brother's full attention. She said, "I can't."

"What do you mean, you can't?" Drew said, angrier than I'd heard him in months. "Jada, you built your own damn house. You can do anything."

If they said anything else, I didn't hear, because I had just gotten an answer to the question that had plagued me.

Yes, it was worth it.

Yes, they were better for it.

Yes, they got it.

They had learned that little bit of fearless that changed everything. And anytime one of them forgot, or let the shadow of the old life creep back over their mind, they would remind each other.

You built your own damn house. You can do anything.

* * *

While I was writing the first draft of this book, I remembered how to be afraid again. Adam had not found us at Inkwell Manor, and I worried what would happen to me and the kids if his memory was refreshed by the book. In fact, I had started and stopped writing the book repeatedly for five years because of this fear. While I worked on the latest draft, and tried to figure out how I would handle renewed contact from him, Adam parked his car at a coffee shop and committed suicide with a knife. We hadn't heard from him directly in several years. It was a horrific end to a tragic, tortured life. And I realized only then how often during an ordinary week I had been afraid and watching over my shoulder for him.

Sometimes people do learn from their mistakes. They do change. Matt came to understand some measure of the trauma he had caused in our lives. He learned. He grew. He became a better person and we are no longer afraid of him.

My dad continues to gather unusual items and find new purposes for them. He visits every year to add a new level of Rube Goldberg–like complexity to the act of starting my lawn mower with his improvements and adjustments. He still brings turkey and cheese but has also added unfathomable quantities of rhubarb to the mix.

Hope graduated number one in her high-school class and was awarded a spectacular scholarship package. By the time she was nineteen she had interned for a former president of the United States and fourteen United States congressmen. She now owns her own consulting agency, which specializes in events, marketing, and online business.

Drew spread his wings all the way to Alaska, where he pursued a degree between snowboarding and climbing mountains. He continued the adventure in Denver while managing an electronic-repair shop. He is now working in the technology industry and will undoubtedly continue planning adventures near and far.

Jada spent time on an off-grid farm, working as the volunteer manager for their sustainable-living organization and gathering knowledge to someday build her own off-grid home. She now creates personalized physical training plans with a focus on people with disabilities, encouraging a healthy lifestyle for those who are often left out while their peers are active on sports teams and neighborhood activities.

Roman is rocking elementary school, with enough confidence to display his own style. He runs his own YouTube channel and has a line of T-shirts and a business plan to become a YouTube gamer star. He is a big part of our family business, and we all suspect we'll be working for him one day.

I write in my library. The window overlooks some of my gardens that are loaded with plants my mother loved, even some that belonged to her parents. I fight with my lawn mower but ultimately enjoy mowing our acre and taking care of everyday household problems. I'll never stop marveling over what we continue to accomplish.

Our dinnertimes and movie times are often interrupted with business chatter and heated discussions. But mostly, we laugh a lot.

It isn't that we aren't afraid of anything, but rather that we are no longer afraid of failure.

What's the worst-case scenario? Yeah, we can handle that.

People often comment on how much Inkwell Manor must mean to us, that we could never possibly sell it. But in the end, the most important thing we learned is that this story—our story—was never about a house.

Acknowledgments

This is the story of me and my children building our house. I have changed the names of most others in the account and I have chosen to omit some of those who were present for privacy or narrative reasons. I've also reordered some events.

Building a book is every bit as tough as building a house. Thanks to those below and the rest of you who tied on tool belts, laptops, or just tied one on in the name of helping me reach the end—which turned out to be the beginning.

Thank you:

My late brother, John Puttkammer, who wanted to but couldn't. Darlene, whose e-mail encouraged beyond the call of duty. Kei and Dorian, for whom I'll always have mom hugs. Scott and Aidan, who are part of Inkwell's spirit. My grandparents, who would have said I was nuts and the aunts, uncles, and cousins who went ahead and said it.

My agent, Jessica, who made me dig deeper and my editor, Rose, who indulged me when I needed to laugh, even when I wasn't funny. And St. Martin's Press, for believing.

Early readers: Sean, Don, Darryl, Jim, and Phil. Jason, who listened when I failed and when I succeeded. Daniel, who lit a match and David, who encouraged, shared, supported, and was generally his amazing writer self.

Hershey, Peek-a-boo, and Inkwell Manor, my best buds when humans were too much or too little.

And to Hope, Drew, Jada, and Roman. If knowing you really can do absolutely anything brings you future grief, I'm sorry, but it was worth it.